*Behenji*

# *Behenji*

## A Political Biography of Mayawati

AJOY BOSE

**PENGUIN**
**VIKING**

VIKING

Published by the Penguin Group

Penguin Books India Pvt. Ltd, 11 Community Centre, Panchsheel Park,
New Delhi 110 017, India

Penguin Group (USA) Inc., 375 Hudson Street, New York, New York 10014, USA

Penguin Group (Canada), 90 Eglinton Avenue East, Suite 700, Toronto,
Ontario, M4P 2Y3, Canada (a division of Pearson Penguin Canada Inc.)

Penguin Books Ltd, 80 Strand, London WC2R 0RL, England

Penguin Ireland, 25 St Stephen's Green, Dublin 2, Ireland
(a division of Penguin Books Ltd)

Penguin Group (Australia), 250 Camberwell Road, Camberwell,
Victoria 3124, Australia (a division of Pearson Australia Group Pty Ltd)

Penguin Group (NZ), 67 Apollo Drive, Rosedale, North Shore 0632,
New Zealand (a division of Pearson New Zealand Ltd)

Penguin Group (South Africa) (Pty) Ltd, 24 Sturdee Avenue, Rosebank,
Johannesburg 2196, South Africa

First published in Viking by Penguin Books India 2008

Copyright © Ajoy Bose 2008

10 9 8 7 6 5 4 3 2 1

ISBN 9780670082018

Typeset in *Goudy Old Style* by SÜRYA, New Delhi
**Printed by: Gopsons Papers Ltd., Noida**

The views and opinions expressed in this book are the author's own and the facts are as reported by him which have been verified to the extent possible, and the publishers are not in any way liable for the same.

# Contents

# Acknowledgements

$\mathcal{P}$eople tend to ask whether this is an official biography of Mayawati. If this means whether she or her party commissioned or officially approved of the book, the answer is a clear no. Nor did I approach her for any help while writing the book. I did so largely guided by my own gut sense that told me political leaders in India today are wary of biographers who claim that they belong to the fast vanishing tribe of neutral journalists. I feared that even though this book was quite objective and largely supportive any effort to co-opt the mercurial lady in the enterprise could swiftly become a hindrance instead of help. If this meant that the book had to do without a heart-to-heart confessional from the BSP supremo (I was pretty certain that Mayawati would not have bared her soul even if promised a publicity brochure masquerading as a book) it was okay by me rather than taking the risk of her insisting on reading the manuscript in return for her seal of approval. Fortunately, I was already familiar with the subject of my book through journalistic encounters with both Kanshi Ram and Mayawati over the years. I am also indebted to Mayawati's own two-volume autobiography that contains a wealth of information provided one has the diligence to go through its two thousand-odd pages that indiscriminately pack together valuable insights, raw data and publicity material. The fact that I went through her autobiography from cover to cover and that too in the unfamiliar language of Hindi deserves a self-congratulatory pat on my own back.

This book would not have been possible without the help and cooperation of scores of past and present associates and peers of Mayawati. I have not been able to directly quote most of them since an overwhelming majority agreed to speak to me frankly only under conditions of strict confidentiality. The valuable information and insights provided by this wide cross-section of politicians, bureaucrats, businessmen, etc., enabled me to build piece by piece, year by year, the evolving saga of Mayawati. In return I have respected the trust they reposed in me.

Although the paucity of existing research on the Bahujan Samaj Party and its leaders Kanshi Ram and Mayawati is shocking, the book has clearly benefited from source material available in certain publications. In the media, *Outlook*, *Frontline*, *Tehelka*, particularly Shivam Vij's illuminating articles, *Seminar*, *Indian Express* and *Times of India* deserve mention. Academic work done by French political scientist Christophe Jaffrelot in his book *India's Silent Revolution—The Rise of the Low Castes in North Indian Politics* and his biography of Ambedkar, *Dr Ambedkar and Untouchability: Analysing and Fighting Caste*, Oliver Mendelsohn and Marika Vicziany in *The Untouchables—Subordination, Poverty and the State in Modern India*, the writings of JNU professor Sudha Pai and her recently edited collection *Political Process in Uttar Pradesh*, and Vivek Kumar and Uday Sinha's monograph *Dalit Assertion and Bahujan Samaj Party—A Perspective from Below* have been most useful. A number of web sites particularly those focusing on Dalit issues also offered surprisingly fresh information and new angles. Wherever relevant, the above sources have been quoted in the book.

I have some individuals and organizations to thank personally. Uday Sinha was a major help in the initial stages. Veteran Lucknow journalists Atul Chandra and Dilip Awasthi provided useful insights. My friend Tani Bhargav did her bit by ruthlessly editing my bad sentence constructions in the first section of the book. The Uttar Pradesh Information Office in New Delhi was most cooperative in supplying photographs.

This book has been a long time in gestation largely because of my insistence of getting the time right for its publication. This is evident from the fact that since it was commissioned by Penguin India, I have had three editors: Nandini Mehta who got tired of waiting for my book and left Penguin to join *Outlook* magazine,

Meru Gokhale who also after some time abandoned the book, publishing, and India to get married to an Englishman in London, and finally Ranjana Sengupta to whom I delivered the manuscript at express speed before she could leave. I know that the wait has been vindicated because in the intervening period the Mayawati saga has grown into a bigger and more developed story. Yet, I do thank everyone in Penguin for bearing with me so patiently and Ranjana particularly for her editorial rigour.

Finally, I thank my family for their support, especially my eldest daughter Aruna who, taking pity at my laborious efforts to plough through pages of Hindi on Mayawati, translated some initial pages into English to help me get on my way.

# Introduction

𝒯he Mayawati story has many dimensions. It is an amazing personal saga of an otherwise nondescript Dalit woman driven by relentless ambition to become one of India's most powerful leaders. At the political level, she has virtually reinvented the games that Indian politicians have traditionally played in the pursuit of power. This is exemplified by her constant political and ideological oscillations that would have been ludicrous had they not delivered such spectacular results. Finally, and perhaps most importantly, Mayawati's rise also reflects the vast social upheaval sweeping away age-old stereotypical caste equations across Indian civil society. This makes a study of her life and times that much more relevant than that of other contemporary political firecrackers such as Narendra Modi, Jayalalithaa and Mamata Bannerjee.

When I first started researching this book nearly four years ago, shortly after Mayawati's third regime in Uttar Pradesh collapsed, many of my friends in politics, bureaucracy and the media felt it would be a waste of time. Some were convinced that the array of corruption charges in the wake of the Taj Corridor controversy against the ousted chief minister would destroy her political career. Others maintained that with Kanshi Ram's debilitating stroke in 2003, the Bahujan Samaj Party (BSP) was in any case sliding downhill and it was a matter of time before his protégé faded into insignificance. And then there were those who were appalled that I had chosen to dignify with a biography 'such a crude, corrupt and completely unscrupulous' politician—a perception of the Dalit firebrand shared by a very large section of the chattering classes till very recently.

I have therefore noted with some bemusement that many of the same people are now lauding Mayawati to the skies after the BSP's stupendous victory in the 2007 Uttar Pradesh assembly polls made her the undisputed empress of India's largest state. All of a sudden she has become the most promising politician in the country. Quite a few go to the extent of predicting she will be the next prime minister. As for my book, I am now showered with praise for my excellent choice of subject and the perfect timing of its publication.

Both the past derision and current hype about Mayawati underline the entirely inadequate understanding about a leader who perhaps represents the ultimate political paradox in India. As the country's most successful Dalit leader, overshadowing even Babasaheb Ambedkar, she has indeed given unprecedented political profile and clout to a community crushed under social prejudice stretching back several millennia. At the same time, her autocratic style of functioning, cynical liaisons across the political spectrum and unabashed flaunting of wealth have made Mayawati perhaps the most controversial political leader in India today. She and her unique brand of politics remain an enigma not just for the layperson but even political pundits.

For a journalist, it is tempting to get carried away by the many controversies and scandals that have surrounded her ever since she came into the limelight. In the beginning when Kanshi Ram first introduced to the public domain a chubby young political greenhorn as his successor, the media grapevine—particularly in the upper-caste-dominated Hindi vernacular press—buzzed with salacious and often openly scurrilous tales about their relationship. For a long time no journalist was ready to accept Mayawati as a serious political leader even if they conceded Kanshi Ram's role as a Dalit prophet. Later, even after she displayed amazing tenacity by repeatedly snatching back the throne of Lucknow, the media continued to focus on her diamonds and mansions, projecting the BSP leader as a vain and capricious upstart who had gatecrashed the world of politics. It is only after Mayawati surprised journalists across the board by achieving the seemingly impossible task of getting a legislative majority in Uttar Pradesh on her own that they have stopped trivializing her. In fact, today as if to compensate for the past, a variety of commentators in print publications and on the small screen tend to paint a larger-than-life picture of the lady.

Perhaps it is this shallow approach by journalists to the fascinating saga of her life and politics that made Mayawati so wary of the media from the outset. Indeed, the biggest challenge of writing a biography of Mayawati is to understand her as a person and not merely as a leader. While there has been considerable coverage of her political career and some analysis of her impact on Dalit society, Mayawati the person is virtually unknown. Except for some stray anecdotes about her personal whims and fancies, Mayawati's private life, both past and present, remains a strictly guarded mystery. More than any other political leader in the country, she has almost made a fetish of avoiding journalists. And in the few interviews and the occasional press conferences, Mayawati has doggedly refused to expose her private persona.

For instance, next to nothing is known about her childhood, familial relationships, friends and lovers since we are dependent on the brief and understandably sanitized glimpses that Mayawati allows us in her autobiography. The only intense personal relationship she seems to have had is with her mentor, Kanshi Ram, and this is invariably projected as a political defining point in her career. The exact contours of this often tempestuous and clearly obsessive relationship remain a mystery, although there are enough people who had the opportunity to observe them at close quarters who suggest that the close personal bond between the two was multi-dimensional.

Indeed, this book is primarily a political biography and makes no claim to lay bare the innermost recesses of Mayawati's mind and emotions. My various encounters with her through the years have been that of a journalist and not a confidant. However, one can also safely assert that no one, not even her closest associates, can lay claim to know the real Mayawati. Interestingly, she is one of the few Indian leaders who discourage personal familiarity from her aides, choosing instead a functional professional relationship. For instance, at least one of her closest associates is yet to introduce his wife to her and does not feel that he is required to do so.

If not much is known about Mayawati's private life, her

personality is at least more accessible, although the varying perceptions of the politicians and bureaucrats who have worked closely with her can be confusing. Obviously, these are coloured by their personal equations with the leader. Those who have turned against her speak of a petty, insecure and vindictive woman who has neither the political vision nor the organizational skills to be a mass leader. They see Mayawati as a creation of Kanshi Ram and an unworthy usurper of his mantle who has taken advantage of the present political disarray in Uttar Pradesh and the lack of an alternative leader among the Dalits. If one were to believe these former colleagues now turned hostile, her success so far is just a matter of phenomenal good luck and it is only a matter of time before she fades away into political oblivion.

Those who are with her, of course, have unflinching faith in Mayawati's leadership. But apart from the faithful, there are quite a few—including several bureaucrats in Uttar Pradesh known for their integrity and competence—who are not ready to join the chorus of denunciation against Mayawati. They maintain that the Dalit firebrand in her four stints as chief minister of the state may have been unconventional but certainly not more corrupt or incompetent than many of her predecessors. In fact, they point out that Mayawati's blunt and direct method of functioning with the state bureaucracy was in many ways preferable to the more venal insidious practices of politically more experienced chief ministers.

Yet, Mayawati's detractors, supporters as well as supposedly neutral observers do concur on certain common traits in her personality. She is unanimously regarded as a rough and ready politician who makes up her strategy as she goes along, rather than plan too much beforehand. Or, as one veteran Lucknow journalist put it, 'She thinks in a straight line, which to her is the shortest distance to get from point A to point B.' All agree that the Dalit leader is fiercely focused and, more importantly, not at all bothered about political conventions or ideological principles.

The fact that she does not quite belong to the political mainstream is underlined by Mayawati's dogged rejection of the debate of secularism versus communalism, which has dominated Indian politics over the past two decades. She has hobnobbed with the Bharatiya Janata Party (BJP) forging coalition governments with them thrice in succession, even going to the extent of campaigning for Gujarat chief minister Narendra Modi shortly after the Gujarat riots. On the other hand, Mayawati has been the sharpest critic of the BJP when she failed to extract her pound of flesh from the latter. Not surprisingly, the Hindu right wing, the communists as well as the Congress are all uneasy at not being able to cast her into a political stereotype and consistently baffled at the many surprises she has sprung on them. Many would call her refusal to spout ideological shibboleths of the Right or the Left as crass opportunism. But it is at least a transparently self-centred approach; more honest, perhaps, than the equally selfish political agendas that other parties practise with far more pretensions.

Indeed, a large measure of her remarkable achievement in a relatively brief period of time has been Mayawati's ability to think and behave in an unconventional manner. While this absence of political scruples has provoked widespread criticism from the media, this has also given the Dalit leader a clear advantage over many of her political peers who are less adventurous in their approach to the rough and tumble of Indian politics. Significantly, her core Dalit constituency has solidly backed Mayawati in her repeated ideological flip-flops even when there seems to be no direct connection between the political games she plays and the larger benefit of the community. As a matter of fact, the childlike faith that Dalits, particularly in Uttar Pradesh, have shown in Mayawati has allowed her the freedom to practise the art of realpolitik more than any other political leader in the history of independent India.

Academics and experts who have followed Dalit movements through the decades are unable to adequately explain the phenomenon of Mayawati's constantly expanding Dalit support base. On the face of it, the lot of the untouchable—as it is of vast sections of marginalized and impoverished masses—remains miserable even in Uttar Pradesh, despite her becoming chief minister of the state as many as four times. Although the first three of these terms in office were rudely cut short, there is not much to suggest that the Dalit leader, now that she has an assured full term in office, will swiftly change the socio-economic profile of her community. The roots of her popularity with the Dalits, therefore, have to be sought at a more symbolic and emotional level. It is the notion of political empowerment of the country's most marginalized group and the dreams of ascendancy that flow from it, that has fired the Dalit imagination.

Mayawati's Dalit supporters are unanimous that what attracts them to her is not what she is but the hope she holds out for the future. They see her as a symbol of political power that not so long ago would have been unimaginable. Having lived off the crumbs from the table for so many centuries, the very idea of a Dalit woman leader sitting at the table—perhaps one day even at the head of it—is a potent brew for the community. The fact that unlike other past scheduled caste leaders, Mayawati no longer depends on the patronage of upper-caste leaders and parties, provides a special appeal that even Ambedkar did not possess. Interestingly, her lack of foreign university degrees and academic brilliance that illuminated the career of the intellectually towering creator of the Constitution, is not a shortcoming but actually an advantage that brings her closer to ordinary Dalits. This 'ordinariness' of such a powerful leader is at once recognizable and reassuring to the community and living proof of their own potential. Babasaheb is up there as an iconic statue on a pedestal, but the very name 'Behenji' represents Mayawati's almost familial relationship with her core constituency despite the giant billboards and cutouts of the Dalit leader that have mushroomed all over the Uttar Pradesh landscape.

The Dalit leader's recent offer to marginalized upper castes like brahmins and banias to join her bandwagon has only added to her mystique. Much as her rival scheduled caste leaders have tried to portray this somersault as a betrayal of the Dalits, it is seen by the community not as a dilution of ideology but instead the assertion of growing Dalit power. The electoral success already garnered by the BSP from such caste alliances in Uttar Pradesh and the widespread expectations that this can be replicated in other parts of the country are only part of the reason why Dalits still repose unwavering trust in Mayawati despite her wooing the upper castes and the espousal of 'sarvajan samaj' instead of 'bahujan samaj'. Dalits who have perceived themselves for so long as a victim community take fierce pride in the fact that their 'Behenji' has so effectively manipulated political levers, that a Dalit-led party is now in a position to offer protection to the past masters.

A palpable illustration of both the kind of influence that Mayawati wields in India today and her importance to the Dalit psyche came six months after she swept back to power in Uttar

Pradesh in the summer of 2007. A Bollywood potboiler, *Aaja Nachle*, marking the comeback to the silver screen of yesterday's heroine Madhuri Dixit, ran into trouble with the Dalit community immediately after release over an offensive portion in the title song that went,'*Bazar mein machi hai maramar; bole mochi bhi khud ko sunhar* (there is so much chaos in the market that even a cobbler is calling himself a jeweller)'. The first Dalit leader off the blocks was Udit Raj of the Justice Party who held a protest demonstration outside a Delhi cinema hall screening the film. But what made a difference was the heavy clout of Mayawati who immediately banned the film in Uttar Pradesh and shot off a letter to the prime minister demanding a countrywide ban as well. Within twenty four hours the film producer, Yash Chopra, had issued an abject apology to Mayawati promising not only to remove the objectionable portion in the title song but also never to use casteist lyrics again. The fact that Mayawati could take on Bollywood, the embodiment of Indian mass culture, and win so decisively on an issue of Dalit pride and sensitivity, would surely not be lost on the community.

Despite her new rhetoric wooing support from the upper castes, Mayawati has been careful not to ignore her core constituency and the symbols that inspire it. This is evident from the frenzied work being done to expand and enhance the giant Ambedkar Maidan in Lucknow ever since her return to power. The gleaming stone being used to build a new boundary wall and other edifices in and around the most noticeable symbol of Dalit power in India which has become a pilgrimage spot for the community are a constant and visible reminder that Mayawati is back in the saddle and with a full majority. The deification of Kanshi Ram, in whose name thirteen ambitious projects with a budgetary allocation of 250 billion rupees, including a hospital, museum, guest house and even a grand garden have been launched, is not just a personal tribute to her mentor but very much a public celebration of the vast financial resources that the Dalit community can now spend in memory of their prophets. For a people denied any kind of religious symbol for centuries, this kind of totemism is very powerful and, perhaps, more relevant than material prosperity.

On the other hand, Mayawati's spending spree on the Ambedkar Maidan and other pet schemes has not gone down well with the upper-caste middle class intelligentsia in Uttar Pradesh who had for a brief while switched their political loyalties to her when she swept back to power. Within six months of the new government, lawyers, journalists, accountants, businessmen and bureaucrats have started grumbling about the Dalit leader, shaking their heads disapprovingly at the wasteful expenditure, lack of serious policy making and, of course, huge corruption that they allege are routine features of Mayawati's fourth stint on the throne of Lucknow. They point out that many of the controversial businessmen associated with Mulayam Singh Yadav whom Mayawati was supposed to punish have managed to switch sides without difficulty. The case of liquor baron Ponty Chaddha is cited as a classic example. He is reported to be flourishing, even more today than during the previous regime, having acquired a stranglehold over the vast liquor trade in Uttar Pradesh. Even Mulayam Singh's close associate Subroto Roy of the Sahara Group, whom everybody expected to be down in the dumps after his political mentor's downfall, is said to have bought peace with the new regime after a lengthy meeting with cabinet minister Nasimuddin Siddique, a key aide of Mayawati.

What the middle class intelligentsia in Lucknow do concede, however, is that the law and order situation has shown a definite improvement after Mayawati took over. This, of course, is not saying much since there was a complete breakdown of law and order bordering on anarchy during the last few years of Mulayam Singh's rule. Yet the security of life and property is something that affects every class and caste and the new government has certainly earned some important brownie points in that regard within six months of coming to power.

It is also impossible not to notice the relaxed air of confidence in state cabinet secretary Shashank Shekhar Singh. In his gleaming white leather and chrome office at the State Secretariat he asserted, 'If we can continue for one more year like this, we will take Delhi.' I would have been tempted to dismiss this as empty bluster if I had not recalled that nearly three years ago, when Singh was languishing in a punishment posting after the downfall of Mayawati's third regime, he had predicted a full majority for her in the 2007 assembly polls.

A dramatic illustration of Mayawati's own self-confidence

today is the way she has sought to defy the NOIDA jinx—an Uttar Pradesh political superstition that has kept all serving chief ministers in the state from visiting the area bordering Delhi during their tenure because of the widely held belief that they would lose their jobs. The jinx started two decades ago when in 1988, the then Uttar Pradesh chief minister, Vir Bahadur Singh, lost his job soon after visiting NOIDA. The next chief minister, N D Tiwari, was also a casualty being voted out in 1989, a few months after his first official visit to the place. In 1995, Mulayam Singh Yadav came to NOIDA as chief minister and within months Mayawati withdrew support to his government. She herself fell victim to the jinx in 1997. After her visit to Noida, the BJP withdrew support to her government. Her successor Kalyan Singh claimed he did not believe in superstition, but was removed in 1999 shortly after visiting NOIDA. Thereafter a visit to NOIDA has been a major bugbear for chief ministers of Uttar Pradesh. For instance in 2002, Mayawati unveiled the foundation stones of Noida's Expressway and Gautam Buddha University from outside the city. BJP chief ministers Ram Prakash Gupta and Rajnath Singh always managed to avoid a trip to the area during their respective tenures. While inaugurating the DND Flyway linking Delhi to NOIDA, Rajnath Singh went to the extent of cutting the ribbon from the Delhi end. The scare about visiting NOIDA was so overwhelming that Mulayam Singh during his last stint in power doggedly refused to visit Nithari even after a public storm erupted over the discovery of mass child graves, simply because the area fell inside the administrative jurisdiction of NOIDA. So Mayawati was making a very significant statement when she went as chief minister to attend the wedding ceremony of the niece of her closest political aide, Satish Mishra, at the NOIDA Expo Centre on 21 November 2007.

Yet, Mayawati's obvious confidence that she will rule Uttar Pradesh for the next many years does not mean that she is resting on her laurels. She is clearly restless for further prizes, particularly the biggest one of all that lies in the capital, Delhi. Ever since the Dalit leader captured power in Lucknow, she has repeatedly declared her ambition of becoming prime minister. This is not just posturing but a serious quest for political power at the centre as her aide, Satish Mishra, acknowledges. He has been put in charge of putting the BSP on the national map and has been touring virtually non-stop across the country to make preparations for the coming Lok Sabha polls. Mayawati herself has also been travelling far and wide choosing to spend the last week of 2007 on a tour of south India where her party barely exists. There she declared her intention of replacing both the Congress and the BJP with the BSP as the main national party of India.

How seriously should we take these assertions? There was an empirical test of the BSP's electoral clout outside of Uttar Pradesh at the end of 2007 when the party contested on its own virtually all the seats in the state assembly polls in Gujarat and Himachal Pradesh. Mayawati had claimed during hectic campaigning in these polls that her party would make a dent in Gujarat and actually hold the key to power in Himachal Pradesh. The results have belied these claims. In Gujarat where the BSP got 2.37 per cent of the vote, it failed to get a single seat while in Himachal Pradesh it managed to win the solitary constituency of Kangra with seven per cent of the overall vote in the state.

Yet, the results show a dramatic jump in voting percentage for the BSP, which was virtually non-existent in these states. Significantly, the Congress blamed Mayawati and her party for its resounding defeat in the hands of the BJP in both states. There is little doubt that in several constituencies in Gujarat and even more so in lower Himachal Pradesh, the BSP vote harmed the Congress, although in some areas it dented the BJP as well. The results confirmed the worst fears of Congress strategists: that the BSP was becoming a major political undercurrent that was eroding the party's base in large parts of the country but in varying degrees from state to state. As the writing is becoming increasingly legible on the wall, some panic-stricken Congress leaders lashed out at Mayawati and the BSP in the aftermath of Congress debacles in Gujarat and Himachal Pradesh. 'Mulayam Singh's government was bad but the Mayawati regime is worse,' alleged Uttar Pradesh party chief Rita Bahuguna.

In response to the war of words unleashed by the Congress, Mayawati fired her own salvo at her first press conference of 2008 in New Delhi. The Uttar Pradesh chief minister said that the United Progressive Alliance (UPA) government at the centre had ignored her repeated appeals for financial resources to develop backward areas in the state. She also accused the central government of deliberately extending corruption cases against her despite the clean chit given to her by the income tax authorities and investigative agencies. The Dalit firebrand went to the extent of accusing the Congress of protecting noted Allahabad Mafioso Atiq Ahmed, who had threatened to kill her. 'If I am murdered, it is the Congress who will be responsible,' thundered Mayawati at the press conference. Interestingly, she sought to differentiate between Sonia Gandhi (in hospital with a respiratory ailment over the end of 2007 and the beginning of 2008) and the Congress adding that it was not clear whether the party supremo was responsible or even aware about the anti-Mayawati campaign. Yet, whatever the personal rapport between Mayawati and Sonia Gandhi may be, this intrinsically hostile political equation between the Congress and the BSP cannot but influence their future relationship.

While the BJP is gloating at the possible advantage to be gained from the woes of the Congress in the face of the BSP challenge, the saffron party itself has little chance of national revival as long as Mayawati holds sway in Uttar Pradesh. BJP leaders privately admit that there is virtually no chance of resurrecting the party from deep coma in the state in time for the next Lok Sabha polls. And without the numbers from India's largest state, and given the BJP's weakness in eastern and southern India, there is no way that it can hope to come back to power at the centre. So even if she does not have the numbers to make a serious bid for power after the next general elections, Mayawati, more than any other contemporary political leader, is increasingly becoming the defining point of national politics.

This book is certainly not a hagiography aimed at painting a rosy picture of Mayawati and her politics. There are enough publicists in India to look after the image building of political leaders. But it is difficult not to be impressed at the tumultuous saga of the Dalit leader who has already redefined the landscape of Indian politics. The probability of her going on to scale even higher peaks of success makes the book an even more worthwhile exercise. Yet, despite her own sterling qualities and a liberal hand from destiny, Mayawati's meteoric rise almost out of nowhere is also a great tribute to the democratic process in this country. Those who tend to rubbish Indian democracy and get impatient with its indubitable flaws should ponder whether there is a historic parallel anywhere else where a woman belonging to the most crushed (the literal meaning of Dalit) community known to mankind has risen through the heat and dust of elections to rule two hundred million people? In fact she may well reach further afield and guide the destiny of a billion more in the not too distant future. And all this without cutting anyone's throat. To my mind this is not only the crowning achievement of independent India but also a political marvel that holds lessons across the world.

*7 January 2008*                                   **New Delhi**

*Section  One*

# ONE

# Early Years

𝓜ayawati's early years are, perhaps inevitably, shrouded by the mythology that has sprung up around her amazing story. Her father claims that she was named Maya because the day she was born he had three strokes of good fortune: a promotion at work, a move to a better department and a tidy sum in accumulated dues. Her mother recalls that barely a fortnight after Mayawati's birth a sadhu predicted that she would become a neta, a great leader.

Her family has many stories calculated to intensify the hype and enhance the aura about her. When she was just three years old, runs one of them, she found a valuable cheque her father thought he had lost. As she grew older, she never forgot to milk the family buffalo even in the middle of her law exams. Her mother speaks of her daughter's incredible culinary skills. Mayawati's many siblings wax eloquent about her courage, wisdom and determination, qualities which were evident even when she was a child.

Not surprisingly, Mayawati, herself, chooses to remember the early memories that complement her present iconic stature. For instance, she recounts these four stories about her childhood in her autobiography:[1]

> As a small child I used to go with my parents to visit my maternal grandparents who lived in Simrauli village in

Hapur district, Uttar Pradesh. One day I was walking with my parents and grandparents past the local river when out came a wolf right in front of us. The adults immediately tried to restrain me by saying that I must stay away from the wolf otherwise it would eat me up. But instead of being scared, I challenged the wolf and said that *I* would eat it up instead. Much to the horror of my grandparents and parents, I chased after the wolf. However, I was stopped from any further adventure by some peasants from nearby fields who brought me back to the adults.

In my early teens, in Fifth or Sixth class, my fourth brother Subhash was born. Within a few days he came down with a terrible bout of pneumonia. He was in desperate need of injections and medicines but unfortunately my father was out of town. The government clinic where we were treated free of charge because of my father's government job, was six kilometres away. My mother was too ill and the rest of us were (still small) children. I knew my brother would die if not taken to the government clinic on time, so I decided to walk him to the clinic since there was no money in the house to hire transport. It was a long, scary journey. Deserted at places, the road cut through a stretch of the Ridge forest. I carried a water bottle from which I gave sips to my brother whenever he cried. I shifted him from right to left shoulder and back. Finally, after a two-hour trek I reached the clinic much to the amazement of the doctors and staff there. They were flabbergasted at my feat. My brother received the proper injection and medicines and quickly improved. I then walked back with my brother reaching home after 9.30 in the night. My mother was waiting anxiously and worried sick. She was thrilled to see us safe and her newly born son looking much better. She gave me a big tight hug.

A middle aged childless couple lived near our house. The wife was the target of all kinds of rumours by people in the colony. They spread stories about her suffering from some dangerous infectious disease. Nobody would speak to her or visit their house. Several years later she was suddenly reported to be pregnant. This only led to even more vile gossip about her. Finally, the day came when the lady was in labour but to her misfortune the husband was away at work. Nobody in the colony was prepared to help despite her loud cries of pain. I was in First or Second Year College and happened to be in the house. I wanted to go to her aid but my mother and other women in the colony insisted that I would be infected by the disease the lady had. Besides, my mother asserted that there was no need for me to get involved with pregnancy since I was unmarried myself. But I didn't heed them and rushed the lady to hospital where she delivered a healthy son now happily married with his own children. When the nurse sought to hand over the newly born infant to the relieved husband who had now arrived at the hospital, he was so grateful to me that he told her to hand the baby over first to 'Behenji' Mayawati without whose help his child would have remained unborn.

We had gone on a large extended family excursion to see Birla Mandir when I was in class two or three. After the entire day there, the time came to go back home. Most of us were returning by bus but a relative had also brought his private car and I was keen to ride in the car. Unfortunately in the confusion of who was going with whom I got left behind. I realised something was wrong when I saw the car driving away without me, the group going by bus having left some time earlier. I chased the car for a distance but how could a small girl catch up with an automobile! Although I ran a considerable distance trying to catch the car I managed to get back to Birla Mandir. Without any tears or tantrums, I patiently waited for my parents to come back for me. They did so after a few hours after discovering that I was missing. When they found me waiting quietly at the gates of Birla Mandir, my parents thanked me for showing such good sense instead of panicking like a little child.

Cynics may question these feats of courage, compassion and duty that Mayawati claims to have achieved at so young an age. Yet her following not only take every childhood story recounted by their leader as the gospel truth, but each of these stories is already part of the folklore surrounding 'Behenji' and have become shining illustrations of role model behaviour. It is quite possible Mayawati herself believes in a heroic childhood and youth, choosing to deny the insecurities, vulnerable moments and the more mundane aspects of what was, after all, a very ordinary early life. But the real point is that these incidents are now like fables and their relevance lies in their contribution to the wider, unfolding Mayawati story.

Mayawati was born on 15 January 1956 at the Lady Hardinge Hospital in New Delhi to Prabhu Das Dayal, a lowly clerk in the posts and telegraphs department of the central government, and a mother, Ramrati Devi, who was illiterate. Although by the time of her birth, her family had moved to Delhi because of Prabhu Das's government job, both parents hailed from Uttar Pradesh. Mayawati's paternal family came from Badalpur village then in Ghaziabad district, but now within the newly created Gautam Buddha Nagar district. Her mother's family came from Simrauli village near Hapur, also in Ghaziabad. Both villages were close to the larger national capital region bordering the capital, New Delhi.

Despite her parent's rural background, Mayawati herself grew up entirely in the Jhuggi Jhopri (JJ) colony of south-west Delhi's Inderpuri—one of the proliferating shanty towns that have for decades housed lower middle class inhabitants across Delhi. The tiny dwelling, shared by the Dayal parents and their nine children—Mayawati's two sisters and six brothers—must have further added to the cramped squalor of her childhood surroundings. It certainly must have helped her to cope with life's challenges as well as opportunities. These survival skills, sharpened in the inner recesses of Delhi's urban jungle, were to serve Mayawati well in her political career.

Significantly, the person whom she loved and respected most as a child was not her father, Prabhu Das, with whom she had a troubled relationship. It was her paternal grandfather Mangal Sen, a former sepoy of the British army who had seen action in Italy during the First World War. Mayawati was her grandfather's favourite, and he made her feel special and wanted. She also admired his wisdom, lofty principles and lack of prejudice. 'He was so principled and progressive that the entire village respected him for his views and came to ask for his advice. Often he was the one who resolved disputes in the village,' recalls Mayawati in her autobiography.

She recounts with obvious admiration that her grandfather refused to remarry despite losing his wife when his son, Prabhu Das, was only six months old. Ignoring the advice of his friends and relatives to marry again, he single-handedly brought up his son. In sharp contrast, Mayawati is openly contemptuous of her own father who was inclined to listen to his relatives and friends when they advised him to acquire a second wife when his wife, Ramrati, produced three daughters in succession. They told him that as the only son of his father it was his duty to have sons who would continue the family name. Many years later Mayawati recalled the sadness and humiliation caused to her mother by her father's desperation for male progeny.

It was Mangal Sen who put his foot down, forbidding his son from marrying again. 'My grandfather said that granddaughters were perfectly capable of continuing the family heritage. He said that if girls are given a good education they can be as capable if not better than sons,' writes Mayawati.

Eventually, a few years later, her mother produced sons with such a vengeance that she gave birth to six in a row. Prabhu Das was overjoyed and boasted about being the father of so many sons. His bias towards his sons was so evident, Mayawati recalls, that his daughters were sent to low-performing government schools for a free education, while the family's small income was spent on educating the boys at private schools and on extra tuition when needed. 'My father was convinced that his sons were his future and therefore needed special grooming. Even though I was the best student in the family, my father did not spend any money on my education.'

Fate provided Mayawati with her revenge in 1993. Her political standing increased sharply once the BSP joined hands with the Samajwadi Party to form the government in Uttar Pradesh. While Mulayam Singh Yadav became state chief minister, Mayawati, the BSP's point person in Uttar Pradesh, closely supervising her party's interests in the state, earned the sobriquet 'super chief minister'. Prabhu Das was besieged in his ancestral Badalpur village by friends, relatives and village elders asking for special favours now that his daughter had become such a VVIP.

When her father came to Lucknow to urge Mayawati to

announce some special schemes for Badalpur she could not help but taunt him, 'But I thought it was your sons who were going to carry forward the family name! Why don't you ask one of them to construct colleges, hospitals and roads in your village?' With obvious satisfaction she recounts in her autobiography that her father begged for forgiveness saying that he had now realized that it was his daughter who was the most important person in his life. Significantly, as her political stars shone brighter with every passing year, Mayawati never cut herself off entirely from her father but kept him at arm's length, often—much to his discomfiture—withholding easy access to her presence. Indeed, it was possibly this equivocal relationship that fired Mayawati's ambition, driving her to achieve more and more, as if to prove to Prabhu Das how much better she was than everyone else.

Mayawati shows far more compassion towards her mother, and her appreciation for Ramrati's unswerving dedication and hard work for the welfare of the family is obvious. She has high praise for her mother's ability to rise above her status as an illiterate housewife and start a dairy in the house to augment the constantly cash-strapped situation of her large family. 'My mother is a simple woman but completely focused on the welfare of her family. It is largely because of her that all us sisters and brothers are well settled in life.'

The gender discrimination faced by Mayawati in her early years and the low status of women in her family and in her immediate society, made her all the more determined to achieve the kind of success that would lift her above the curse of social prejudice. This need was also fuelled by overwhelming feelings of humiliation and vulnerability as a Dalit that she had felt from her childhood, feelings she describes vividly in her autobiography.[2]

> Even as a small child, there was no escaping the curse of being a Dalit! My parents would often take me by bus or train to my grandparents in the village. On the way they would start talking with other passengers who, as soon they heard the name of the village, enquired further to which specific mohalla—Brahmin, Jat, Thakur, Gujjar etc we were going. The moment my parents mentioned Chamar mohalla, passengers belonging to other castes shrank back and stopped talking to us. At first these

people who behaved in such a strange way confused me. When I asked my mother she explained that people were divided into castes and sub-castes, and they lived in segregated clusters in the village. She also told me that our Chamar caste was considered low, unclean, and treated unkindly by upper castes. From a very early age, I learnt to hate the caste system with all my might.

An admiration for the great Dalit icon, Baba Bhimrao Ambedkar, became another impetus to succeed in life and combat the curse of the caste system. Every year on 14 April, along with her entire family, she attended functions held across Delhi to mark Ambedkar Jayanti—the birth anniversary of the Dalit leader and architect of the Indian Constitution. She heard leaders and scholars from the community speak on Ambedkar's life and writings. This celebration of Ambedkar has become routine practice over the past several decades in most urban—and increasingly rural—Dalit families; it is akin to the religious rituals observed by other segments of Indian civil society. It is one reason why Dalits, perhaps more than any social group, are intensely aware of their rights under the Constitution and are also ready, from a very young age, for political mobilization.

Yet, Mayawati's early exposure to Ambedkar's call to destroy the caste system produced a response that went beyond the reaction of an average Dalit child. Even before she fully grasped Ambedkar's politics and social philosophy, the awe and respect accorded to the Dalit icon mesmerized her. While she was still in middle school, Mayawati asked her father whether people would praise and respect her if she, too, fought against social injustice like Ambedkar. It is interesting to note that even as a teenager she craved public adulation.

Prabhu Das shrewdly sought to direct his daughter's desire for fame for practical benefit, instead of just dismissing it as childish prattle. 'Of course you, too, can be like Baba Ambedkar. But first you have to finish school and college, then pass the Indian Administrative Service (IAS) exams, become a collector and only then as a government bigwig will you be able to rise in society and fight for your community. Only then will you get success and fame,' he told his daughter. The scheduled caste government clerk was uttering a mantra familiar to all his peers. They believed that the road to success was to become government officers through the reserved caste quota.

It became Mayawati's mission in life. With single-minded dedication she decided to pursue the goal of passing the IAS entrance exams to become a district collector whose hands wielded the levers of official power. Mayawati was so impatient for this to come to pass that she asked her father if she could take her high school exams early. Prabhu Das, ready to take advantage of his daughter's enthusiasm, found out that she could actually take a combined exam for the classes nine, ten and eleven at her government school. In an incredible spurt of scholastic effort, if not ability, Mayawati leapfrogged three school years, passing the school-leaving board exam in 1972.

This enthusiasm to get through school did not necessarily mean that Mayawati was a scholar. Academic standards at her government school were notoriously low. Passing the board exam prematurely should not be mistaken for the feat of a prodigy. Mayawati's modest academic abilities are underlined by her graduation from Kalindi College, ranked fairly low among Delhi University's colleges, where she graduated with a third division in the not very academically rigourous BA (Pass) course.

Interestingly, the few who remember Mayawati in college find it difficult to recall any early pointers of her subsequent stardom. For instance, the administrative officer of Kalindi College, J.B. Anand, who admitted her, remembers a shy, tongue-tied sixteen-year-old, clutching on to her father when she came for admission. 'Such a timid girl! She seldom mixed with others and was reticent; in fact she was even scared of the teachers. I am at a loss to explain this complete turnaround. There has been a drastic change in personality. *Din or raat ki farak hai* (the difference between day and night)!' he declared in an interview after Mayawati triumphantly swept to power in Uttar Pradesh for the fourth time.[3]

Her low profile in college and lack of scholastic flair is not surprising. An overwhelming majority of Dalit students keep their head well down in colleges where they are made to feel like interlopers in a club that they do not really belong to. The fact that large numbers of them still flock to colleges despite the inhospitable environment is an eloquent testimony to their hunger for the success they hope to acquire through an academic degree. Dalit students use their reserved quotas in colleges, competitive exams as well as government offices with quiet determination, traversing a path that rarely crosses those taken by other sections of society. College was hardly the arena for Mayawati to display her innate abilities or skills. On the other hand, there is little doubt she was far from being a cerebral giant like Ambedkar who, regardless of his social background, impressed everyone by the sheer weight of his intellect from an early age. In this respect, to the average aspiring Dalit student who struggles through education, Mayawati is a far more realistic role model than the intellectually brilliant father of the Indian Constitution.

After her graduation in 1975, Mayawati immediately enrolled for a one year Bachelor of Education (BEd) course which she completed the following year from a Ghaziabad college affiliated to Meerut University. She then went on to study law in Delhi University. This was the final preparatory step in her attempt to clear the entrance exam for the Indian Administrative Service. Each stage was calculated. The BEd degree allowed her to become a teacher in a government primary school. The law degree was a useful backup in case she failed to make it to the IAS. It remains a tried and tested route for young Dalits who want to get ahead, using every resource and opportunity available.

Mayawati's pursuit of the holy grail of the IAS did not mean that she was just a mere careerist. She had increasingly become aware about Dalit issues and the inequities of the caste system. She devoured Ambedkar's books 'soaking up his writings like a blotting paper' as a profile in a newspaper described her as doing at this time.[4] As she grew into a young woman, the bewildered anger at being despised as a chamar that she had felt as a child while travelling with her parents to her ancestral village in Uttar Pradesh had been replaced by a full-blown hatred for a social order that even in supposedly cosmopolitan Delhi, humiliated her constantly in a myriad overt and covert ways.

It was not long before Mayawati was sucked into radical Dalit politics. She belonged to the seventies generation of young, urban, educated Dalits who were agitated by what they perceived as a historic betrayal of their caste by the Congress. They squarely blamed the party for the Dalits' continuing social and economic oppression and deprivation, despite using them as a loyal vote bank in successive elections over several decades. The nineteen-month Emergency, imposed in the mid-seventies by Indira Gandhi egged on by her son Sanjay, had further alienated Dalits. They were among the worst sufferers in the forcible sterilization and demolition drives in urban centres like Delhi. Anti-Congress feeling among politically conscious Dalits was compounded by the troubles faced by veteran scheduled caste leader, 'Babuji' Jagjivan Ram, considered by Indira Gandhi to be politically suspect even though he was a member of the cabinet during the Emergency. This finally forced him to quit the Congress on the eve of the landmark 1977 general elections. The Emergency regime's astounding electoral debacle left the Congress in tatters and its image was tarnished even further among the Dalits.

At the same time, the hopes that Jagjivan Ram may have raised among Dalits of creating a political alternative vanished very quickly. Although it was his defection—along with H.N Bahuguna—from the Congress to the Janata coalition that provided the final push to the Emergency regime, 'Babuji' was humiliated and marginalized in the aftermath of the Janata Party's victory. Various upper caste factions headed by the powerful Jat leader, Charan Singh, closed ranks against Jagjivan Ram, scuttling a bid to make him the new prime minister. The credentials of the first non-Congress government at the centre were thus swiftly destroyed for the Dalits. The political plight of Jagjivan Ram, till then the tallest scheduled caste leader in India after Ambedkar, was henceforth cited by radical Dalit groups as palpable proof of the futility of lower castes depending on mainstream political parties dominated by upper castes. At the same time, it is worth pondering what might have transpired had Ram been made prime minister in 1977. A Dalit prime minister would have had a huge impact on the national political scenario and inducted Dalits into the social mainstream. The history of Mayawati, the BSP and quite possibly Indian politics itself may well have turned out quite differently

The disillusionment of Mayawati and other young Dalit radicals was not just limited to the post-independence leadership of mainstream political parties. They traced the betrayal of lower castes back to Mahatma Gandhi's ambiguous attitude towards the caste system. Indeed, Gandhi's denial of Ambedkar's demand for a separate Dalit electorate in 1932 is seen as the original sin. In page after page in her autobiography Mayawati spits venom at 'manuvadi' Gandhi, whom she considered from her early days in politics as being one of the prime perpetuators of the ancient social stratification system of Hindu civil society created by King Manu. She is convinced that by forcing Ambedkar to retreat from the demand for separate electorates, Gandhi, through his usual threat of a fast unto death, had deliberately stopped the untouchables from becoming a significant independent political force (a status then being offered by the British Raj), thus leaving them vulnerable to continued oppression by the upper castes. Dalits like Mayawati are unimpressed by Gandhi's social work in untouchable colonies, partly because they regard it as patronizing charity but also out of suspicion that it was all just a ploy to keep the untouchables on board while maintaining the existing caste system. Nor do they acknowledge his support to the policy of reservation—this despite the obvious benefits that have accrued from the policy, not the least of which has been the phenomenal success of the BSP. This was based to a great extent on first, the support of scheduled caste government employees in the reserved quota, and later, through electoral wins in reserved constituencies in Uttar Pradesh. Instead, Mayawati lauds Ambedkar for battling against Gandhi and other upper-caste leaders of the freedom struggle and credits him for whatever rights Dalits have in independent India, rights that are enshrined in Ambedkar's handiwork—the Constitution.

Mayawati, along with an overwhelming majority of Dalits, finds the term, 'Harijan' (God's children), which Gandhi used for the untouchables, offensive. This is widely perceived among the Dalit community as patronizing eyewash that perpetuates segregation of untouchables, instead of emphasizing their assimilation into mainstream Hindu society. Whatever Gandhi's motives in coining the term 'Harijan' (even his periodical bore the same name), it is no longer used by political leaders for fear of causing offence to scheduled caste constituencies. Interestingly, Mayawati mentions another reason for hating the term: apart from its exclusivist connotation, she points out a parallel analogy is that of 'Devdasis' (God's slaves), a term used to describe women who danced in temples and who were sexually exploited by resident Brahmin priests; their illegitimate children would logically be called 'Harijans' (God's children).[5]

Considering the depth of her animus for the term 'Harijan', it is perhaps fitting that it proved—quite inadvertently—to be the catalyst, which pitchforked her into political stardom. The venue was a three-day conference organized by the Janata Party at Delhi's Constitution Club in September 1977 to discuss ways and means of fighting caste prejudice. It was an attempt by the newly formed political party, particularly its socialist faction, to mobilize support among lower castes. The irrepressible Raj Narain, then health minister and at the height of his political fame having defeated Indira Gandhi from Rae Bareilly in the just concluded general elections, was one of the chief speakers. Quite unmindful of the furore he might create, the minister in his speech consistently referred to the untouchable caste as 'Harijans'.

Mayawati was in the audience, with BA and BEd degrees and a government primary school teacher's job under her belt, and was simultaneously studying law at the Delhi University while preparing for the IAS exam. Mayawati, like many other scheduled caste students, had already participated in many Dalit political rallies; in fact she had won considerable appreciation for her impassioned speeches. She was scheduled to speak at the Janata Party conference after political bigwigs and senior scheduled caste leaders had had their say.

Mayawati was horrified at the way Raj Narain offended his audience by using the hated term 'Harijan' and appalled that most Dalit leaders and activists present just grumbled among themselves but did not protest. When her turn came to speak, Mayawati lashed out at Raj Narain, his party and government, as well as at the entire political mainstream. She said that despite the offensive connotation of 'Harijan', a senior government minister had repeatedly used the term, insulting all Dalits in the audience. This made a mockery of a conference which purported to discuss how to end caste prejudice. Mayawati pointed out that Ambedkar had used not 'Harijan' but 'scheduled caste' in the Constitution, yet upper castes continued to provoke the Dalits using this offensive term. The young Dalit radical also did not miss this opportunity to condemn Gandhi's followers, who needed to be exposed as those who perpetuate the caste system while pretending to fight it.

Such a bold and fiery speech by a Dalit girl barely in her twenties, electrified the audience. 'Down with Raj Narain', 'Down with the Janata Party' rent the air and gave way to slogans hailing the memory of Baba Ambedkar. Leaders and activists from various organizations representing scheduled castes crowded around Mayawati and congratulated her for showing such courage. Among them were members of the Backward and Minority Communities Employees Federation (BAMCEF)—a new organization making waves across the Dalit community because of its unconventional leader and his radical message. The leader, Kanshi Ram, would soon hear of this young Dalit schoolteacher who had created such a stir at the Constitution Club. The stage was set for perhaps one of the most significant encounters in Indian politics.

TWO

# Kanshi Ram

*K*anshi Ram was a visionary Dalit activist and organizer who, in the seventies and eighties, almost single-handedly changed the idiom of Dalit politics; in fact, he may well have altered the language of Indian politics forever. Before we get to his first historic meeting with Mayawati, it is important to understand that any political appraisal of Mayawati and the Bahujan Samaj Party must recognize the crucial role played by this mentor and founder. Without the initial momentum created by Kanshi Ram in the organizational sense as well as the strategic direction he gave it, the BSP might never have become the formidable force it has today. Indeed, it may not have even existed. His indefatigable pursuit of a wider coalition of the economically exploited and socially oppressed was indispensable when Dalit and radical politics were floundering. For much of his activist career, Kanshi Ram remained an unarmed prophet. Only in the last decade of his life, despite several years marred by a crippling stroke, did he see the enormous potential of what he had set in motion.

On 15 March 1934, in the Khawaspur village of Ropar district in Punjab, Kanshi Ram was born to a lower middle class Sikh family that had converted from the Chamar caste. Significantly, he was not subjected to much social discrimination during his childhood or youth. There are two reasons for this. Firstly, much like Ambedkar, Kanshi Ram's father, Hari Singh, came from a family of soldiers, which automatically opened both economic and social avenues. As a matter of fact, all Hari Singh's brothers saw action in the Second World War. He was the exception since an adult male had to stay home to tend the family's four-acre agricultural land. Interestingly, Hari Singh, though semi-literate himself, educated his three sons and four daughters. Only Kanshi Ram chose to complete his graduation.

The other reason for the comparative absence of social discrimination in Kanshi Ram's early years is because he belonged to a Sikh family. In the Sikh community converted Dalits do not share the same status as upper-caste Sikhs, but do not suffer relentless humiliation and oppression that Dalits face in Hindu society. Kanshi Ram referred to this in a later interview to French political scientist Christophe Jaffrelot[1] declaring, 'the teachings of the Sikh gurus were more egalitarian' and that 'converted Chamars at least had some upward mobility.' As a young Sikh from a family of soldiers, he was largely unaware about his caste while in school or in a college in Punjab.

Only in 1956 after Kanshi Ram graduated with a BSc degree from Government College, Ropar, and joined central government service through the scheduled caste reserved quota, did he began to experience caste prejudice. This intensified after he shifted in 1958 to Kirkee near Pune in Maharashtra, following a brief sojourn at the Geological Survey of India office in Ropar. Hoping to improve his prospects, the young, shaven Sikh had eagerly taken the job of a laboratory assistant in the Kirkee munitions factory of the Defence Research and Development Organization (DRDO). He was in for a shock when he saw first-hand for the first time the social oppression and economic exploitation suffered by Maharashtrian scheduled castes such as the Mahars and Matangs.

It did not take Kanshi Ram long to be diverted from a career in government. His outrage at the discrimination suffered by his fellow scheduled caste employees was fuelled by a belated realization about the stigma of his caste. A colleague at the munitions factory, D.K. Khaparde, played an influential role in Kanshi Ram's journey towards activism. Khaparde, a Mahar Buddhist, was a committed Ambedkarite. He introduced the young laboratory assistant from Punjab to Ambedkar's writings. This proved to be a turning point in Kanshi Ram's life. He read and reread Ambedkar's *Annihilation of Caste* again and again, three times in one sleepless night. He also read *What Gandhi and the Congress Have Done to the Untouchables*, Ambedkar's bitter and sweeping indictment of what he perceived as the betrayal of the untouchables by the leader of the freedom struggle and his party. 'These two books influenced me the most,' Kanshi Ram told Jaffrelot.[2]

He later discovered Jyotirao Phule, the nineteenth-century revolutionary social reformer from Maharashtra who fought against social and economic oppression of lower and untouchable castes. It was Phule, while launching his Satyashodak Movement in the Bombay Presidency in 1873, who first spoke of the need to mobilize the 'bahujan samaj', the majority of the people, who constituted the entire social spectrum outside the upper castes. The writings of Ambedkar and Phule, as well as the movements launched by them, opened up an exciting new world of issues and ideas for the young laboratory assistant.

His growing consciousness about caste conflict did not remain at a purely theoretical level for Kanshi Ram. Along with Khaparde, he began to participate in agitations for the rights of scheduled caste employees in the government and to improve their working conditions. He was in serious trouble in 1964 with his employers for playing a proactive role in an agitation by scheduled caste staff demanding special leave for the birthdays of Dalit icons like Ambedkar, Valmiki and Buddha. This clash with an administration dominated by upper caste officers provoked Ram and Kharpade to actively consider forming an organization that would protect scheduled caste government employees from harassment and discrimination.

Conflicting reports exist about when Kanshi Ram quit his job and became a full-time activist. Some suggest that he did so as early as 1964, shortly after participating in the agitation by scheduled caste staff for more holidays. It is more likely, however, that while Kanshi Ram spent most of the late sixties on activism rather than his job, he actually resigned in 1971 after even a bigger row with the administration. Ram, hot-headed from an early age, prone to being physically violent, reportedly slapped a superior officer after the latter refused to appoint a young scheduled caste woman candidate despite her fulfilling the required qualifications. He did not even bother to attend the disciplinary proceedings. He chose to quit government service.

Kanshi Ram had a government job at the age of twenty-two,

but after one-and-a-half decades took the plunge into full-time activism. He wrote a twenty-four-page letter to his mother in the village declaring that he was taking sanyas and severed all links with his family, vowing not only to remain unmarried but also to never return to his village home for family functions such as weddings, birthdays or funerals. Kanshi Ram announced to his mother that henceforth the rest of his life was dedicated to the uplift of the downtrodden.

Kanshi Ram's first challenge was to form an organization to give his ideas and beliefs concrete form. In the mid-sixties he had become a member of the Republican Party of India (RPI), the main Dalit organization in India, claiming historic links to Ambedkar's Scheduled Caste Federation, whose strongest base was in Maharashtra. But he was bitterly disillusioned by the endemic factionalism within the party and the consequent defections to the Congress. He also found the RPI exclusivist in its political approach, limiting its reach to mainly Mahar Buddhists. The party was simply not interested in crafting a wider constituency of the oppressed. Kanshi Ram felt that the RPI was straying from Ambedkar's vision because it focused on a small sect of Dalits. From the very outset, he knew that success lay in mobilizing large numbers of people and that only by uniting a whole range of oppressed communities could the stranglehold of the upper castes be loosened.

Kanshi Ram formally adopted Ambedkar's famous slogan, 'Educate, Agitate, and Organize' as the motto of his campaign, but drew inspiration from Phule's concept of 'Bahujan Samaj'. In fact, despite Ambedkar's firm rejection of a racial basis to the caste system, Ram found Phule's explanation of the caste system, the result of India's indigenous majority being enslaved by a far smaller group of foreign Aryan invaders, a far more potent rallying call to build a larger constituency. Jaffrelot points out the similarity of such tactics to those adopted by Dravidian parties in the south to isolate the Brahmins which had proved spectacularly successful.

Kanshi Ram used racial pride and the cold logic of numbers to convince his audience. 'The Bahujan Samaj accounts for eighty five percent of the votes. It is a shame that the foreign Aryans constituting fifteen percent are ruling over the eighty five percent. . . . The Aryans have exploited us. An Aryan ruler can never work for our betterment . . . When our ancestors from the Bahujan

Samaj were ruling over this country, India was known world wide for its prosperity. The Bahujan Samaj can rule this country even today . . .'[3]

He reiterated this theme at public meetings through his entire life, even after the mid-nineties when the BSP had mellowed in its approach to upper castes and started giving them election tickets. Addressing an election meeting in Maharashtra on the eve of the 1999 Lok Sabha polls, Kanshi Ram mocked the upper caste leadership of the BJP for raising doubts about Sonia Gandhi's Italian birth. He accused them of being the 'original foreigners' who enslaved the indigenous Dravidian people of this country. 'Now is the time to push these Aryaputras out of the county,' he declared.[4]

Along with the untouchables and the lower and backward castes of Hindu society, Kanshi Ram also included the various religious minorities as a part of the Bahujan Samaj. His view of Indian society, later expounded with a sketch in his book *Chamcha Age* shows brahmins, kshatriyas and vaishyas constituting ten to fifteen per cent of the population at the top of the social structure built out of various castes.[5] This upper-caste minority are described as the beneficiaries of the system controlling all the five major sources of power: political, economic, bureaucratic, feudal and cultural. The rest, constituting eighty five to ninety per cent of the population, are described as victims of the system and divided into four categories: intermediate castes, other backward castes, scheduled castes and scheduled tribes. Kanshi Ram saw his mission in stitching together a rainbow coalition of victims of the caste system who once united, could sweep away the domination of the upper castes through sheer weight of numbers.

Although his head was bursting with ideas of a mass movement, Kanshi Ram realized that he had to make a beginning amongst his peers—government employees. On 14 October 1971, Kanshi Ram created his first organization with the somewhat unwieldy name of 'Scheduled Castes, Scheduled Tribes, Other Backward Classes and Minorities Employees Welfare Association'. From the mid-sixties he and Khaparde had been in regular contact with scheduled caste government employees who shared their world view working in and around Pune. It was they who formed the core membership of the new organization. Ram, however, insisted that the leadership of the association should reflect the larger strategic vision of untouchables, tribals, backwards and minorities coming together to form an alliance, a bahujan samaj to fight the upper castes. Accordingly, the first five vice-presidents chosen to assist him in running the organization were a mahar, an adivasi (tribal), a mali (gardener—from the backward castes), a Muslim and a Christian.

The association was duly registered with the Pune charity commissioner. Its stated objective was 'to subject our problems to close scrutiny and find out quick and equitable solutions to the problems of injustice and harassment of our employees in general and the educated employees in particular'. However, it remained a far cry from Ram's attempt to mobilize a wider constituency. The association's openly Ambedkarite ideology and the limited circle from which he and Khaparde could recruit, ensured that the members were mainly Mahar Buddhists—the same handicap that had afflicted the RPI. In fact, most were scheduled caste employees from the departments of defence and the post and telegraphs—the two government departments where Ram and Khaparde made friends and influenced people.

Yet despite its limited reach, the organization grew rapidly due to Ram's boundless energy and enthusiasm. Within a year there were more than one thousand members and the Association opened a full-fledged office in Pune. News of Kanshi Ram and his fledgling organization spread not just in Pune and across Maharashtra but also reached the capital, New Delhi. The organization's first annual conference in 1972 was addressed by the then defence minister, Jagjivan Ram, the biggest Dalit leader in the country at that time.

It was not long before Kanshi Ram felt the need for a wider national canvas to play out his agenda. His next step was to create a national platform for scheduled caste government servants. In 1973, by holding a three-day conference in New Delhi, he and his colleagues turned the Association into a national federation. It was rechristened the All India Backward and Minority Communities Employees Federation (BAMCEF). Although still quite provincial considering that almost seventy per cent of the delegates to the New Delhi conference were from Pune, this new national organizational plank with a catchy acronym—BAMCEF—was a step forward towards a grander design. Within three years a functioning office was established in Delhi. BAMCEF was relaunched with greater fanfare on 6 December 1978, the anniversary of Ambedkar's death, with two thousand delegates marching in a procession to the Boat Club lawns in the heart of New Delhi.

Kanshi Ram quite deliberately kept the stated objects of the new federation essentially the same as those of the earlier association to avoid harassment of government employees by the authorities. Strict government service rules forbade employees from political activities of any kind. On the other hand, they could legitimately participate in an organization that advanced the welfare of government employees.

In reality, the raison d'être of BAMCEF was quite different. It organized educated members of the bahujan samaj not merely to advance their own interests, but to provide leadership to their communities. It specially targeted the upper band of lower castes that had managed to get into the government by taking advantage of the reserved quota. Kanshi Ram was clear about the purpose of organizing this elite. It certainly was not to merely engage them in agitations concerning the workplace. They were to be the vanguard of a social movement that involved the entire Bahujan Samaj and were expected to sacrifice their own personal careers if necessary for the sake of the community. In fact, Ram and other BAMCEF leaders openly chastised the majority of the educated elite for betraying the ideals of Phule and Ambedkar and abandoning their less privileged caste brothers and sisters.

A BAMCEF bulletin in 1974 reflected the new rhetoric:

As all the avenues of advance are closed to them in the field of agriculture, trade, commerce and industry, almost all the educated persons from these [oppressed] communities are trapped in government services. About two million educated oppressed Indians have already joined various types of jobs during the last 26 years. Civil service conduct rules put some restrictions on them. But their inherent timidity, cowardice, selfishness and lack of desire for social service to their own creed have made them exceptionally useless to the general mass of the oppressed Indians. The only ray of hope is that almost everywhere in the country there are some educated employees who feel deeply agitated about the miserable existence of their brethren.

Through the seventies and till the mid-eighties Kanshi Ram scoured the country using BAMCEF to establish a wide network of contacts. He would describe this network of contacts as the 'talent bank', 'think bank' and 'financial bank' of his movement. Not surprisingly he began this gigantic exercise in Maharashtra and adjacent regions. During his frequent train trips from Pune to Delhi, Ram would often get down at major stations like Nagpur, Jabalpur and Bhopal along the way. There he would just walk into government offices and contact likely sympathizers among lower caste employees and simply harangue them into joining his organization.

Once he had moved to Delhi in the late seventies he widened his net, eagerly pushing into his native Punjab, Haryana and Uttar Pradesh. Virtually all who met him were struck by his persuasive arguments and messianic zeal. There was little doubt that he was quite different from the average Dalit leader and his message even more unique. When Kanshi Ram entered the scene, Dalit leaders came in two models. One was the wild-eyed radical who spoke of blood on the streets in a language close to Naxalite groups and their message of armed revolution by the wretched of the earth. In sharp contrast were scheduled caste leaders who had joined the political mainstream—mainly the Congress party and affiliated organizations. They helped in preserving and consolidating the loyal scheduled caste vote bank that had remained in the party's pocket since independence.

Neither model particularly enthused the educated elite in the community. There was admiration for the idealism and fire of young Dalit radicals who, following the example of the Black Panthers in the United States, organized themselves as the Dalit Panthers in 1972. But most scheduled caste employees found the Dalit Panther agenda not just risky, but also utopian and unlikely to work in a stable democracy like India. On the other hand, they secretly despised mainstream scheduled caste leaders despite running after them for favours and patronage. Such leaders were widely seen as 'Uncle Toms' selling out Dalit interests in return for political crumbs from the upper caste table.

Kanshi Ram proposed a third path. It did not call for drastic revolutionary methods but nor did it mean tame collaboration. The BAMCEF's bid to create a network connecting educated lower castes across the country was seen as a necessary launching pad in preparation for a mass movement on behalf of the Dalit community. It struck a responsive chord among many government employees in the reserved category who saw that BAMCEF offered a proactive role for the Dalit educated elite in the struggle to gain dignity and justice denied for centuries to the community, but did not require them to violate either service rules or the law, thus risking dismissal and perhaps arrest.

The network of the BAMCEF grew steadily in the seventies and even more rapidly in the first half of the eighties when the organization claimed to have as many as 9,200,000 members including 500 PhDs, 15,000 scientists, 3,000 medical graduates and 7,000 other postgraduate and graduate degree holders. A majority were said to be from Maharashtra and Uttar Pradesh where Ram not only attracted Ambedkarites but also socialists searching for a new social movement.

Despite the rapid growth of his organization, the going was not easy for Kanshi Ram, particularly in the initial years. Typically, funds were a huge problem, considering the near impossibility of getting moneyed backers for an outfit whose whole purpose was to rock the boat of the establishment. He had no option but to ask his own cadres to contribute two per cent of their salaries. Many years later Ram admitted the huge difficulties he had faced in collecting funds for BAMCEF. Speaking at a public meeting on 14 April 1999 at the Constitution Club lawns in New Delhi, Ram recalled:

> The collection drive from BAMCEF cadre was a complete failure. I used to get receipts for collection of funds printed but could not even recover the cost of printing. We started running up losses. On the other hand there were leaders who used to collect the money from other members and keep it in their own pocket. People started complaining about the bungling of money that they had donated for the movement. It became very embarrassing for me.[6]

A lesser man might have lost heart. But Kanshi Ram was both extremely determined and prepared to wait. As he explained to his audience at the Constitution Club, it was not that his cadres did not want to donate money. They simply were not used to giving money for their own movement, and they were also fed up with unscrupulous leaders who simply pocketed their donations. It was therefore not surprising, he pointed out, that the donation drive never took off. Ram learnt his lessons about fund collection the hard way and would pass them on to his protégé Mayawati. This is perhaps the reason why they later managed to raise such phenomenal amounts of money from their own flock without having to depend on industrialists like other politicians.

Money was just one problem. The larger question remained: was this the best way to mobilize the target audience in the bahujan samaj? Kanshi Ram valued the network of educated scheduled caste elites. They would play a crucial role as core supporters of the BAMCEF and its later political avatars. But Kanshi Ram recognized that the membership of his organization was a miniscule fraction of the bahujan samaj. As much as ninety per cent of BAMCEF members were scheduled castes, mainly mahars from Maharashtra and chamars from north India. Barely ten per cent were tribals and other backward castes. As for religious minorities, he had managed to recruit very few for his organization.

Moreover, Kanshi Ram did not much care for the average-educated scheduled caste government employee who formed the bulk of the BAMCEF membership. The educated elite was cut off from the rest of their community and severely constrained by their narrow personal interests. Kanshi Ram realized that confining his movement to this group hampered its scale and thrust. First, the preponderance of scheduled caste employees in the organization impeded the growth of a coalition of oppressed communities which could potentially mobilize eighty-five per cent of society. The present configuration confined the movement to urban areas, although economic exploitation and social discrimination by upper castes was felt most acutely in the villages. He also had to contend with government service rules that restricted members of BAMCEF to focus on employees' welfare and not involve themselves with larger social and political issues. Most importantly, he was far too interested in the big picture to remain as the leader of a narrow group of scheduled caste government servants.

Nevertheless, as BAMCEF expanded in north India, particularly across the country's largest state Uttar Pradesh, Kanshi Ram's quest to mobilize the bahujan samaj met with some encouragement. Educated kurmis, a backward caste that had economic clout but felt socially ostracized by the upper castes, showed interest in his agenda. Many were socialists disillusioned with the manner in which various political parties had sold out the interests of backward castes such as kurmis.

The spread of BAMCEF across north India and its inroads into the kurmi community in Uttar Pradesh whetted Kanshi Ram's appetite for a political outfit which would enable him to wage a no-holds-barred social movement with the promise of one day capturing state power. A golden opportunity was presented by the electoral humbling of the Congress in the 1977 Lok Sabha polls and the partial collapse of the party's Dalit and minority vote bank in north India. He could sense that the unprecedented loss of power by the Congress at the centre had opened up infinite political permutations and combinations.

Despite a provincial background and a complete absence of political tutelage, Kanshi Ram possessed an amazing capacity to think big. Kanshi Ram scored over other Dalit leaders with sharper intellects, demagogic flair or even more fire in their belly because of his larger vision and a driving ambition to make it big on the national stage. The fact is that as early as the seventies and eighties, when Kanshi Ram and his movement barely registered on the national radar, he dared to dream of a nationwide political alliance of oppressed communities and groups that would capture power through the electoral process. This rare quality distinguished him from his peers and forced him to think out of the box. Had this not been so, he may well have remained just another local Dalit leader.

Kanshi Ram combined his visions of grandeur with a down-to-earth pragmatism that saved him from overreaching himself. He may have believed in an impossible dream of a just and equitable society for the oppressed, but his ear remained close to the ground and he was always on the lookout for opportunities that came his way in the Indian political jungle. Another unusual characteristic was his dogged refusal to accept traditional shibboleths, Dalit, radical or otherwise. Despite the affinity of his politics with victims of social discrimination and economic exploitation, Kanshi Ram, unlike the Left, for instance, pointedly stayed away from public gestures and campaigns on these issues. In conversations with politicians and journalists he did not hide his contempt for the many collective efforts led by leftists and liberals within Parliament and outside to demonstrate and agitate on behalf of minorities, the working class and even lower castes. He and his party did not participate in a single one. Kanshi Ram had his own blueprint for a social revolution, which he pursued with single-minded focus. He had little time or inclination for he regarded as token political posturing. This won him few friends in Left and radical circles. But his fiercely independent stance, free from any established norm of ideological behaviour allowed him to twist and turn, improvize and manipulate to gain maximum advantage in the constantly changing political scenario.

Kanshi Ram was an extremely persuasive individual who was able not only to make acquaintances but lifelong friends who helped in every way they could. One of his first friends in mainstream politics was Dr Chinta Mohan, a scheduled caste Congress member of Parliament from Andhra Pradesh. His South Avenue flat in New Delhi became Kanshi Ram's shelter whenever he was in the capital in the early eighties. The Congress MP was also useful later in negotiating with the party leadership. Another close friend from the early eighties was Malaylee journalist T.V.R. Shenoy, who headed the New Delhi bureau of *Malayala Manorama*. Many years later Shenoy, who was close to BJP leaders, played a key role in helping Kanshi Ram craft alliances between the BSP and the BJP in Uttar Pradesh.

Shenoy has fond memories of Kanshi Ram. 'He was easily one of the most extraordinary people I have met in my life. Not only was he honest and dedicated, but also, unlike other politicians, Kanshi Ram was simply not interested in personal power. He only wanted political power as a tool to fulfil his ideological mission. That way he was really like a latter day Gandhi!'

By the late seventies as BAMCEF increased its activities in north India, Kanshi Ram recognized the need to concentrate his organizational energies. He realized that Ambedkar's legacy in Maharashtra was a double-edged sword and the internecine war between various factions of the RPI along with the exclusivist urban-centric radicalism of groups like Dalit Panthers, made it difficult for his agenda to make major headway in the state. Kanshi Ram also knew that despite his pioneering work in Pune and other cities and towns of Maharashtra, his Punjabi origin would remain a handicap and he would always be considered an outsider.

In north India, particularly Punjab and Uttar Pradesh, the prospects appeared far more encouraging. In Punjab, which had perhaps the largest percentage of scheduled castes in the country, Kanshi Ram saw himself doing a 'return of the native'. Indeed in a relatively short period of time he managed to set up an extremely active BAMCEF unit in Punjab where, despite the buffer provided by the Sikh faith, Dalit Sikhs appeared ripe for the plucking.

Uttar Pradesh was even more tempting—the largest state by far and the nerve centre of national politics. The state also had a huge population of chamars, the most politically conscious Dalit group in the state. Kanshi Ram was convinced that it was Uttar Pradesh that held the key to the ultimate success of his movement. The fact that he got the support of some other backward castes like kurmis, increased his resolve to spread the organization's wings in the state.

However, Kanshi Ram was pragmatic enough to realize he himself was not the ideal public face for a mass movement in Uttar Pradesh, despite his success in making friends and influencing people in individual and small group encounters with scheduled caste and backward caste communities. He knew that just as in Maharashtra, his target audience would see him as a Punjabi interloper. Kanshi Ram needed somebody with local credentials, preferably from the chamar sub-caste, who would serve as mascot for his movement. He was also conscious that such a mascot must possess not only considerable personal charisma but also project an image both contrary to, and distinct from, the average political *neta*.

This search for a new kind of leader to attract a wider constituency of oppressed communities in Uttar Pradesh may well have played on Kanshi Ram's mind when his followers brought back news of Mayawati's bold public rebuff to Janata leader, Raj Narain, at the Constitution Club meeting in New Delhi in September 1977. His enthusiasm grew once he made further enquiries about the twenty-one-year-old schoolteacher. She had already acquired a reputation of being a fiery speaker who had the gift of calling a spade a shovel. The fact that she was not already formally involved with any particular activist group or political outfit was an added advantage. Most importantly, she was from the chamar community, which was vital in Uttar Pradesh. It is not known whether Kanshi Ram had a premonition even before he met her that Mayawati was the right person for his movement in the country's largest state. But there is little doubt that a plan was already forming in his mind considering the alacrity with which he pushed for a personal meeting with the virtually unknown Dalit girl barely out of her teens.

# THREE

## *Behenji and Saheb*

*I*t was after nine on a winter night in 1977. Mayawati settled down after dinner with her pile of books to study for the IAS entrance examinations. It was a nightly ritual for the twenty-one-year-old schoolteacher who was enrolled in the first year of the LLB course in Delhi University. Her parents and other siblings were preparing to retire for the night. But Mayawati would study till after midnight. She was determined to leap over the daunting hurdle of the IAS exams and become a district collector. This had been her unwavering goal ever since she was a schoolgirl when her father told her that the way to fame and power lay in becoming a government officer.

Suddenly there was a loud knock on the door of their house. It was an unusual interruption because relatives and friends rarely dropped by so late at night. When Mayawati opened the door, she found much to her surprise, a BAMCEF leader whom she recognized from previous Dalit public meetings. A balding middle-aged man wearing crumpled clothes and a muffler round his neck accompanied him. It was her first encounter with Kanshi Ram.

Mayawati and her family were thrilled by this unexpected visit. Kanshi Ram was already a respected name with the urban Dalit community across the country. He and his organization BAMCEF were widely recognized as a rising phenomenon in the Dalit movement. It was a great honour to have him pay a personal visit. Even Prabhu Das, who was initially annoyed at the knock on the door and the sound of strange voices late at night, was impressed and sat down quietly to listen to what Kanshi Ram had to say.

The Dalit leader came straight to the point. Ignoring Prabhu Das, he spoke directly to Mayawati. Pointing at the pile of books scattered around her table, Kanshi Ram asked, 'You seem to be busy studying a lot of books! What is it you want to become after so much study?'

Pleased at this attention from such a senior Dalit leader, Mayawati announced somewhat piously, 'I am studying to pass the IAS exams and become a collector so that I can serve my community properly.' Her father also piped up, starting to boast how he had been grooming his daughter to become a big officer so that she could be a pride to the Dalit community.

But Kanshi Ram waved Prabhu Das aside. Once again he addressed Mayawati directly.

'I think you are making a big mistake,' he declared. Kanshi Ram went on to explain why he felt that Mayawati would not be able to serve her community as well as she thought by becoming a collector. He pointed out that collectors and other government officers, whether in the states or at the centre, merely carried out orders given by ruling political parties and leaders in power. 'Our community has produced many collectors and officers in recent years. But we have not been able to provide the right type of political leaders to point these collectors and officers at the correct direction,' he asserted.

And then Kanshi Ram said something that sent an electric charge through Mayawati and completely floored her father.

'Your courage, dedication to the Dalit cause and many other sterling qualities has come to my notice. I can make you such a big leader one day that not one but a whole row of collectors will line up with files in front of you waiting for orders. You can then truly serve the community and get things done,' the Dalit leader predicted.

That evening Kanshi Ram spent over an hour with Mayawati at her house discussing various social and political issues. Not surprisingly, the conversation focused on the exploitation and discrimination suffered by Dalits through history and also about those leaders and movements that fought back. They agreed that mainstream political parties were dominated by upper castes and collaborated in their domination of Dalits and other oppressed communities. Both lamented the collapse of the Dalit movement after the death of Baba Ambedkar and Mayawati nodded vigorously in agreement as Kanshi Ram expounded his theory about the *bahujan samaj* and the need for a rainbow coalition of the oppressed to fight the establishment more effectively.

Prabhu Das who was quite politically conscious also participated in the discussion. He was in two minds about the meeting. It was of course a great honour for the family to have a big Dalit leader praise Mayawati to the skies and he also broadly agreed with many of Kanshi Ram's views. But he disapproved of the way Kanshi Ram was diverting his daughter from the tried and tested path of the IAS exams and the guaranteed privileges of a gazetted government officer. Prabhu Das, like many Dalits of his social standing viewed the IAS as the ultimate ladder of success. He was not willing to have his ambitions for his daughter sidetracked by what he considered just idle political chatter.

But Mayawati's entire world had been turned upside down in just one hour. All of a sudden her earlier mission in life had evaporated. The words of Kanshi Ram echoed inside her head long after he had left the house. She saw the logic of what he said about the limited role of a government officer in a society where political parties and leaders called the shots. But was she capable of living up to his great expectations? Flattering though it surely was for the twenty-one-year-old schoolteacher and IAS aspirant, Kanshi Ram's visions of political grandeur for her may well have appeared a bit fanciful on that winter night in 1977.

It was certainly the defining moment of Mayawati's life and career. So far, her father had guided her on the well-trodden path to success. This was the first time she was being asked to take a risk by abandoning the certainties of a career in administrative service. Despite her innate pragmatism, there was something in Kanshi Ram's vision that made Mayawati feel like throwing caution to the winds. Part of the temptation to believe the Dalit leader no doubt lay in his adulatory remarks about her. He made her feel much bigger than she had ever felt before. But there was also the irresistible tug of the brave new world of political adventure that could never be matched by the safe enclosure of government service bound by rules and regulations.

Hitching her wagon to Kanshi Ram's star posed huge challenges to Mayawati in the coming months and years. This not only meant the abandonment of the IAS dream that she had cherished. It also required defiance of her father, till then the central figure of authority in Mayawati's life. As his daughter was sucked more and more into Kanshi Ram's movement, Prabhu Das, who had otherwise encouraged his family to be politically conscious, bitterly resisted her participation in a movement that began to consume all her energies. It is not that there were drastic changes in Mayawati's life overnight. She was shrewd enough to continue with her government schoolteacher's job and attend evening classes at Delhi University for her law course. But it became increasingly clear to her whole family including Prabhu Das that Mayawati's new priorities were being shaped by Kanshi Ram. Her schoolteaching job and law course did not occupy much of her interest or attention, which now was completely focused on organizational work for the BAMCEF. As for the IAS, much to her father's annoyance, she seemed to have lost all enthusiasm for becoming a collector after the job was so comprehensively rubbished by Kanshi Ram.

The growing displeasure of Prabhu Das at his daughter's obsession with Kanshi Ram and his politics was understandable. Independent Dalit politics did not seem to have much of a future in the late seventies and early eighties. Kanshi Ram and the BAMCEF may have created ripples among certain sections of urban Dalits, but hardly represented a political force or even an established organization with adequate resources. Prabhu Das found that most of his relatives and friends agreed that Mayawati was being naïve and foolhardy to abandon her own career prospects to pursue a political path that had little or no chance of success.

Prabhu Das manifested a fair degree of personal ego and proprietary interest in Mayawati. As her father and mentor he felt directly responsible for her welfare and was not ready to be shoved aside by some strange man who had walked into their lives one winter night. He developed a fierce animosity towards Kanshi Ram who he felt had ulterior motives in leading his daughter astray with false promises of political stardom. He resented the fact that Mayawati no longer turned to him for advice but hung on to every word Kanshi Ram said. Stung by this fall in his daughter's esteem Prabhu Das turned increasingly hostile to her involvement with politics.

At first he tried to persuade Mayawati to give up her obsession with political activism. When this failed, he suggested that if she was indeed determined to become a politician, she should at least join an established party like the Congress that had adequate resources and a national profile. 'You won't even become a local municipal corporator if you hang around losers like Kanshi Ram,' Prabhu Das taunted his daughter.[1]

Her father's hostility towards Kanshi Ram and his jeers about her lack of political prospects only served to put Mayawati's back up. She had been strong-willed and obstinate from her childhood and considered her father's response to her new interests as gross interference in what was, after all, her own life and career. It is possible the almost daily fights that started erupting between Mayawati and Prabhu Das over her growing involvement with Kanshi Ram may well have driven her even more decisively to the latter.

The tug of war between Kanshi Ram, Mayawati and her father continued for quite a few years. Meanwhile, Mayawati continued with her law course as well as the schoolteaching job, the salary of which she saved every month. Interestingly, it was Prabhu Das who had suggested that she accumulate her schoolteacher's salary so that it could be used for her marriage dowry. However, for Mayawati, who had no intentions of getting married let alone paying dowry, the savings provided crucial financial autonomy from her father should she need it one day.

Finally, matters came to a head between father and daughter one day. One of their usual shouting matches about Kanshi Ram, BAMCEF and the IAS got nastier and nastier till Prabhu Das served his daughter an ultimatum. 'Either you stop meeting Kanshi Ram, give up this silly politics and start preparing again for the IAS exams, or else leave my house immediately,' he shouted.[2]

Prabhu Das had delivered the ultimate threat. He was banking on Mayawati's vulnerability as an unmarried girl who would be too fearful at the thought of leaving her father's house. But he grossly underestimated his daughter's courage and determination. Without tears or recrimination Mayawati took out the money put aside from her schoolteacher's salary, packed a few clothes and belongings into a suitcase and simply walked out of the house that she had grown up in.

Having taken the plunge in the heat of the moment, Mayawati

had no idea what to do next. She had been unable to consult Kanshi Ram as he was out of town on tour. In desperation, she took shelter in the BAMCEF office in Karol Bagh, not very far from her father's Inderpuri house. Fortunately, Kanshi Ram was back soon. Mayawati told him about her dramatic decision to abandon her home for him and his politics. She said that she had decided to dedicate her life to the movement.

For Kanshi Ram it was further proof of Mayawati's personal courage and commitment to the movement. Many years later in an article written for a Dalit web site, he wrote admiringly of the 'uncommon courage' she displayed by leaving her father's shelter and joining him in his political quest.[3] He was also impressed at Mayawati's capacity for hard work and long hours. 'Early morning she was going to teach in the school, work in the (BAMCEF) office whole day and go to study law in the Law College in the evening,' Kanshi Ram recalled.

The Dalit leader offered her his own living quarters—a rented room quite close to the BAMCEF office—as he said he himself was almost always out of Delhi on tour. Once again Mayawati showed a rare audacity by accepting Kanshi Ram's offer, although she must have known that the thought of a young unmarried girl moving into the room of a middle-aged bachelor would create quite a controversy in her circle, which it of course did. However, she brought her favourite brother, Siddharth, along to live with her for security.

This was the beginning of an amazing relationship that has been the subject of much speculation and considerable gossip for over two decades. There were several dimensions to this encounter that lasted over two-and-a-half decades between two very exceptional personalities. It began when she was a naïve young political activist in her early twenties, starry-eyed about her middle-aged mentor and guide. The relationship ended with his death as a helpless, bedridden invalid looked after devotedly by his now fully established protégé. Their association was fundamentally political in nature, giving birth to the BSP and helping it grow to the formidable force that it is today. But there is no denying that the two also shared a strong emotional bond as well. And they did live in close physical proximity to each other from the day Mayawati moved into Kanshi Ram's room in Karol Bagh.

Unfortunately, much of the interest in the Kanshi Ram-

Mayawati relationship has been of the prurient kind. Right from the beginning their close association had been the target of sexual innuendo even among some of their colleagues in the BAMCEF, Dalit Soshit Samaj Sangharsh Samity (DS4) and the Bahujan Samaj party. In fact, in her autobiography Mayawati admits that there were widespread rumours among fellow activists after she left her father's house and moved into the room Kanshi Ram had hired. Finally after the insinuations got really offensive, Mayawati writes, she went to Kanshi Ram one day and told him that it would be better if with her accumulated salary she bought an independent room (no landlord in any lower middle class Delhi colony would have dreamt renting out a room to an unmarried girl).

There was also huge pressure on Kanshi Ram. He was blamed by Mayawati's rivals for showing her undue favour as she became more and more prominent in the movement, superseding older and more senior colleagues. Indeed, till a brain stroke completely crippled the Dalit leader in 2003, many politicians and journalists were convinced that her main asset was an older man's weakness for a much younger woman. That is why there was a widespread impression after Kanshi Ram's stroke that this also spelled the end of Mayawati who was seen as merely his creature. It is only after the BSP continued to prosper in leaps and bounds under her stewardship, even improving when Kanshi Ram was totally incapacitated, was there a grudging acceptance in political and media circles about Mayawati's own abilities.

Both were extremely touchy about any suggestion of a physical relationship. Mayawati vehemently reiterated on more than one occasion that Kanshi Ram was like an elder brother or even father figure to her and that the insinuations about them were despicable. He, too, was infuriated by journalists, many of them undoubtedly motivated by upper caste antagonism, who baited him on the subject of Mayawati. There was one particularly ugly encounter at his MP's bungalow in New Delhi, where visiting journalists found women's undergarments hung out to dry on a clothesline on the lawn. Kanshi Ram was visibly angry when a few journalists, instead of raising political issues, pestered him with questions about what women's undergarments were doing in a bachelor's house, whether they belonged to Mayawati and the nature of his relationship with her.

Nevertheless, there was no denying the strong personal chemistry between Kanshi Ram and Mayawati, vouched for by all those who came in contact with them. And as is often the case, it was the intensity of their quarrels that often underlined the emotional bond. The bickering, according to old associates, sometimes turned so explosive that those within earshot trembled. Kanshi Ram's hot temper, blunt language and propensity to use his hands when provoked, were legendary. Mayawati, too, was no pushover. She gave as good as she got, never shy of using the choicest expletives. From all accounts it was the lady who usually won the argument.

More than anything else, Mayawati was extraordinarily possessive about Kanshi Ram. She felt threatened by anyone who got too close to him. There were innumerable people he brought into the party who ultimately had to leave because she hounded them out. Although Kanshi Ram from the very start held Mayawati very high in his esteem and made no secret of his admiration, strangely enough she remained insecure about him for a very long time, in fact until she finally established complete control over the organization. Old associates recall how when Kanshi Ram would be sitting in the living room of his house speaking to a visitor, Mayawati would find an excuse to come into the room virtually every five minutes.

The two were quite different in temperament. Kanshi Ram was highly sociable, loved to chat with politicians and journalists, and trusted people with whom he shared ideas and beliefs. Mayawati, on the other hand, was an introvert who felt political chit-chat was a waste of time. She was also distrustful of virtually everybody in Kanshi Ram's circle of contacts, friends and acquaintances. She spent enormous effort and time to find out whom he met and what they discussed. Later, if he did not tell her about the meeting or discussion, Mayawati would surprise him with the details and quarrel with him for keeping her in the dark.

The story of Rashid Alvi, a Muslim leader from Uttar Pradesh who was initially close to Kanshi Ram and later endeared himself to Mayawati, is a good illustration of her obsessive relationship with her mentor. It was Kanshi Ram who had inducted Alvi into the BSP and Mayawati, who regarded all such recruits with a fair degree of misgiving, treated him warily at first. But quite inadvertently, one day Alvi managed to break the ice and gained her confidence. The Muslim leader had organized a public meeting in Jaipur, Rajasthan, and invited Kanshi Ram to address it. The latter accepted but much to Alvi's chagrin, the Dalit leader failed to show up. Alvi was even angrier when he learnt from his sources that Kanshi Ram had indeed come to Jaipur but spent the day with a lady journalist. Infuriated at this callous rebuff, Alvi rushed off to Mayawati and complained bitterly about the way he had been humiliated. It was only after he had unburdened his heart to Mayawati was he understandably apprehensive about how she would react to this outburst. Much to his surprise, she was extremely sympathetic, praised him for bringing the matter to her notice, and promised to take it up personally with Kanshi Ram. She also asked him to report similar incidents to her without fail in the future. Interestingly, from then on Alvi moved closer and closer to Mayawati and at one stage became one of her confidants. It is another matter that some years later, she dumped him after she felt that he had got too big for his boots.

Although Kanshi Ram would occasionally get annoyed at this constant monitoring of his social circle and daily activities by Mayawati, he was by and large indulgent of her interference. Virtually none of his friends and colleagues liked her very much and there was persistent pressure on him to dump what many felt was a needless hindrance to his personal life as well as his politics. On the other hand, Mayawati slowly but surely prised Kanshi Ram away from his old mates, often on the plea of medical advice that he desist from too active a social life. Indeed, particularly in his later years, she was far more proprietary about him than any protective wife. In this tug of war between his friends and Mayawati, he clearly chose her and ultimately abandoned some of his closest associates because they could not get along with her. Kanshi Ram's fondness for her was evident in special gestures made to her sometimes in public and the manner in which he tried to accommodate her insecurities.

Yet, despite Mayawati's constant meddling in Kanshi Ram's life, there was no questioning her personal loyalty and attachment to him. As a matter of fact, there are close observers of the duo who believe that she cut down his feverish social routine at the end of the nineties mainly out of the protective instinct of a loved one. They feel that the cerebral disease that ultimately consumed him in 2006 had started having its impact on the BSP leader several years earlier, and he may well have been suffering from the onset of dementia that affects both physical and mental behaviour. It is possible that while many of his friends and acquaintances misunderstood the signals, it was genuine concern and not proprietary interest that forced Mayawati to slowly isolate her mentor from the outside world. This became visible after he was reduced to a helpless invalid by a sudden cerebral stroke in 2003. For the three years he lived after that in her house, Mayawati nursed him with rare devotion, quite often washing and feeding him personally with a tenderness that underlined the depth of her feelings. By then Kanshi Ram had nothing to give her and what she did was clearly out of purely personal attachment. Allegations by some members of Kanshi Ram's family that she was mistreating him were, therefore, a complete travesty of the truth and obviously manipulated by her political opponents.

As to whether Kanshi Ram and Mayawati actually had a physical relationship, this to a large extent becomes irrelevant except for the purpose of salacious tittle-tattle considering what they shared was much more sweeping and had far wider implications than a mere affair. This is not least because while the personal element was no doubt a key catalyst, it was the political association between the two that acquired such huge significance. For without Mayawati's mass charisma, Kanshi Ram could not have brought about the momentous political changes that happened with the potential of even bigger events around the corner. And we do know that without him to open up the world of politics, she would have gone on to be just one of the many scheduled caste officers in government service.

Kanshi Ram and Mayawati perfectly complemented each other politically. He traversed the country with dogged determination attracting recruits to his movement by meeting individuals and small groups of people. She had a gift of speaking directly to the masses particularly the chamars of Uttar Pradesh who adopted her as their sister—'Behenji'. He subtly manipulated other politicians and parties into back-room deals that helped the BSP to clamber on top. She used rough-and-ready methods to break these deals after they outlived their utility so that the party could move on. He poached political parties to recruit a procession of new converts to his cause, seeking tactical advantage from their support but aware of their dubious loyalty on a long term basis.

She was the guardian angel who ensured, through strong-arm tactics if necessary, that no other leader hijacked the party and movement from under their feet.

Kanshi Ram always saw the big picture and was constantly thinking of stratagems to spread the movement across the country. Obsessed with making the BSP a national party, it was he who insisted that the party fight elections in virtually every corner of the country to add vital votes to its all-India kitty so that the Election Commission gave it the required recognition. His mind was a databank crammed with statistics of electoral performances through the decades by various parties and he could reel them off whenever he needed to score a point in an argument. Not satisfied with simple explanations or a one-dimensional approach, Kanshi Ram was not satisfied till he exhausted all possible solutions to a problem or challenge.

Mayawati, on the other hand, was designed as a special missile for a specific target. Her task was to deliver the Dalit vote bank in the country's largest state and she single-mindedly wooed her constituency. Whether riding a cycle in her initial days as a political novice or being ferried by an imported helicopter as she is today, Mayawati has tended to focus her energies in one direction not allowing herself to be diverted from the primary job. 'She thinks in a straight line taking the shortest distance from one issue to the other,' said an observer.

The single-minded zeal with which Mayawati took on the daunting challenge of conquering Uttar Pradesh suited Kanshi Ram very well. There are suggestions he was forced to stay away from the state after Mayawati warned him not to meddle in her patch, but the truth is that right from the outset, Kanshi Ram was nervous about tackling such a large state where he had no roots, and preferred to hand it over to somebody more suitable. As a matter of fact, he chose Mayawati with the specific intention of filling the leadership vacuum in Uttar Pradesh where none of the Dalit and backward caste leaders he had recruited really fitted the bill. Several years later, Kanshi Ram recalled the resentment among more senior party members over his choice, '. . . her seniors became furious . . . put pressure on me for giving opportunity to Km. Mayawati. So much so that most of them left the movement. I do not know where they are today, whereas Mayawati kept improving along with the movement.'[4] The fact that she plunged into the job with so much enthusiasm not only gave momentum to his movement in the state, but also left him free to build bastions in different parts of the country where there was potential to do so.

It is this team of 'Behenji' and 'Saheb', as they called each other, that by merging their individual strengths and skills into a lethal combination, built brick by brick a political edifice that would later shake up Uttar Pradesh and create waves in the country. They had occasional political differences but on the whole Kanshi Ram and Mayawati worked together in remarkable harmony. The stunning success of their joint enterprise belied constant media speculation about a major rift between the two. Had their political partnership been flawed or impaired by turf battles—as some commentators suggested—it would not have turned out so fruitfully nor would the BSP have scored its repeated electoral triumphs.

When Kanshi Ram invested so much trust in a young Dalit schoolteacher with no political experience and persisted in backing her against his other associates, he was taking a huge gamble. 'We did feel at that time he was getting carried away by his personal feelings about Mayawati against his better political judgement,' said an old associate of Kanshi Ram, adding, 'she has proved us wrong.' Had the outcome been different, he would have been the subject of endless ridicule for throwing away his movement for the sake of a younger woman. The fact that his faith in Mayawati was vindicated so spectacularly must have provided immense satisfaction to the Dalit messiah in his final years.

The ultimate symbolism of this relationship, which is unparalleled in the political history of not just this country but perhaps anywhere else in the world, is to be found in the eerie inner cavern of the 102-foot-high pyramid-shaped Bahujan Samaj Prerna Kendra in Lucknow. There, two extremely lifelike statues of Kanshi Ram and Mayawati, each nearly twelve feet high, stand next to each other under the shadow of a statute of Babasaheb Ambedkar. Kanshi Ram's statue is dressed in his usual attire of bush shirt and pants, while Mayawati's sports cropped hair, a dupatta around her neck and clutches a handbag. And on the wall, engraved in deep blue lapis lazuli is Kanshi Ram's last will and testament. It reads:

My bones and ashes are not to be thrown in the Ganga or Yamuna after my death. I want them to be kept in this inspiration centre. May God give long life to Mayawati. I wish that after her death, her bones and ashes too be kept beside mine in this inspiration centre. I hope her parents/brother/sister/all relatives and members of BSP will ensure fulfilment of my will. This will always be a symbol against the Manuvadi system of society and inspire the Bahujan Samaj to respect and devotion towards this memorial.

# FOUR

# The Quest for Political Power

$\mathcal{K}$anshi Ram had realized by the late seventies that BAMCEF was incapable of delivering his vision of a bahujan samaj. In this he differed seriously from most of his senior colleagues in the organization, including old friend and co-founder D.K. Khaparde. For them the first priority was to organize the educated intelligentsia of the scheduled castes, scheduled tribes, other backward classes and minorities into a vanguard dedicated to, and capable of, changing the social system. Khaparde was of the view that until this vanguard was in place it was suicidal to attempt a mass movement, particularly one aiming at electoral politics. The failure of the Republican Party to carry forward Babasaheb Ambedkar's legacy was a result of putting politics before social reform. Khaparde also worried that participation in politics would inevitably compromise and distort basic ideological principles and that would defeat the entire purpose of the bahujan movement.

Kanshi Ram, on the other hand, obsessesively quoted Ambedkar's 'political power is the master key.' He was far too ambitious to be satisfied with running what he knew would never be more than a group of do-gooders with grandiose visions of social change but without the clout to implement them. He also feared that limiting their enterprise to the educated elite of the bahujan samaj restricted it to a fraction of the Dalit community. For more than a decade they had failed to enlist recruits in any numbers from the other backward castes or minorities. Kanshi Ram was also weary of discussing the perfidy of upper castes within a small circle of people, all of whom agreed with each other. He was impatient to proceed with launching a grassroots struggle to challenge the establishment. 'I want to get my teeth into real mass politics instead of going on discussing strategy and tactics,' he told his journalist friend Shenoy in the early eighties.

Mayawati gave Kanshi Ram the courage to move on from BAMCEF. He was delighted to find in her a kindred spirit who yearned for success, albeit driven perhaps more by personal ambition than by the political vision that compelled her mentor. Despite her lack of organizational experience and ideological depth, the young schoolteacher emboldened Kanshi Ram to move forward. Had Mayawati not had this invigorating effect on him, he may have balked at snapping ties with BAMCEF compatriots like Khaparde, even though considerable strain existed over who actually held the reins of the organization. Her unquestioning faith and confidence in him as well, as her youthful fervour for political adventure regardless of the attendant risks, impelled him incontrovertibly towards the larger world of mainstream politics.

During the late seventies and early eighties north India witnessed great political turmoil. The Congress had been ousted from power at the Centre for the first time since independence by a motley coalition of the entire Opposition, many of whose leaders had been under arrest during the Emergency and were fresh out of jail. But despite the initial euphoria of restoring democracy in the country, the new political entity, the Janata Party, did not last long. It collapsed under the weight of its own contradictions, nudged along by the manoeuvrings of the deposed Indira Gandhi and her rogue son, Sanjay. One by one the heroes of March 1977 fell tarnished to the ground. As noted earlier, Jagjivan Ram, the scheduled caste leader who crossed over to the Opposition before the elections, was the first to be humiliated. Soon prime minister Morarji Desai and his government were pulled down by the ambitious home minister Charan Singh, backed by a socialist bloc that was incompatible with the more conservative components of the Janata Party. Along with Desai fell erstwhile rightwing Jana Sangh leaders like Atal Behari Vajpayee, whose membership of the Hindu fundamentalist sect Rashtriya Swayamsevak Sangh (RSS) became the catalyst for the collapse of the Desai government.

The successor Charan Singh government propped up by Indira Gandhi and the Congress, crumbled after she pulled the plug within a few days. Mrs Gandhi continued to twist the knife, demolishing her political opponents in the mid-term elections that followed. Only Charan Singh propped up by a coalition of intermediate and backward castes, garnered a few seats in north India.

Interesting trends within the bahujan samaj were emerging. On the Dalit front, the leadership gap widened in the late seventies and early eighties. The Republican Party, heir to Ambedkar's legacy, further disintegrated under pressure from radical new groups such as the Dalit Panthers. The Panthers fizzled out despite their fiery rhetoric, unable to become a significant force to further Dalit interests. Meanwhile the 1980 Mandal Commission that recommended an additional twenty-seven per cent reservation (over and above the 22.5 percent reservation for scheduled castes and tribes) for other backward classes in both government jobs and institutions of higher education, galvanized the backward castes. These were straws in the wind for Kanshi Ram and they added momentum to his fledgling movement. Most importantly, the field was clear for anybody to fill the political vacuum caused by the Janata Party's inability to provide a national alternative to the Congress behemoth.

Despite the sweeping electoral return by Indira Gandhi and the virtual decimation of the Opposition, Kanshi Ram remained unconvinced of the seeming invincibility of the Congress. It was completely misleading. The old vote banks of the Congress among the scheduled and backward castes as well as the minorities were not as rock solid as they appeared. Their return to the Congress was due to mainstream political parties failing so palpably to provide a feasible political alternative. This did not mark a genuine revival of the ancien regime and its obsolete politics of patronage. With the sudden and untimely death of Mrs Gandhi's favourite son and political hatchet man, Sanjay, in a plane crash barely six months after she stormed back to power, the inherent weaknesses of the Congress became even more apparent.

Kanshi Ram's first major initiative to mobilize sections other than educated scheduled caste employees was conducted in 1980 even before he relinquished BAMCEF. Between April and June that year, the BAMCEF launched its most ambitious venture so far. It was 'Ambedkar on Wheels', a mobile oral and pictorial account of Ambedkar's life and views. It also showed the historical background of the iniquities of the caste system and disseminated information on the contemporary oppression and exploitation of Dalits. The roadshow travelled to thirty-four destinations across nine states of north India. It was an impressive display of organizational skills and mobilization of funds and gave a foretaste of the kind of mass movement that he had dreamt of for all these years. Mayawati's tireless participation was in no small measure responsible for the huge success of 'Ambekdar on Wheels' among Dalits and backwards, many of them poor and illiterate.

By the end of 1981, Kanshi Ram announced a mass platform. It was called 'Dalit Shoshit Samaj Sangharsh Samiti' inventively nicknamed 'DS4'. The new organization rallied around an evocative slogan *'Thakur Brahmin, Bania Chod, Baki Sab Hai DS4'* which pointed out that if you left out the main upper castes of thakurs, brahmins, and banias, what remained were the DS4.. Dalit Shoshit Samaj was a synonym for the bahujan samaj, Kanshi Ram's target audience. Although technically not a political party, the DS4 unlike the BAMCEF actively sought to mobilize a larger body of Dalits, backwards and minorities on major issues that concerned them. It served as a crucial bridge between Kanshi Ram's trade union days as leader of BAMCEF and his emergence as a full-fledged politician.

Significantly, one of the first events organized by the DS4 was a People's Parliament on the lawns of the Boat Club in New Delhi on Christmas Day in 1982. Kanshi Ram explained the rationale for this unique exercise in the BAMCEF magazine, the *Oppressed Indian*: 'People's Parliament will provide them the opportunity for debate and discussion on their burning problems which are side tracked in the National Parliament. Such a debate and discussion if conducted on a large scale over the length and breadth of the vast country can definitely influence the National Parliament. Besides such a debate by the People's Parliament without power will be a constant reminder for the oppressed and exploited masses to make the National Parliament a truly representative one as early as possible.'

The People's Parliament was held shortly after Kanshi Ram published his ideological treatise, *Chamcha Age*, a booklet which was a vitriolic attack on the scheduled caste elite that lambasted them for selling out the interests of their community for personal advancement describing them as 'chamchas' or stooges. 'A tool, an agent, a stooge or a chamcha is created to oppose the real, the genuine fighter,' he declared.[1] Ram chose to publish it on the eve of the golden jubilee of the 1932 Poona pact that the Congress was planning to celebrate with much fanfare. The controversial booklet lashed out at the historic truce between Ambedkar and Gandhi on the former's demand for separate electorates for untouchables. Kanshi Ram wrote that Gandhi with his threat of a fast unto death had blackmailed the Dalit leader into giving up his demand. Asserting that this was a calamity that sealed the political fate of scheduled castes and initiated the chamcha age, it denounced all those who accepted Gandhi and his successors in the Congress. This was yet another indication of his determination to target the Congress as the main enemy of the people.

Another interesting aspect of the treatise was its emphasis on an alliance between the Dalits and other backward castes to combat their common oppressors—the upper castes. Kanshi Ram pointed out that after failing to implement his separate electorate demand for Dalits after the country became independent, Ambedkar had spent his last few years trying to broad base his movement with an alliance with other backward castes. Significantly, the booklet empathized more with the plight of the backward castes pointing out that they did not even have the benefits of reservation as compared to the 22.5 per cent reservation for scheduled castes and tribes 'even though their representatives remained chamchas of the ruling castes'.

Kanshi Ram also outlined a plan of future action in this booklet, which was widely distributed to activists of the BAMCEF and the DS4. His strategy to challenge the caste system offered both a short and a long-term solution. The short-term solution was social action for which the DS4 was deemed the ideal vehicle. Kanshi Ram spoke about the formation of Awakening Squads that would spread out all over the countryside mobilizing the Dalit Shoshit Samaj on general and specific issues. Curiously, the strategy called for a wide range of social movements incorporating 'mild to wild' activities. To quote: 'By and large social action should be mild, but continuous without any break. It may be in one form or another, may be for one cause or another. To make it meaningful and effective occasionally it will have to be wild, but non-violent. It will all depend upon the types of struggles.'

The long-term solution Kanshi Ram prescribed was political action with the formation of a political party. He said that since all the national parties were controlled by upper castes and perpetuated their stranglehold over society, the Dalit Shoshit Samaj was helpless despite having eighty-five per cent of the votes. 'It is widely felt that we must have our own political party. In the past some efforts were made, but without success. Recently we have conducted some experiments towards building such a party. Such experimentations known as Limited Political Action will be further conducted till we feel sure of forming a political party of National level on our own. Through such a party of the Dalit Shoshit Samaj political action for putting an end to the chamcha age will be launched.'

Armed with this ideology expounded by Kanshi Ram in *Chamcha Age*, the DS4's Awakening Squads spread out across north India. There were several campaigns launched including a forty-day-long 'cycle march' in March 1983 when a hundred leaders and activists cycled a distance of 3,000 kilometres criss-crossing seven states around the capital New Delhi. The march called 'The miracle of two feet and two wheels', captured the imagination of rural Dalits and backwards who were used to netas visiting them in a long procession of cars. When criticized for using outdated conveyance for political mobilization in an era of automobiles and planes, Kanshi Ram retorted, 'Trucks, tractors, buses, cars and rail are all in the hands of capitalists and those who are holding power. They can use them conveniently as and when they need them for their own benefit. The very same facilities cannot be available to the oppressed and exploited people. They cannot organize their agitation around these machines. (The) bicycle is the best weapon for them in their agitation. If their two feet are all right they can reach any place to make their presence felt.'[2] Indeed, through the eighties, the bicycle became the favourite mode of transport for both leaders and workers of the DS4 and later of the BSP. Mayawati herself became an expert cyclist and though she is only seen today descending from a helicopter, old-timers remember her on a cycle with her pigtail flying, scouring the dusty mud paths of the Uttar Pradesh countryside in the eighties.

The DS4 existed for less than three years, but it will be remembered for launching a highly provocative and aggressive propaganda campaign against the upper castes the like of which have not been seen in north India before or after. Considering the lowly economic and social status of Dalits across north India and the small number of activists that the organization had in its initial stages, it required enormous courage and determination to have taken up such confrontationist postures against rural elites well entrenched for centuries. Indeed, this very no-holds-barred combativeness helped the DS4 send ripples across the region, particularly in Uttar Pradesh and also in Punjab.

Activists of the DS4 were able to get away with their provocative war of words against the upper castes without being physically assaulted by the latter largely because they limited themselves to a propaganda exercise. Kanshi Ram and Mayawati shrewdly avoided any kind of mass agitation that would bring them into direct conflict with either the state machinery or the upper castes. This also placed the Congress—the main target of DS4 propaganda—in a dilemma over its response to this challenge that threatened to rob the party of its scheduled caste vote bank. Had the DS4 like other radical groups sought to fight street battles or caste wars on behalf of the Dalits and other oppressed communities, the Congress could have used the police and courts to break the back of the bahujan movement. But there was no way in a democracy to stop a campaign whose only purpose was to capture minds. The extraordinary vision of the caste pyramid being turned upside down and the in-your-face manner with which this message was conveyed demanded immediate attention. What also helped was a series of pithy slogans that reverberated in the Uttar Pradesh countryside for nearly two decades until Kanshi Ram and Mayawati decided to soften their approach to upper castes.

The most controversial one, '*Tilak, taraju aur talwar, isko maro joota char*' called upon the Dalits and backwards to use their shoes to beat the brahmin represented by the distinctive mark painted on his forehead, the tilak, the banya symbolized by the taraju or a pair of scales and the thakur represented by the talwar or the sword. Upper castes were stunned at the audacity of the slogan even as it impressed the lower castes for the same reason. More than two decades later when trying to woo support from a section of the upper castes, Mayawati would deny any link with this particular slogan. But there is no denying the widespread use of the slogan by cadres of the DS4 as well as the Bahujan Samaj Party well into the late nineties. Equally effective in capturing the Dalit imagination were the meetings in the early days when Kanshi Ram would begin his speech by declaring that if there were any upper caste members of the audience they should leave for their own safety.

Other popular slogans were 'Vote *hamara, Raj tumhara, Nahi chalega, Nahi chalega* (We have the votes, but you have the power, this won't do, this won't do)'and '*Jiski Jitni Sankhya Bhari, Uski Utni Bhagedari*'—those with the largest numbers should be the best represented. Another voiced the need to simultaneously capture both the political establishment as well as the bureaucracy—'Vote *se lenge* PM/CM, *Aarakshan se lenge* SP/DM'—which targeted the posts of prime minister and chief minister through elections and the posts of superintendent of police and district magistrate through the reservation quota.

Was part of the virulent rhetoric against the upper castes mere political posturing by Kanshi Ram? His close journalist friend T.V.R. Shenoy insists that even in the early eighties, two decades before Mayawati actively wooed brahmins for electoral advantage, Ram in private conversation spoke about an ultimate alliance between brahmins and Dalits against the intermediate castes whose economic and political clout was increasing every day. At the same time, his speeches and writings in that period clearly targeted the upper castes that because of historic reasons were obvious objects of hate to the bahujan samaj.

The DS4 concentrated its efforts in some key north Indian states, most notably, Uttar Pradesh, Madhya Pradesh, Punjab and Haryana. Of these it was Uttar Pradesh and Punjab that appeared to hold the most promise. Uttar Pradesh, the country's largest state was clearly a prime target not just because of its size but also its caste break-up. The state had a sizeable Dalit population dominated by the chamar sub-caste to which both Kanshi Ram and Mayawati belonged. Apart from the Dalits, there were also a large variety of other backward castes as well as a sizeable Muslim minority and even a partial combination of the three segments would be decisive in electoral outcome. As for Punjab, the sheer proportion of Dalits—nearly twenty-nine per cent of the population—was higher than in any other state in the country and clearly fertile ground for the bahujan samaj's political efforts.

In Uttar Pradesh, Kanshi Ram was delighted to have already broken the ice with other backward castes and minorities. He enlisted the dynamic Kurmi leader, Jang Bahadur Patel, who later became president of the Uttar Pradesh unit of the Bahujan Samaj Party. He befriended Dr Masood Ahmed, a lecturer from Aligarh Muslim University, earlier with the Congress but known to be looking for an alternative since the early eighties when Indira Gandhi flirted with soft Hindutva. Kanshi Ram was very keen on a triumvirate by incorporating Mayawati as leader of the Dalits, Patel representing the backward castes and Dr Ahmed mobilizing Muslims to lead the charge in Uttar Pradesh. Many years later, Patel and Ahmed would abandon Kanshi Ram and his cause because they fell out with Mayawati, but in the early eighties as the DS4 found its feet in Uttar Pradesh, the emergence of all these leaders from diverse sections of the bahujan samaj gave an added impetus to the movement.

In Punjab, the DS4 made rapid progress in mobilizing the Dalit Sikh community which had been a loyal vote bank for the Congress for many years; now they were looking for an alternative. The fact that Kanshi Ram himself came from Punjab also helped the organization. In a relatively short period of time, it made a mark for itself particularly in the Doaba area including the Congress bastions of Jullundur, Hoshiarpur, Kapurthala and Nawasahar. Considering the importance of the Dalit vote bank for the Congress in the traditional see-saw battle with its main political rival, the Akalis, party leaders who would have otherwise been quite dismissive of the DS4, began to worry at what appeared to be a dangerous subversion of the party's electoral prospects.

However, the dramatic advent of extremist violence across Punjab in 1983 cast a long shadow on the state. The spiral of terrorist killings that marked the rise of Sikh fundamentalist leader Sant Jarnail Singh Bhindranwale, disrupted every kind of normal activity in Punjab including the campaign launched among Dalit Sikhs by the DS4. Very soon this bloody turn of events snowballed into a political cataclysm with the storming of the Golden Temple by the Indian Army dealing a major blow to the fledgling Dalit movement in the state from which it never did quite recover. In the bitter aftermath, Sikh religious fundamentalism overwhelmed public consciousness in Punjab, making it difficult for political leaders and groups that sought to highlight social discrimination and exploitation. Having failed to gather full momentum at the outset, Kanshi Ram and his politics never fulfilled their potential in the state despite its vast scheduled caste population even after the tide of religiosity ebbed later in the state.

The cataclysmic events in Punjab were only a harbinger of even grimmer days ahead beyond the state. Prime Minister Indira Gandhi's assassination by her own Sikh bodyguards, the ghastly anti-Sikh riots that followed and Rajiv Gandhi's sweeping victory in the Lok Sabha polls overwhelmed every other development in the country. Not surprisingly, Kanshi Ram's formal transfer from social action to politics with the formation of the Bahujan Samaj Party (BSP) on 14 April 1984 went almost unnoticed in media and political circles, obsessed as they were with the larger picture.

Indeed, mainstream politicians as well as the media largely ignored the huge meeting in New Delhi attended by several lakh Dalits that greeted the launching of the BSP. This had been preceded by cross-country cycle processions by DS4 leaders and activists for a hundred-day non-stop countrywide campaign that incorporated as many as seven thousand meetings on the way. Nobody paid much attention to these frenzied preparations as Kanshi Ram and Mayawati (who promptly resigned from her teaching job to become a fulltime politician) started their political quest. The birth of the BSP created barely a blip on the national radar screen giving little indication of the formidable force it would become in Indian politics.

Barely had the party been formed, than a series of national catastrophes overtook India: Operation Bluestar, the Bhopal gas disaster, Indira Gandhi's assassination and the anti-Sikh riots. The BSP's entry into the electoral fray in the 1984 Lok Sabha polls could not have come at a more inopportune moment. There was a tidal wave of nationwide support for Rajiv Gandhi and the Congress in the aftermath of the Indira Gandhi assassination, sweeping the ruling party to a record victory. In an election where even major political parties were decimated, a fledgling party like the BSP stood little chance to win its spurs.

Strictly speaking, the 1984 poll was not Kanshi Ram's first foray into electoral politics. Earlier, even before the BSP was formed, the DS4 had propped up as many as forty-six independent candidates in the Haryana assembly elections of 1982 and several dozen more in the Uttar Pradesh assembly polls of 1983. They failed to make much of an impact except to raise eyebrows at the DS4's provocative election graffiti that appeared in Dalit hamlets and urban ghettos. But with the birth of the BSP in the summer of 1984, the Lok Sabha polls at the end of the year provided the arena for the formal political debut of Kanshi Ram's movement.

The 1984 Lok Sabha poll was the first time that Mayawati and Kanshi Ram contested any kind of elections. Since the BSP was as yet unrecognized by the Election Commission as a political party and not allotted a symbol, both contested as independent candidates—Mayawati from Kairana parliamentary constituency in Muzaffarnagar district of western Uttar Pradesh, and Kanshi Ram from Janjgir constituency then in Madhya Pradesh but now in the state of Chhattisgarh. Interestingly, that both were unreserved constituencies underscores the BSP's still tentative relationship with the Dalit electorate.

Considering the odds, the twenty-eight-year-old political debutante put up a creditable performance in her first electoral foray. Although she was beaten easily by the winner, Akhtar Hassan of the Congress who got 2,36,094 votes and the runner up Shyam Singh of the Lok Dal who bagged 1,38,355 votes, Mayawati came third with 44,445 votes beating the Janata Party candidate who managed a mere 9,376 votes and other independents all of whom got a few thousand votes each. Kanshi Ram also lost from his constituency in Madhya Pradesh, receiving around nine per cent of the vote.

Undaunted, Mayawati was back at the hustings next year in a high profile parliamentary by-election from Bijnore (reserved) constituency in Uttar Pradesh. The triangular contest included Jagjivan Ram's granddaughter Meira Kumar and emerging Dalit leader Ram Vilas Paswan. She came third once again but managed to increase her votes to over sixty thousand in an election that saw Meira Kumar squeezing past Paswan by barely five thousand votes. In fact, the large number of Dalit votes, which traditionally went to the Congress, were garnered by Mayawati, and this was, perhaps, one of the main reasons for the narrow margin of Meira Kumar's victory. This was a big blow to the Congress that had projected her as the political legatee of Jagjivan Ram, the foremost post-independence scheduled caste leader. On the other hand, the entire mainstream Opposition had banded together to prop up Paswan, who thereby had the support of the sizeable upper caste

population in the constituency. Despite her second successive
electoral defeat, Mayawati could take heart from the fact that as
an unknown independent candidate from a party still unrecognized
by the Election Commission, she had held her own in such a high
profile contest between political heavyweights.

In May 1987, Mayawati tried her luck once again in a
parliamentary by-election, this time from Haridwar (reserved)
constituency. The BSP was now recognized by the Election
Commission as a political party and she contested on her party
symbol. Although failing to win, she managed a respectable tally
of over one lakh thirty thousand votes, not far behind the winning
Congress candidate. Sweeter still was her truimph in relegating
Ram Vilas Paswan, also a contestant, to third place. Paswan lost
his deposit and never contested from Uttar Pradesh again. This
was further indication that the BSP was steadily improving its
prospects in Uttar Pradesh and Mayawati herself gaining public
stature.

Kanshi Ram was the biggest admirer of Mayawati's progress as
the BSP's political spearhead in Uttar Pradesh. He was quite
overwhelmed at the distance she had covered since she resigned
her schoolteacher's job in 1984 and plunged into politics as a full-
timer. Several years later he would describe his protégé's great leap
forward in some detail:

> General elections to the Parliament were held in December
> 1984. She decided to contest. There was no chance for
> anybody in the Bahujan Samaj Party to win that election.
> Everybody advised her not to contest that election because
> as a government servant she was required to lose the job.
> Again her courage was put to test. She picked up courage
> and left the job to fight that election. After that election,
> she was jobless, but her seniors were safe in their job.
> Keeping her condition in mind, I gave her support and
> more and more opportunities in the organization. In 1985,
> she was told to prepare the parliamentary seat of Bijnore
> for the by-election. She went from village to village and
> prepared the seat well to increase the vote bank from
> 5700 votes to 65,000 within a period of one year. Another
> by-election in the nearby seat of Haridwar came next. She
> prepared it so well that she came second to the ruling

Congress Party. By securing 1,36,000 votes she improved
the vote bank of BSP 14 times, from 9,000 in the general
election to 1,36,000 in the by-election. I was happy with
her performance in these by-elections. But her seniors
became furious. They put pressure on me for giving
opportunity to Mayawati. So much so that most of them
left the movement. I do not know where they are today,
where as Mayawati kept improving along with the
movement.[3]

The next year Kanshi Ram himself decided to jump into another
high profile contest that pitted Vishwanath Pratap Singh, who
had resigned over the Bofors scandal from both Rajiv Gandhi's
cabinet and the Congress. He stood against the official party
candidate, Sunil Shastri, son of the late prime minister Lal
Bahadur Shastri. They were to fight in a parliamentary by-election
for the Allahabad seat vacated by filmstar-turned-politician Amitabh
Bachchan who had decided to leave politics in the stormy
aftermath of the Bofors controversy. With a united Opposition
projecting Singh as its leader and a back-to-the-wall Congress
pushing the entire party machinery to make a stand at Allahabad,
the by-election had acquired larger than life proportions. Displaying
characteristic impudence, Kanshi Ram chose to stick his finger in
and stir the pot in Allahabad knowing fully well that if nothing
else he and the BSP would get huge nationwide publicity in the
bargain.

The results vindicated Kanshi Ram's self-confidence. While
Singh romped home with over two lakh votes, the Congress
candidate Shastri could not even manage one lakh votes, even as
the BSP leader got almost seventy thousand votes most of it
snatched from the traditional Dalit vote bank of the ruling party.
All of a sudden the national media started noticing the BSP for
the first time. Several newspapers and periodicals while covering
the rise of the V.P. Singh phenomenon, also noted the crucial
subversive role being played by the BSP in closing the lid on Rajiv
Gandhi and the Congress. The fact that the Congress had lost so
many Dalit votes to the BSP, first in Bijnore and now in
Allahabad, underlined the latter's growing political clout at least
as a spoiler for the ruling party in Uttar Pradesh. While the
dangers posed by the new party to Congress electoral prospects in

some north Indian states was visible even earlier, for instance in Punjab, where the ruling party's defeat by the Akalis in the 1985 state assembly polls was partially influenced by Dalit Sikh votes taken away by BSP-supported candidates, it is only after Bijnore and even more so the Allahabad parliamentary by-election, that there was some recognition in media and political circles about the increasing importance of the BSP.

As the BSP's determination to hurt the electoral prospects of the Congress became more and more palpable, the latter became increasingly fearful at what was threatening to develop into much more than a minor annoyance. Congress leaders began to question the source of the BSP's funding. How did it manage to contest so many elections and by-elections, considering that the party claimed to represent only the very poorest sections of society? There were even allegations that the CIA—a favourite Congress bogey from the early seventies—was secretly funding the new party. BSP leaders laughed away these charges. As Kanshi Ram pointed out at one public meeting, 'List all the traitors exposed in various spy scandals after independence. You won't find a single lower caste person; they all belong to the upper castes!'

It was not just the Congress that was getting jittery about the rise of the BSP across north India in the eighties. The RSS, which had its own plans for reviving the BJP in the region, was getting worried about this unexpected challenge from political outsiders. Writing in the *Oppressed Indian* in April 1985, Kanshi Ram pointed out, 'The measure of the BSP's success in uniting such victims of Brahminism can be assessed from the fears of the RSS. The annual reports of the RSS released on 15th March 1985, devoted a full para to such a success of the BSP in uniting the oppressed and exploited caste groups and securing brotherhood against them. . . . In the eyes of the RSS such a success of the BSP is the greatest danger to the Hindu fundamentalist.' That this was not an idle boast was confirmed by the RSS chief Balasaab Deoras who was quoted by the *Illustrated Weekly of India* in 1988 describing the BSP as ' one of the real problems for the RSS in north India'.

The repeated electoral forays in Uttar Pradesh were also accompanied by a sustained public awareness campaign in the state, mostly spearheaded by Mayawati. Travelling on cycle or on foot, she relentlessly toured the countryside, occasionally addressing several meetings in a single day. Her audience comprised Dalits, lower backward castes and poor Muslims—the very bottom of the social and economic heap in rural Uttar Pradesh. They had never ever seen a leader like Mayawati before. Many village women marvelled at the unprecedented sight of a young girl still in her twenties striding confidently into a domain where women kept a very low public profile. The village folk were astounded at the authority with which she spoke as if she owned the place. An account in her autobiography describes the way Mayawati roused her audience at public meetings during a padyatra in Nainital in September 1986. It gives us a fascinating glimpse of how she built a mass base among the poor and exploited in Uttar Pradesh that served her so well in later years.

Mayawati began by posing a question addressed to her largely Dalit audience and traditional Congress voters. 'Can you name me even one Dalit family in this village or in the surrounding region who has prospered because of the various economic welfare schemes like pig herding, rickshaw pulling, leather tanning, etc., initiated by the Congress government over the past forty years?' There was complete silence since nobody could think of any Dalit family they knew who had prospered. Mayawati remarked, 'So, you do admit that the Dalits have been fooled by the Congress.' The audience replied after some hesitation 'Yes, the Congress has fooled of all of us.'

Mayawati fired her second question, 'In every election since the first one in 1952, ninety-five per cent of the Congress votes have been from Dalits and only five per cent from the brahmins. But in states ruled by the Congress or at the centre, only five per cent of the ministers are Dalits and nearly fifty-five per cent of them are brahmins! Out of the twenty-two state chief ministers in the land, not even one is a Dalit. Why do you think this is so?' The crowd roared back, 'You are right. We have been fooled by the Congress.'

She then asked, 'We all know that upper caste manuwadis do not want Dalits to eat well, dress well or do well, so do you think a machine can be built in Delhi or in some other part of the country that can suddenly change the hearts of all these upper-caste ministers and leaders so that they will help Dalits to prosper?' By then the crowd, quite agitated, shook their heads vigorously saying, 'That is impossible! They hate us too much, they will never want us to do well!'

Her next question was, 'Today, Dalits have managed to get a few doctors, engineers, IAS officers from their community thanks to the reservations enshrined in the Constitution by Babasaheb Ambedkar. Do you think he would have been able to do anything for the Dalits if he did not form his own organization and joined a manuwadi party?' The audience replied, 'No way! They would have never let him do it.'

Finally, she would pose the crucial question, 'So, don't you want that eighty-five per cent of the population who are the oppressed and exploited form their own party? Are you not waiting for the day when this overwhelming majority take power in their own hands and change their destiny?' Thunderous slogans of 'Kanshi Ram you fight on, we are all with you' and 'Mayawati you fight on, we are all with you' brought the meeting to a close.

Significantly, both Kanshi Ram and Mayawati carried on a sustained campaign through the eighties demanding the implementation of the Mandal Commission report submitted in 1980. They sought to do so well before a controversy erupted over the report in 1990 after V.P. Singh as prime minister of the shaky Janata Dal government announced its implementation in a bid to checkmate political opponents like Devi Lal. With Rajiv Gandhi and other Congress leaders maintaining a diplomatic silence on Mandal Commission report, Kanshi Ram and Mayawati held a series of demonstrations and meetings across north India agitating for reservations in higher education and government jobs as recommended by the commission. The campaign intensified as the country headed for another general election in 1989.

In hindsight, the BSP's emphasis on backward caste reservations on the eve of the 1989 polls presents an interesting contrast to the parallel campaign against the Congress by other Opposition parties led by rebel Congress leader V.P. Singh. Singh and his camp followers, however, chose to highlight corruption in high places as symbolized by the Bofors scandal. It is significant that the man who played the Mandal card in such a big way after he came to power was hardly concerned about backward caste reservations while campaigning to oust the Congress regime. This just goes to prove that Mandal was a tactical sleight of hand played by the thakur leader rather than a fundamental ideological belief. For Kanshi Ram and Mayawati, on the other hand, the backward castes were a core component of the bahujan samaj they sought to lead. This made the reservations promised to backwards by the Mandal Commission report a vital political issue, not a mere tactical ploy.

The BSP did not ignore the Muslim community either. They held many meetings in the mid- and late eighties in the Muslim villages and ghettos of north India in a bid to mobilize the minority community. It held 'Bhaichara Banao' (Build Brotherhood) programmes not only in Dalit and backward caste localities, but also in Muslim areas. This included a well-attended meeting in Delhi's Jama Masjid on 15 December 1987 where Mayawati gave a fiery speech urging Muslims to join the alliance of Dalits and backward castes. She received a loud ovation as she described the plight of Muslims after independence. 'Only two per cent of Muslims are now employed in the government as compared to thirty-three per cent before 1947. And when Muslims after being denied employment try to make their own living by starting shops and businesses, these upper caste manuwadis get sleepless nights. So they regularly organize riots wherever Muslims are trying to prosper—in Allahabad, Bhiwandi, Aligarh, Jamshedpur. . . . All the riots are a manuwadi conspiracy to get Dalits, backward castes and minorities like Muslims and Sikhs to fight among themselves so that they don't unite under one banner and challenge the rule of the upper castes!' Interestingly, in the same meeting held more than a year before the Babri Masjid and Ram Janambhoomi became a matter of public controversy, Mayawati made a strong plea for the mosque to be handed over to the Muslims accusing upper caste Hindus for snatching away the minority community's historic right to the site.

The 1989 Lok Sabha polls gave Kanshi Ram and Mayawati the opportunity to test the success of these sustained efforts in north India to enlist support from the different communities of the bahujan samaj which they had undertaken from the early eighties. It was a performance with which they could be justifiably satisfied. In an election where the big story was, of course, the ouster of Rajiv Gandhi and his Congress party, and the formation of the V.P. Singh-led minority Janata Dal regime supported by both the Left and the right wing BJP, the BSP's maiden entry into Parliament was a small but important sidelight.

The BSP managed to win three parliamentary seats including the Bijnore (reserved) constituency in Uttar Pradesh from where

Mayawati romped home getting 1,83,189 votes, winning by a comfortable margin of nearly ten thousand votes over her nearest Janata Dal candidate. She also contested the Haridwar (reserved) seat, and though she was unsuccessful, still managed to get over a lakh votes. The BSP also won from Azamgarh in Uttar Pradesh and from Phillaur in Punjab. In both states it was an impressive performance by a party of meagre financial resources that had started from scratch just a few years ago. In Uttar Pradesh the BSP received nearly ten per cent of the vote, beating the BJP which had less than 7.5 per cent to the third place behind the Congress and the Janata Dal. In Punjab too, the BSP came third garnering a handsome 8.62 per cent. Madhya Pradesh, where the new party appeared to have prospects, gave it 4.28 per cent of the vote, though it failed to win a seat. On a national scale, the BSP contested 245 seats, won 2.07 per cent of the national vote and three seats in Parliament.

The results from Uttar Pradesh were particularly encouraging. Apart from the two seats the BSP won, it managed to get more than twenty per cent of the vote in at least half a dozen seats, and more than 15 per cent in another dozen. In the state assembly polls held along with the Lok Sabha elections, the BSP managed to win thirteen seats and roughly the same percentage of votes as in the Lok Sabha. Though Kanshi Ram himself lost from the East Delhi constituency, the good results from Uttar Pradesh and Punjab and the reasonable performance in Madhya Pradesh was a vindication of his gamble to abandon the safe haven of pure social activism and enter mainstream politics. For Mayawati it was a personal feather in her cap, fulfilling her long-cherished dream of entering Parliament—and added to this was the satisfaction of spearheading the BSP's good showing in Uttar Pradesh.

Parliament opened a new world for Mayawati. For the first few weeks, she was awestruck at the elaborate procedures governing the two Houses. Although, the thirty-three-year-old political novice hardly knew anybody in Parliament, she was eager to learn from anyone who was willing to teach her the many parliamentary rules and regulations. With characteristic fortitude she did not let the imposing façade of parliamentary democracy and its complicated rules intimidate her. For instance, she was fascinated by the practice—mostly adopted by Opposition MPs—where the lawmakers would rush to the well of the House when they were prevented by the Speaker from raising certain issues. Soon, Mayawati became an ardent exponent of this tactic and her first stint in Parliament is remembered for her noisy interventions.

On most occasions, Mayawati's charges to the well of the House were provoked by atrocities against Dalits reported from different parts of the country. Ajay Singh, minister of state for railways and Janata Dal member of Parliament from Agra, remembers a harrowing onslaught by Mayawati on his very first day in Parliament. Ignoring the Speaker's pleas to maintain parliamentary decorum, she rushed to the well charging Singh—who belonged to the Jat community—of personally raping twenty-three women in Agra in a Jat raid on Jatav localities in the city. The outlandish allegation completely flummoxed Singh, still new to his parliamentarian and ministerial duties, and provoked much laughter in the House. Recovering his wits, Singh, a former student of Delhi's elite St Stephen's college, tried to make light of the matter with the wisecrack, 'Behenji, I have one wife and can barely handle her! What chance of me trying to tangle with two dozen women?' The House dissolved in laughter for the second time, but the sarcasm did not impress Mayawati who kept up her barrage of abuses and accusations.

Her rough-and-ready ways in the House raised eyebrows and provoked criticism from traditionalists in Parliament who felt that she was a typical example of the deteriorating standards of parliamentary debate. Mayawati's oiled and plaited hair and casually dressed appearance reportedly affronted or amused other more 'sophisticated' women members of Parliament, most of whom came from royal houses and aristocratic families. They even complained she sweated too much and asked a senior MP to advise her to use a stronger perfume!

Mayawati's first stint in Parliament was short-lived. The chronically unstable V.P. Singh-led Janata Dal regime, dependant on both the Left Front and the right-wing BJP, collapsed in less than a year. It was replaced by an even more miniscule ministry led by the Janata Dal rebel faction leader, Chandra Shekhar, and supported from the outside by the Congress—a replay of the disastrous Charan Singh-led experiment barely a decade ago. This, too, crumbled in no time bringing the curtain down on the eleventh Lok Sabha and forcing mid-term general elections on the country.

Not only did Mayawati lose her seat in Parliament, the BSP was also quite overwhelmed by the political turmoil sweeping north India. On the one hand, V.P. Singh's sudden and dramatic decision to implement the Mandal Commission report to quell the revolt inside the Janata Dal, provoked caste battles on the streets. While Janata Dal leaders including V.P. Singh, Ram Vilas Paswan and Sharad Yadav donned the mantle of backward caste messiahs, upper-caste students, with covert backing from sections of the BJP and the Congress, carried out a violent agitation across north India. All of a sudden the BSP was nowhere in the picture, despite being amongst the first political parties to raise its voice on behalf of the backward castes. The Janata Dal, by virtue of being in government and because its organizational network was far larger than that of the BSP, comprehensively hijacked the Mandal issue.

To complicate matters further for Kanshi Ram and Mayawati, the BJP initially stunned by V.P. Singh's Mandal card, recovered hastily to play the Kamandal—the Ram Janambhoomi—card with party leader Lal Krishna Advani setting out on his infamous rathyatra. The movement to demolish the Babri Masjid and build a Ram temple in its place picked up further momentum after Mulayam Singh Yadav, the then chief minister of Uttar Pradesh, ordered the police to fire upon a group of Hindu holy men marching towards the disputed shrine. This resulted in heavy casualties and provoked a huge backlash in the majority community. Significantly, a prime objective of RSS and BJP strategists, as they sought to exploit this unprecedented Hindu fervour, was to win back the loyalty of the backward castes and divert them from a battle with the upper castes on the reservation issue. Once again, the BSP was caught on the wrong foot and watched helplessly as backward castes, including a large segment of kurmis who earlier seemed to be tilting towards the bahujan movement, turned into Ram bhakts and karsevaks overnight.

More drama was added to an already surcharged political atmosphere by the assassination of Rajiv Gandhi by a Tamil Tiger suicide bomber in the middle of the Lok Sabha mid-term polls in the summer of 1991. Although the Congress seemed to be in serious trouble in north India finding both the Mandal and the Kamandal issues too hot to handle, the assassination helped the party to snatch back power at the Centre by the skin of its teeth. Riding on a sympathy wave triggered by the loss of yet another

Gandhi to a terrorist strike, the Congress managed to get around forty to fifty bonus seats that allowed it to form a government with the help of smaller parties and groups. Quite a few of these extra seats were from Uttar Pradesh with Dalits and some poorer backward castes going back to their old political patron in a knee-jerk emotional response.

All these factors contributed to the disappointing show by the BSP in the 1991 Lok Sabha elections. Instead of improving on its encouraging performance in 1989 it came down from three to two seats, one from Uttar Pradesh and the other from Madhya Pradesh. Mayawati lost from both her constituencies Haridwar and Bijnore. In Haridwar she got barely 22,000 votes slipping to fourth place, her performance in Bijnore was a bit better with more than one-and-a-half lakh votes but still nearly a lakh less than the BJP winner. In Uttar Pradesh, the BSP's vote percentage slipped from ten to 8.4 even as the BJP climbed to an amazing 32.5 per cent yielding the party fifty-one parliamentary seats from the state. Similar results in state assembly polls held along with the Lok Sabha elections saw the BSP's tally coming down from thirteen to twelve seats and the vote percentage slipping several decimal points. Kanshi Ram's entry into the Lok Sabha from Etawah constituency as the sole BSP winner from Uttar Pradesh was the only good news.

Although the BSP did manage to win the Ferozepur seat when Lok Sabha polls were held in Punjab in 1992, there was a sense of disquiet within the party. With passions running high all over north India on the Mandal and Kamandal issues, the novelty of the BSP had faded a bit. Mayawati herself was rattled by the comprehensive defeats in both her constituencies. Desperate to get back into Parliament, she fought a Lok Sabha by-election at the first opportunity. This was from Bulandshahr in western Uttar Pradesh in November 1991. But she lost again, managing to get barely 67,000 votes and coming third—way behind the BJP winner and Congress runner-up. She managed to pester Kanshi Ram into giving her a ticket from Hoshiarpur for the 1992 Lok Sabha polls in Punjab, the only time she has contested outside Uttar Pradesh. Unfortunately, she lost yet again, although considering she was an outsider to the state, it was a creditable performance to get more than 90,000 votes and come second.

In the early nineties, the prospects for the BSP, or for that matter any other party except the BJP, seemed grim. Riding high on the Ram Janambhoomi movement, the BJP had swept both the parliamentary polls and the state assembly polls in Uttar Pradesh held in 1991. The party seemed invincible particularly in Uttar Pradesh where it formed a stable majority government led by Kalyan Singh, belonging to the Lodh backward caste—a clever ploy by the upper caste-dominated BJP to further consolidate support from the backward castes who had already been co-opted into the movement for the Ram temple.

Just when the Sangh Parivar appeared set to launch itself across the country after capturing the largest state, it made the fundamental mistake of allowing a frenzied mob of Hindu zealots to demolish the Babri Masjid in December 1992. The demolition, in flagrant violation of a Supreme Court order, was widely criticized by the national media and attracted the wrath of the central government ruled by the Congress. At one stroke, the demolition removed—along with the dilapidated mosque—the most potent symbol with which it had mobilized different sections of Hindu society. As a matter of fact, some commentators even suggested that the then prime minister, Narasimha Rao, reputed for his Machiavellian cunning, had deliberately allowed the mob to demolish the Babri Masjid to kill two birds with one stone—get rid of the disputed shrine and the BJP's most potent political mascot.

The immediate impact of the demolition was certainly negative for the BJP, which lost key governments in north India. The Kalyan Singh government in Uttar Pradesh was the first to go, the chief minister resigning before he could be sacked by New Delhi. Soon BJP governments in several other north Indian states followed suit. Although the demolition further communalized the political atmosphere, the isolation of the BJP made it easier for other parties to sink their differences and come together in a concerted bid to counter the saffron surge.

This is precisely what happened in the run up to the mid-term state assembly polls in Uttar Pradesh held in 1993. Two regional forces, Mulayam Singh Yadav's Samajwadi Party and Kanshi Ram's BSP struck a historic alliance to tame their common enemy—the BJP. The two leaders had already tasted personal electoral success by joining hands in the 1991 Lok Sabha polls. They helped each other to win in adjoining parliamentary constituencies—Kanshi Ram from Etawah and Mulayam Singh from Jaswant Nagar—in an election where the BJP rode high in most constituencies. Apart from the tactical compulsion of containing the BJP, there were ideological bonds as well: both parties were strong votaries of Mandal politics and the policy of caste-based reservations.

Mulayam Singh and Kanshi Ram struck a deal at a secret meeting at the Ashoka Hotel in October 1993. The deal was clinched in the room of industrialist Jayant Malhoutra, perhaps the first businessman to have taken the gamble of investing in Kanshi Ram and the BSP. Malhoutra claimed that his assistance to Kanshi Ram was motivated by concern to help bring about a 'soft landing' for India after the inevitable clash between the haves and the have-nots.[4] Another industrialist, Sanjay Dalmia, who was close to Mulayam Singh, also played a key role in brokering the deal. The two industrialists had familial connections and knew each other well. This further helped to cement the political arrangement. Significantly, both were rewarded for their efforts within a few months with Rajya Sabha seats: Malhoutra was nominated by the BSP and Dalmia by Samajwadi Party in early 1994.

The prime minister Narasimha Rao and the Congress party, who were determined to short-circuit the advance of the BJP at all costs, blessed the arrangement. Kanshi Ram kept Mayawati away from the deal-making exercise perhaps fearing that his volatile protégé could complicate the delicate negotiations. This enabled the BSP president to be fairly magnanimous in the seat-sharing with the Samajwadi Party. In fact, Mulayam Singh acknowledged this generosity in conversations with local journalists at that time. Even during the election campaign, Mayawati, considering that she was the public face of the BSP in Uttar Pradesh, did not play a very high-profile role sticking mainly to her turf in the western part of the state. In hindsight, these pinpricks dealt to her ego before the 1993 polls may well have played a role in fomenting trouble for the alliance after it came to power.

However, as an electoral combine the alliance was a phenomenal success. The combination of Dalits and a whole range of backward castes, backed by a consolidated Muslim vote desperate to see the back of BJP rule in Uttar Pradesh, ultimately proved too powerful even for the seemingly unstoppable Hindutva juggernaut.

Although the BJP managed to emerge as the single largest party with 177 seats, this fell well short of a majority. The party watched helplessly as the Samajwadi Party with 109 seats and the BSP with sixty-seven seats crafted a coalition government with the help of the Congress, smaller parties and independents. Isolated from the political mainstream in the aftermath of the demolition, the BJP could not make a similar bid despite being the largest party.

Mulayam Singh Yadav became chief minister and the BSP bagged eleven ministerial portfolios in a cabinet of twenty-seven. Although Mayawati did not join the government she was given the more powerful task of supervising the functioning of the alliance. Overlooking the claims of several more senior leaders in the BSP, Kanshi Ram gave a carte blanche to Mayawati to do whatever was required to ensure that the new government in Lucknow pursued the BSP agenda. In less than a decade after its birth, the party was in a position to actually dictate government policy and that too in the country's largest state. Kanshi Ram had finally managed to grasp at least a part of the master key.

# FIVE

# A Doomed Alliance

*Pragati disha, Nav nidhi ki dhor,*
*Vir Mulayam chahun dish oar,*
*Kanshi Ram ka lag gaya zor,*
*Vir Mulayam, chahun dish oar*

(The beacon of progress is lit by the first rays of the sun,
Brave Mulayam you are hailed from all directions,
The strength of Kanshi Ram is with you,
Brave Mulayam you are hailed from all directions)

𝒯his was the chorus of a song written by a Mulayam Singh Yadav acolyte (who also happened to be a former aide of controversial godman Chandraswami) to mark the victory of the SP–BSP alliance in Uttar Pradesh in December 1993. It was Yadav who had insisted that the songwriter put in at least one line about Kanshi Ram as a political sop to his ally. The song was sung at a massive victory rally, one of the largest ever in Lucknow. The several hundred thousands who attended came in two groups. One, supporting Mulayam Singh, was rowdy and full of swagger. The Samajwadi Party leader himself had to shriek at a particularly boisterous section and tell them to stop dancing and sit down when Kanshi Ram rose to speak. The second group, the BSP congregation, huddled together silently. Many were barefoot and not equipped for the Lucknow winter. For most of them it was their first trip to a big city like the state capital. Yet even if they were overawed by the occasion, their eyes glinted with the jubilation of a Dalit victory.

Upper castes in Lucknow trembled at this show of strength. The full implications of a full-fledged social revolution delivered through the ballot box were beginning to sink in. It was not a reassuring sight for an entrenched elite which had enjoyed uninterrupted political power for so many centuries. The contrast between the SP and the BSP supporters carried a message. From the outset it was clear that while the two social streams had collaborated to end the political dominance of the upper castes, they were fundamentally dissimilar in character and spirit.

The coalition government between the SP and the BSP in Lucknow meant different things to its three main protagonists, Kanshi Ram, Mulayam Singh Yadav and Mayawati. For Kanshi Ram it was a huge leap forward towards the fulfilment of a hitherto elusive mission to bring together Dalits, backward castes and Muslims on the same political platform. He disliked the political heritage of Mulayam Singh Yadav and his Samajwadi Party with its past links to Jat patriach Chaudhary Charan Singh whose pathological antipathy to Dalits, particularly chamars, was no secret. But what mattered to Kanshi Ram was that his new political partnership had brought a whole flock of backwards and Muslims to what had been primarily a Dalit enterprise. He clearly believed that this experiment in Uttar Pradesh could be replicated elsewhere in the country. He rushed off with great enthusiasm to start a nationwide campaign leaving Mayawati in charge of the fledgling coalition in the state.

Mulayam Singh, a shrewd politician widely regarded in Uttar Pradesh as the successor of Charan Singh who had been the first to politically harness the rising economic clout of the backward castes in the state, cared little for Kanshi Ram's ideological vision. The Samajwadi Party supremo had crafted a purely tactical alliance with the BSP that had miraculously put him back on the Lucknow throne when it seemed he had lost it forever to the Sangh Parivar. Schooled in a completely different political tradition to both Kanshi Ram and Mayawati, he was openly contemptuous of their unconventional methods of running a movement and party. Much like his mentor Charan Singh, he believed that Dalits were incapable of providing political leadership and needed to be led rather than followed. While recognizing the vital importance of keeping Kanshi Ram and his protégé in good humour, he never took them too seriously. Mulayam Singh was fairly confident that with his experience in making and breaking parties, he would in time be able to lure away most of the BSP legislators to his party and gobble up Kanshi Ram's flock.

For Mayawati, the new government opened the door to realize her personal ambitions. Having been entrusted with the job of coordinating the alliance, the young Dalit leader, then still in her thirties, saw this as an opportunity to build her own image. She welcomed Kanshi Ram's decision to stay away from Uttar Pradesh and concentrate on building the movement in the rest of the country. In fact, it is more than likely that her mentor deliberately chose not to interfere in the state sensing that she had already marked it out as her own turf. Not surprisingly, within a few months of the new alliance coming to power, the local media was already calling Mayawati 'super chief minister', a title that gave her evident pleasure.

For the first couple of months the alliance worked reasonably well. A common ideological bond between the two parties was their support to the Mandal Commission report and the policy of extending reservations in government jobs and educational institutions to backward castes. They joined hands to implement Mandal report quotas in Uttarakhand, the hilly north-eastern region of Uttar Pradesh that later became a separate state. This was done despite bitter opposition from the BJP and upper caste members of the Congress who pointed out that only two per cent of the population in the region belonged to the backward castes.

For Mayawati, the alliance in Uttar Pradesh proved immediately beneficial. Thwarted in her efforts to get re-elected to the Lok Sabha in the 1991 general elections and in subsequent by-elections, she could now get back into Parliament riding on the back of the BSP's numbers in the state assembly. She was elected to the Rajya Sabha in January 1994, barely two months after the coalition came to power in Uttar Pradesh. However, Mayawati was no longer as excited about parliamentary proceedings as she had been when she first entered the Lok Sabha in 1989. She now had the country's largest state as her political fiefdom and was busy holding public meetings across Uttar Pradesh to consolidate and expand the hold of the BSP.

Interestingly, at least in the first few months of the alliance, there was little to indicate the fight that would soon erupt between the chief minister Mulayam Singh and Mayawati. In fact, in meetings and encounters with the media immediately after the formation of the government she fiercely defended the alliance, denying newspaper reports that strains had developed between the two parties. Instead she blamed the 'manuwadi' media for carrying out a campaign of falsehoods at the behest of the BJP, which she said had been trying to create a rift between the SP and the BSP from even before the assembly elections. She was also critical of the Congress and the Janata Dal who were also accused of being 'manuwadi' although both had declared unconditional support to the government. She said that they had no other option but to support the SP–BSP alliance because it was the only force that could stop the BJP which was otherwise poised to take over the country.

Mayawati was particularly critical of Janata Dal leader Vishwanath Pratap Singh. She said Singh had, along with Muslim clerics such as Imam Bukhari of the Jama Masjid in New Delhi, indirectly helped the BJP in the elections by taking away Muslim votes from the SP–BSP alliance particularly in western Uttar Pradesh. Obviously, the fact that the BSP did poorly in the assembly polls from the region, which was directly under Mayawati's charge, still stung. Addressing a series of public meetings in Muslim-dominated areas of the region she admonished the community for electing so few BSP and SP candidates, warning them that the only way to keep the BJP away from power was to give wholehearted and unanimous support to the SP–BSP alliance.

It is also significant that in the initial phase of the alliance Mayawati actually downplayed the spate of atrocities on Dalits that had already started all over Uttar Pradesh, which would later become a trigger for the collapse of the coalition. Addressing a rally at Mathura in February 1994 she accused the BJP of instigating some of the incidents in order to give the government a bad name. The media was also blamed for exaggerating the scale of violence against the lower castes and spreading 'false' stories about differences between the Samajwadi Party and the BSP. Mayawati claimed that the atrocities against Dalits were far less than those committed during previous Congress and BJP regimes. Her defence of the SP–BSP alliance in its early months provides an interesting contrast to her righteous indignation not long afterwards at Mulayam Singh and his Yadav kinsmen for unleashing a reign of terror against Dalits. These were the kind of political and rhetorical volte faces that would come to characterize the BSP.

At the time Lucknow was abuzz with political conspiracy theories. One of them was sparked off by a bizarre incident at Mayawati's residence in September 1994. A youth claiming to represent *India Today* magazine came to interview her but instead offered the BSP leader fifty lakh rupees to pull down the Mulayam Singh-led coalition government. Maywati smelt a rat and called the police. The youth later confessed that he was not a reporter but had been sent by some Congress leaders to bribe her. Mayawati claimed that he had mentioned the name of an Uttar Pradesh legislator who was close to Chaudhary Charan Singh's son, Ajit Singh, who was at that point with the Congress party. It is interesting to note that even as late as September 1994, Mayawati was more concerned about the threat to the coalition government from the Congress and BJP, than a war with the Samajwadi Party.

In March 1994 Mayawati created a nationwide controversy by firing another salvo against Mahatma Gandhi. What triggered this outburst still remains a mystery though some political analysts saw it was a deliberate bid to attract public attention in a repeat performance of the tantrum she had thrown about Gandhi in 1977 that had first put her under the spotlight. Others maintain that she had simply lost her cool after persistent questioning by hostile journalists who delighted in baiting Mayawati at that time in the hope of provoking a controversial quote. Whether deliberately or inadvertently, she obliged the media after repeated questions about her frank opinion about the Mahatma and what he meant to Dalits.

'His actions have retarded our progress. Gandhi called the Dalits, Harijan—children of God. I ask, if Dalits are the children of God, are the others children of the devil? If Gandhi was so fond of the word why didn't he call himself a Harijan? Why didn't he prefix Harijan to his own name?' Mayawati thundered while speaking to the media in Lucknow in the first week of March 1994.

As most mainstream political leaders are highly laudatory about Gandhi, these remarks were certainly unconventional; but the manner in which the local and national media played up Mayawati's diatribe against the Mahatma and the inordinately strong reaction in political circles was excessive. After all, both during the freedom struggle and after independence, politicians from both the Left and the Right have voiced far harsher opinions against Gandhi. Considering Mayawati's exact words, it was sheer mischief on the part of sections of the media to twist her remarks and to suggest that she had called Gandhi either satanic or the son of Satan. Therefore, there was little rationale for some politicians to express demands for Mayawati's arrest under the Terrorist and Disruptive Activities (Prevention) Act (TADA) and even less to warrant a public denunciation of her as a 'political illiterate' by so eminent a political personality as former prime minister Chandra Shekhar. The exaggerated reaction in media and political circles indicated that the steady rise of the BSP and its passage to power in collaboration with the Samajwadi Party in the country's largest state had indeed got under the skin of the upper-caste establishment.

Mayawati did not appear particularly perturbed at the wave of hostility against her from journalists and politicians. She doggedly refused to retract her remarks on Gandhi. In fact, she made several more critical comments about the Father of the Nation at meetings, press conferences and media interviews. She was, however, careful not to use any unparliamentary language about the Mahatma, which—to be fair—she had never done even in the past. Mayawati's defiant mood is well illustrated by the excerpts below from an interview in April 1994 in *Maya*, a Hindi periodical published in Uttar Pradesh:[1]

> *Maya*: You go on criticising Mahatma Gandhi. What is the political strategy behind this?
>
> **Mayawati**: I want to inform people that the caste system supported by Gandhiji is the reason for the plight of Dalits today. Gandhi was not for the Dalits but against them. He insulted Dalits by calling them Harijans. When Baba Saheb Ambedkar tried to do some good for the Dalit community, Gandhi invariably put obstacles in his way. When Baba Saheb tried to get a separate electorate for the Dalits Gandhi forced him to withdraw his demand by going on an indefinite hunger strike. Gandhi always used false pretences to claim he was a friend of Dalits, but it was actually Baba Saheb who was the true friend.

*Maya*: But don't you think that Gandhiji went on that indefinite strike to stop the division of Hindu society, which would have happened if different sections of the community demanded separate electorates?

*Mayawati*: What Hindu society are you talking about? Those days Dalits were not allowed to enter temples. They were not allowed to draw water from wells. They could not study along with other castes. Naturally, Baba Saheb felt that Dalits and oppressed people could never lead a life of dignity in Hindu society. That is why he wanted a separate electorate.

*Maya*: But the situation has changed today. Don't you consider Dalits as Hindus?

**Mayawati**: I don't want to get into that dispute. Our Constitution guarantees freedom to practise any religion of your choice. I consider humanism and charity to others as my faith. I do not believe in blind faith or in rituals.

*Maya*: You have this attitude to religion when your party is accused of encouraging casteism?

**Mayawati**: Our party is trying to end the caste system not to perpetuate it. It is the manuwadi system that wants to perpetuate it and Gandhi was a supporter of this.

*Maya*: Do you consider Gandhi as a great man? Please answer either yes or no.

**Mayawati**: Look, don't try to trap me. I consider only Baba Saheb Amebedkar as a great man so the question does not arise whether I do so about Gandhi. I just want to make it clear that Gandhi was not only against Dalits but also against backwards. That is why he opposed Sardar Patel who came from a backward caste although he had the majority. On the other hand, Gandhi supported Nehru who was in a minority just because he was a Brahmin.

*Maya*: Your comments on Gandhiji have provoked severe criticism from all quarters in the country. In particular, former Prime Minister Chandra Shekhar has denounced you.

**Mayawati** (*sounding agitated*): Yes, he has called me political illiterate. I want to remind Chandra Shekhar about the time he called Kanshi Ramji and me when he wanted our advice while forming his government. He had a long discussion about the formation of his cabinet offering Kanshi Ram the post of deputy prime minister and Mayawati the post of Home Minister. So when you need someone that person suddenly becomes capable! Today, Chandra Shekhar is just an MP. He is afraid that he could even lose his deposit in the coming elections. So that is why he thought he must do his share on the Mayawati controversy. I well know the extent of his political clout today. How many people does he have with him?

The aggressive posture adopted by Mayawati on the Gandhi controversy and her refusal to budge an inch on the issue was wholeheartedly endorsed by Kanshi Ram. He was urged by a lot of his political friends and contacts to defuse the controversy by persuading his protégé to retract her remarks on the Father of the Nation. But the BSP president insisted that she had done nothing wrong and was merely echoing Ambedkar's own sentiments on Gandhi. He even challenged the government to arrest Mayawati under TADA. Speaking to correspondents a few days after the furore erupted over remarks, Kanshi Ram declared: 'If Mayawati is arrested they will be doing us a big favour. My party will then take to the streets to debate the unfinished agenda between Ambedkar and Gandhi. We will also get the opportunity to discuss what successive Congress leaders like Nehru, Indira Gandhi and Rajiv Gandhi have done for the Dalits. So please let them arrest Mayawati!'

Faced with this in-your-face defiance by the BSP leadership, the Congress led by the cautious prime minister P.V. Narasimha Rao quickly backed off from a confrontation on Mayawati's remarks on Gandhi. The last thing the Congress High Command wanted was to open a new battlefront that could cause further erosion of the party's already dwindling Dalit vote bank. Janata Dal leader V.P. Singh who felt that aggravating the controversy would only help the BJP and other upper caste opponents of his own political agenda adopted a similar policy. Janata Dal leaders, including Ram Vilas Paswan, were bitterly opposed to Mayawati and eager to launch a full-scale war against her, but were instructed to refrain by the party leadership. BJP leaders Atal Bihari Vajpayee and Lal Krishna Advani did mildly criticize Mayawati's remarks, but the Sangh Parivar conscious of its own dubious history on Gandhi, largely operated from behind the scenes by egging on the media's Mayawati-bashing campaign.

For Mulayam Singh Yadav, Mayawati's controversial remarks and the subsequent furore were yet another example of the 'irrational' behaviour of his alliance partner. He was careful not to criticize Mayawati in public although he clearly distanced himself from her remarks by stating that he was a great admirer of the Mahatma. In private conversations with politicians and journalists the chief minister pointed to what he felt was the 'complete lunacy' of attacking a historical figure as revered as the Father of the Nation. Given the social background and political heritage that Mulayam Singh Yadav came from, his lack of empathy for the deep-rooted compulsions of the Dalit psyche to exorcise the ghost of the Mahatma and the symbolic relevance of Ambedkar's clash with Gandhi many years ago was unsurprising. Instead, the episode only confirmed the stereotype planted in Yadav's mind by Charan Singh that Dalits were incapable of providing stable political leadership or organization.

Although there were many reasons for the ultimate collapse of the alliance, this was the most fundamental—Mulayam Singh's inability to understand the psyche of the BSP leadership. When he first formed the government in alliance with the BSP, he was pleasantly surprised at the accommodative approach of Kanshi Ram on ministerial posts in sharp contrast to the hard bargaining on such matters he had experienced with other parties and leaders so far in his political career. The BSP leader even admitted to an associate of Yadav with disarming candour that since most of his party legislators were inexperienced first-timers they would not be able to manage senior ministries.

Kanshi Ram was completely unlike the usual Indian politican and would take great delight in scandalizing political and media circles with politically incorrect and irreverent statements. Even though those close to him described the BSP leader as an incurable romantic driven by an overarching ideological vision, he would, on occasion, deliberately make the most cynical remarks which were clearly aimed at shocking politicians and journalists.

'He was very contemptuous of the fake, pious declarations made by other netas and wanted to project a different image from them,' his journalist friend Shenoy explained.

Despite his deep commitment to the uplift of the scheduled castes, he could be as disparaging about them as an upper caste bigot. Seema Mustafa, a journalist with the *Asian Age* recalls that at a Delhi farmhouse party around the time the government was being formed in Uttar Pradesh, Kanshi Ram shocked her by his unusual reaction when asked why there were so few Dalits in his cabinet. 'He pointed at his feet and said that chamars had been living down there and could not expect to reach up here overnight, pointing at his head,' the journalist said, adding that she was absolutely flabbergasted at the crude and dismissive manner in which the leader refered to his own caste and core constituency.

Mulayam Singh did not have the time or inclination to understand the complexities of the BSP leader's personality or political style. He used familiar and standard methods to keep the deal between their two parties going. Even before forming the government, he had asked industrialist Sanjay Dalmia to 'look after' Kanshi Ram and Mayawati. Dalmia was already well known to Ram through a friendly Sikh journalist who used to work in a weekly newspaper run by the industrialist. The Samajwadi Party leader mistakenly assumed that this arrangement was sufficient to keep the BSP leader and his protégé happy. Such a close relationship between industrialists and political leaders is a common phenomenon, not confined to Uttar Pradesh alone but prevalent across India and perhaps the world. The connection thrives in a country where politics requires an endless supply of funds and business empires need political backing to flourish.

The other move by the chief minister to maintain good relations with the BSP was the choice of his principal secretary, Panna Lal Punia, a Dalit officer of the 1971 IAS batch. Although from Rohtak in Haryana, Punia displayed extraordinary skills in influencing politicians in Uttar Pradesh. He was also a shrewd administrator who could get things done, by hook or by crook. His record over the past one and-a-half decades speaks for itself. He held the position of principal secretary in Mulayam Singh's regime (1993-1995) as well as during three successive stints of Mayawati's rule in 1995, 1997 and 2002-2003; he also held key positions with two out of the three BJP chief ministers: Ram Prakash Gupta

(1999–2000) and Rajnath Singh (2001–2), losing his clout only when Kalyan Singh (1997–9) moved him to a punishment posting in the state administrative tribunal. In 2003, Punia, along with Mayawati, was charged by the CBI with amassing vast amounts of wealth. Not long after this, he joined politics and unsuccessfully contested the 2007 Uttar Pradesh assembly polls on a Congress ticket.

Mulayam Singh was quick to spot the advantage of having a Dalit officer with such diverse skills. While the chief minister personally dealt with Kanshi Ram, he left Punia to handle the more volatile and demanding Mayawati with instructions to get as close to her as possible. The bureaucrat's brief was to bring back as much information from the BSP camp as possible. But ultimately, Kanshi Ram and Mayawati turned the tables on the Samajwadi Party leader, managing to hijack the Dalit official to their side.

Nothwithstanding these arrangements, relations between the two parties had deteriorated sharply by the middle of 1994. There were several specific reasons. The atrocities on Dalits were becoming far too widespread for Mayawati to ignore, although at first she did try, as we have noted earlier, to play them down. Although quite a few of the atrocities were being committed by the upper castes, particularly thakurs, there were increasing cases of upper backward castes, especially the Yadavs, behaving in the same violent manner against Dalits. Explaining this phenomenon, French political scientist Christophe Jaffrelot wrote: '. . . the backward castes who were anxious to improve their social status and keep the scheduled castes in their place, reacted violently to their efforts to achieve social mobility. The OBCs' and the Dalits' class interests are clearly antagonistic in some regions in Uttar Pradesh: while in east UP the OBCs and the scheduled castes have a common enemy: the old elite made up of upper caste landlords, elsewhere, the scheduled castes are often landless labourers or cultivators with a very small amount of land who work for OBC farmers. While conflicts about the wages of agricultural labourers and disputes over land ownership have always been acute, they became more frequent when both groups—the Dalits and the OBCs—became more assertive after the 1993 elections.'[2]

The sharp rise in atrocities on Dalits in Uttar Pradesh after the SP–BSP alliance came to power is underlined by statistics enumerated by the National Commission for Scheduled Castes and Scheduled Tribes. It listed 1,067 cases of atrocities in Uttar Pradesh in its 1989–90 report, which grew alarmingly to 14,966 such cases in its 1995 report. Significantly, many of the clashes were provoked by the new sense of self-confidence and assertiveness among Dalits in the state. One common cause for tension between Dalits and other castes was the new drive by the former to build Ambedkar statues in their urban ghettos and rural clusters. This served several purposes for the recently emboldened Dalits according to Jaffrelot: '. . . to propagate the Ambedkarite iconography, and thereby to generate a kind of pan-Indian bahujan "imagined community", and to assert the bahujans' control over land and polarize the upper and lower castes, just as the building of new Hindu temples and Muslim shrines could be used to crystallize communal solidarities.'

Trouble erupted in Meerut in March 1994 when the forcible removal of an Ambedkar statute by some upper castes from a public park provoked angry Dalit demonstrations in the town. The largely Yadav constabulary cracked down on the demonstrators, opening fire to disperse them and killing at least two Dalits in the process. Caste riots also broke out in Fatehullapur in Barabanki district where Yadavs claimed that local Dalits had installed a statute of Ambedkar on a plot occupied by the former. In the first four months alone of the new coalition government, as many as sixty incidents of violence related to installation of Ambedkar statues were reported from different parts of Uttar Pradesh, resulting in several deaths and injuries, the overwhelming majority of the victims being Dalits.

The unending violence gave Mayawati the excuse to interfere in the government, a task that she clearly enjoyed as is evident from the account included in her autobiography of her April 1994 interview to *Maya* magazine.

*Maya*: People accuse you of interfering more than you should in the Mulayam Singh-led coalition government.

**Mayawati**: When the government was first formed, Kanshi Ramji told chief minister Mulayam Singh that he had full freedom to run the government as long as he looked after the interests of the Dalits, (the) oppressed and Muslim minority on whose behalf we had been elected to power. He had promised to do so. The bureaucracy was supposed to be adjusted so that the bahujan samaj was no longer neglected. But he (Mulayam) instead removed the few bureaucrats from the bahujan samaj who had been placed in senior positions during the previous governor's rule and BJP regime. That is when Kanshi Ramji ordered me to go to Lucknow from time to time and check on the Mulayam Singh government. After all if we are partners in the government, it is our responsibility to ensure that the government is functioning properly.

*Maya*: Is that why you have been given the name of 'Super Chief Minister'?

**Mayawati**: What can I do if people think I am the super chief minister! My job is to maintain harmony between the two parties. That is why I have to occasionally hold discussions with Mulayam Singh. I have also to give him some instructions.

*Maya*: But when you speak against your own coalition government, it is only natural that the press and public think that there are strains within the alliance?

**Mayawati**: The press and public should understand what is my intention. Why should I want to topple a government where we share power? I want the government to do well.

Mayawati's evident pleasure at being refered to as the 'Super Chief Minister' is underlined by her claim that she held discussions with the chief minister, and on occasion gave him instructions. In reality, Mulayam Singh, who was in any case uncomfortable with women politicians, studiously avoided her and most of her interaction with the government was through his principal secretary, P.L. Punia. It was the bureaucrat who had to deal with the long list of demands that Mayawati would regularly send for urgent implementation. A lot of them were related to grievances by the BSP's Dalit constituents, including, of course, the growing cases of violence and harassment against them. Other demands were linked to transfers and posting of Dalits in various government departments. The lack of government funds for BSP ministers and functionaries was another constant complaint.

A senior official working in the Uttar Pradesh chief minister's office at that time described the scene in the following manner:

'The atmosphere in the chief minister's office would change as soon as a new list by Mayawati was received. The tension on the principal secretary's face was evident, as he would rush around trying to see what could be done. I think he tried his best to address most of the demands. But the chief minister had his own political compulsions and could not annoy his supporters and vote banks. Punia, although very powerful, had to keep in mind all these considerations.'

There was some action taken by the chief ministers's office in starting criminal proceedings against those found guilty of atrocities against Dalits. Even Mayawati acknowledged this in the April 1994 interview to *Maya* magazine. But this was clearly not enough to stop the violence as the number of atrocities continued to mount through the year. There was also little scope for Mulayam Singh to be accommodative about the demands for postings and transfers in government jobs, inundated as he was by demands from his own supporters and friends. As for funds, the bulk of the chief minister's discretionary fund was reserved for his party functionaries at various levels. Although these funds were stretched by unprecedented margins running into many crores (for which the Yadav leader would later face legal investigation), only a tiny fraction reached his coalition partner.

'For instance, even a village pradhan belonging to the Samajwadi Party stood a better chance of getting more money from the chief minister's discretionary fund than a BSP cabinet minister,' remarked an official.

The occasional meetings that the chief minister held with Kanshi Ram did not resolve the growing differences between the two political allies. Instead they made matters worse. The BSP leader would use these meetings as exercises in one-upmanship with Mulayam Singh. He never went to meet the chief minister, insisting the latter come and call on him at the state guest house. Kanshi Ram would then keep the Samajwadi Party leader waiting in the reception lobby, sometimes for over half an hour. He would finally come down looking dishevelled, casually dressed in a banian and lungi, in a visible gesture of contempt for his alliance partner who would be attired, of course, in formal chief ministerial regalia. The fact that all this happened in front of newspaper correspondents and photographers, only added to the chief minister's embarrassment.

Mulayam Singh quietly swallowed these insults, choosing not to react publicly despite persistent needling by the local media. But behind the scenes he accelerated efforts to lure away leaders and legislators of the BSP. This was not all that difficult since many were already resentful at being marginalized by Mayawati who had become all-powerful in Uttar Pradesh. These included most of the veteran leaders who had helped Kanshi Ram build the BSP organization from the days of BAMCEF and DS4. Among the big names alienated by the meteoric rise of Mayawati in the party were Dr Masood Ahmed, the first Muslim leader to leave the Congress to join the bahujan samaj movement in the early eighties; Jang Bahadur Patel, a key kurmi leader who had popularized the BAMCEF with the backward caste community; and Raj Bahadur, the senior-most Dalit leader and president of the state unit of the BSP. Not surprisingly, Mulayam Singh made rapid inroads into the BSP party organization, subverting its legislators.

The first big shock for Kanshi Ram and Mayawati came in the 1995 panchayat elections. Out of the fifty districts where elections were held, as many as thirty, that is sixty percent of the total, were captured by the Samajwadi Party, nine by the BJP, five by the Congress and only one by the BSP. The results made it clear that even at the grassroots level it was the Samajwadi Party and not the BSP that had gained after the formation of the SP–BSP government. By the middle of 1995, the chief minister had already tied up a dozen BSP legislators, including several top leaders who were ready to cross over to his side when given the signal. It was just a matter of time before he got a sufficient number of BSP legislators to ensure that he had adequate strength in the state assembly to do without an alliance with the BSP. Significantly, the shrewd Samajwadi Party leader had already lured away several legislators from both the Congress and Janata Dal.

Mulayam Singh's plan to steadily cut the ground away from under the feet of the BSP was based on the assumption that maverick Dalit leaders like Kanshi Ram and Mayawati had little option but to sink helplessly to their political doom. He was convinced that leaders who condemned Mahatma Gandhi in public would find little support from mainstream parties or the media. In any case, the Samajwadi Party leader had put both the Congress and the Janata Dal on the backfoot by breaking their state units.

As for the BJP, the chief minister was absolutely certain that the ideological gulf between the advocates of Hindutva and those of the bahujan samaj would prevent the Sangh Parivar from supporting the BSP. What the Yadav leader clearly underestimated was the extent of the paranoia that his growing power in Uttar Pradesh generated among all other political parties as well as within the upper-caste establishment. He did not realize that even the BJP, regardless of its upper-caste Hindu bias and the strong antipathy of its local leaders to Mayawati, was desperate enough to prop up the BSP if only to cut him to size and check the rising political clout of the intermediate and backward castes.

Also outside Mulayam Singh's calculations was the personal chemistry between Kanshi Ram and the BJP's strongest leader, Atal Bihari Vajpayee. In fact, Vajpayee was one of the first senior political leaders to become friendly with the BSP leader soon after he entered the Lok Sabha in the 1991 general elections. The two held long political discussions and Kanshi Ram was a regular visitor to Vajpayee's residence. The astute BJP veteran was one of the earliest to recognize the growing importance of the BSP's brand of politics in Uttar Pradesh and—to a lesser extent—in other north Indian states. Having seen the ease with which the BSP, in combination with the Samajwadi Party, stopped the BJP juggernaut despite the momentum gained from the Ram Janambhoomi movement, Vajpayee felt it was important to cultivate Kanshi Ram. His view was supported by his senior party colleague, Murli Manohar Joshi, as well as the recently appointed RSS chief, Rajendra Singh (Rajju Bhaiya), who was from Uttar Pradesh and politically very shrewd, unlike a lot of his other colleagues in the Sangh.

Interestingly, a completely different view was held by the other BJP stalwart, L.K. Advani, and his Uttar Pradesh protégé, Kalyan Singh. Both were convinced that the forces of Hindutva in the state were strong enough to triumph on their own without allying with antagonistic parties like the BSP and its controversial leaders. It is an interesting coincidence that the two important BJP leaders who were bent on pursuing a closer relationship with the BSP were both brahmins. Indeed, sources close to both Vajpayee and Kanshi Ram indicate that as early as the early nineties the two leaders had discussed a tactical alliance between the brahmins and Dalits to counter the rising clout of the intermediate and the more upwardly mobile backward castes. This was particularly relevant at that time when the bulk of the brahmins in Uttar Pradesh had crossed over from the Congress to the BJP. The divisions within the BJP over the BSP had another dimension. It was at this point, after his rathyatra, that a larger-than-life Advani was eclipsing senior party leaders, including Vajpayee and Joshi. The internal battles of the BJP played a crucial role in determining its relationship with the BSP right from the beginning and continued to do so in the years ahead.

As the summer of 1995 approached, the strains within the SP–BSP alliance moved towards breaking point. Mulayam Singh was working at a feverish pace to break the BSP and hijack the government. To complicate matters further for the BSP, just at that point Kanshi Ram fell seriously ill, partly due to exhaustion from his travels across the country, and also because of medical complications brought on by chronic acute diabetes and hypertension. But even from his sick bed the BSP leader managed to tie up an alliance with the BJP, putting his personal relationship with Vajpayee to good use.

Vajpayee, with support from Joshi and the RSS chief, was able to browbeat the unwilling Advani and Kalyan Singh to go along with a secret plan to prop up a BSP government. Interestingly, this plan also had the tacit support of the senior leadership of both the Congress and the Janata Dal—both parties had seen their legislators poached upon by Mulayam Singh. It is significant that the main go-between the ailing Kanshi Ram and concerned BJP and other party leaders was industrialist Jayant Malhoutra, now a BSP-supported Rajya Sabha member of Parliament, and not Mayawati who appeared to have been kept in the dark about such a plan till the last moment. This indicates that Kanshi Ram at that point still did not trust his protégé's skills as a fixer, preferring the services of a professional wheeler-dealer like Malhoutra.

The BJP leadership was keen to make Kanshi Ram the new chief minister but his frail physical condition was hardly conducive to such a punishing job. They had already given him a letter of support but were waiting for him to recuperate. By the end of May news reached Ram that Mulayam Singh was about to break the BSP and there was no time to lose in staking claim for an alternative government. Kanshi Ram summoned Mayawati to his hospital bed and revealed his plans. He described that moment in an article on Mayawati several years later.[3]

On one side I was under pressure to make changes in U.P. and on the other side I was sick, facing health problems. At that time, Mr Jayant Malhoutra was with us. Km. Mayawati and Mr Malhotra took me to hospital. In the hospital, doctors tested me thoroughly. On the basis of these tests Mr Malhoutra told Km. Mayawati that Kanshi Ram was facing a serious problem. And because of such a problem his father died in a London hospital. Km. Mayawati became nervous. Many thoughts might have come to her mind. "What will happen to her if Kanshi Ram dies? Who will guide her? Who will help her in the movement?" The nurse attending to me told me that Km. Mayawati was weeping outside my room. I called Km. Mayawati inside the room and asked her, "Mayawati would you like to be the CM of U.P.?" She could not decline my words. She thought my health problem had become serious. And that was why Kanshi Ram was uttering something irrelevant. I convinced Km. Mayawati that I was in a position to make her the CM of U.P. I showed her all the relevant papers and told her to go to Lucknow and hand over those papers to the Governor of U.P. He will give the oath and majority will be tested within 15 days on the floor of the house. She did that on 1 June 1995.

When word reached Mulayam Singh on the afternoon of the first day of June that Mayawati had just met the Uttar Pradesh Governor Moti Lal Vora and withdrawn support to his government laying claim to form a government with the support of the BJP, he is reported to have been livid with rage. Not with Mayawati and Kanshi Ram, but with himself for delaying a split in the BSP. This crucial mistake was partially caused by his excessive trust in his principal secretary, P.L. Punia, who had given him no warning of an imminent counter-attack by the BSP leadership. In fact, just a few days ago at the Samajwadi Party national executive, Punia had been quite non-committal when asked by Mulayam Singh and his aides about the latest developments in the BSP. The chief minister was vaguely aware of a joint conspiracy brewing between the BJP, Congress and Janata Dal to destabilize his government with the help of Kanshi Ram, but he was quite sure that these plans could not be immediately implemented because of the latter's confinement to a hospital bed. Whether Punia was unaware of the BSP plan to withdraw support or he knew but deliberately kept quiet, remains a mystery. The fact that the principal secretary made such a smooth transition in the change of regime keeping his post intact suggests that he had developed his own links with the BSP. As the *Indian Express* commented in a profile of the bureaucrat in August 2003, 'When Mayawati became chief minister just hours after that "guest house incident", anybody who was somebody in Mulayam raj found himself in the doghouse. Punia was the one exception. He stayed put on the fifth floor of the state secretariat, as the chief minister's aide.'[4]

Mulayam Singh was completely flummoxed at the combined Opposition agreeing to substitute him with someone he had dismissed so far as a hysterical Dalit woman. This was an unexpected and outrageous development. His surprise and anger at being ousted by her may well have contributed to the suspension of the Samajwadi Party leader's better judgement. 'The problem was that Mulayam Singh had a very low opinion of Mayawati. And many of the BSP legislators were already in his pocket. I think in the heat of the moment a decision was taken to scare the hell out of the BSP so that it backed off from laying its claim to power. What happened afterwards would never have happened if Mulayam stopped to think,' recalled an old associate. Indeed, Samajwadi Party goons may not have dared to cross the limit to the extent they did had Kanshi Ram been present in Lucknow on the fateful day of 2 June 1995.

The exact culpability of the Samajwadi Party chief minister in the attack on the Lucknow guest house by his party legislators and activists is not known. It is difficult to establish whether he meant to murder Mayawati as she has repeatedly accused him of over the past decade. An enquiry by a senior IAS officer, Ramesh Chandra, immediately after the 'guest house incident' led to a charge sheet against Mulayam Singh and seventy-four others. This sparked off a decade-long legal wrangle that is yet to be completely resolved. However, there is little doubt that without a green signal from the chief minister, his party legislators and activists would not have thrown caution to the winds and raided the Lucknow state guest house where Mayawati and her party legislators had assembled. Nor could the local administration, including police officers, have so studiedly looked the other way during the attack on the guest house.

Strong political logic linked the chief minister to the attack. Having refused to step down from his post after the BSP withdrew its support on 1 June 1995, Mulayam Singh had to immediately prove that he had the required majority to continue in office. For this he had to break the BSP, which meant the support of at least one third of the sixty-nine legislators that the party had in the state assembly, to avoid violating the anti-defection law. The chief minister had already managed to get letters of support from fifteen BSP legislators led by the state party president, Raj Bahadur, by 2 June 1995 but still needed eight more to make the magic figure of twenty-three, one-third of the total sixty-nine party legislators. The plan clearly was to use some rough-and-ready methods involving both physical intimidation and bribery to quickly enlist the support of the BSP legislators he so badly needed. In a parallel, more sinister, move there appeared to be a deliberate bid to scare, publicly humiliate, if not physically harm, the chief ministerial aspirant, Mayawati, to traumatize her into submission.

Interestingly, a number of administration and police officials in Lucknow were shifted by the government on the night of 1 June 1995 after the BSP withdrew support from the Mulayam Singh led SP–BSP coalition ministry and Mayawati staked her claim to form a new government with the support of BJP, Congress and the Janata Dal. A controversial police officer, O.P. Singh, was brought in hurriedly as senior superintendent of police, Lucknow. Singh had a grievance against Mayawati who had transferred him twice in the recent past for alleged malpractices. The police officer would have played a key role in the anarchy that prevailed at the state guest house in Lucknow on 2 June 1995.

The following account of the incident is culled from eyewitness accounts of legislators, administration officials, police officers and constables, and others who deposed before the Ramesh Chandra Enquiry Committee and whose depositions were included in the report.

On the afternoon of 2 June, Mayawati had summoned a meeting of BSP legislators to discuss the developing political situation within the common hall of the state guest house where she was staying in suites 1–2. After the meeting had finished, the BSP leader had retired to her suite with a select group of party legislators for further discussions. The rest of the legislators remained in the common hall. Shortly after 4 p.m. a mob of around 200 Samajwadi Party legislators and activists attacked the state guest house. They were shouting, 'The chamars have gone mad, we have to teach them a lesson,' along with other slogans which expressed threats to maim and kill BSP legislators and their families. Most of the slogans were blatantly casteist, uttered with the intent of inflicting maximum humiliation. They also shouted, using filthy and abusive language.

The legislators in the common hall hurriedly closed the main door, but this was smashed open by the frenzied mob. They then set upon their hapless BSP victims, slapping and kicking them. At least five BSP legislators were forcibly dragged out of the state guest house and put into cars that took them to the chief minister's residence. There they were asked to join the BSP rebel faction led by Raj Bahadur and sign a piece of paper pledging support to the Mulayam Singh government. Some of them were so intimidated that they signed on the dotted line. The legislators were confined there till late at night.

Even as BSP legislators in the state guest house were being trussed up and taken like chickens to the slaughter house, another bizarre drama was unfolding in front of suites 1–2 where Mayawati was sitting with some BSP legislators. A few legislators had managed to escape from the mob outside and taken refuge in the suite. The last one in was senior BSP leader R.K. Chaudhury escorted by Constable Rashid Ahmed and Chaudhury's personal security guard, Lal Chand. The latter instructed the occupants in the suite to lock the door from inside and hardly had they done so, when a section of the mob burst through the corridor and started pounding on the door.

'Drag the chamar woman out from her hole,' hollered the mob, which included some elected legislators as well as a few women. As they hammered on the door, the mob screamed filthy abuses giving graphic details of what would be done to Mayawati once she was dragged out. The situation was fast getting out of hand.

What saved Mayawati was the courage of two relatively junior police officers, Vijay Bhusan, the station house officer (SHO), Hazratganj, and Subhash Singh Badhel, the SHO, (VIP), who, along with some constables, managed to push the mob back a bit with great difficulty. They then formed a wall in the corridor so that no one could get past. The angry crowd, however, continued to shout slogans and abuses, threatening to drag Mayawati out of the suite.

Apart from this brave and timely move by some individual police officers, most other officials present, including the state guest house management and security staff, did nothing to stop the complete bedlam that continued for over an hour. It is also shocking that, according to the depositions of several BSP legislators and some policemen, the senior superintendent of police, Lucknow, O.P. Singh, was present when the legislators were being abducted and Mayawati's suite attacked. According to eyewitnesses, he just puffed away on his cigarette. Mysteriously, soon after the attack began, electricity and water supplies to the guest house were snapped—another indication of connivance by the administration.

A semblance of order was restored only after the arrival of Rajiv Kher, district magistrate, Lucknow, who showed nerve as well as presence of mind by taking a firm stand against the mob. Along with Rajiv Ranjan Verma, the superintendant of police, City, the district magistrate first managed to push those members of the mob who were not legislators out of the guest house building. Later, when more police reinforcements arrived, he managed to push everyone, including legislators from the Samajwadi Party, outside the compound of the state guest house. Even though this required him to order a lathi charge on the legislators, he went ahead ignoring warnings from the chief minister's office against taking any action against the Samajwadi Party MLAs. At 11 p.m. the district magistrate was summarily issued transfer orders for doing his duty without fear or prejudice.

The situation inside the guest house slowly started returning to normal late in the evening as more and more security forces were rushed to the spot after interventions from the governor's office, the central government, and senior BJP leaders. With security inside and outside the building considerably tightened, the mob still shouting abuses, threats and slogans, finally melted away. But it took repeated entreaties from the district magistrate and other officials that the danger had passed and they could open the door to convince Mayawati and her flock of party legislators who had barred themselves inside suites 1–2. It was late at night before they finally opened the door.

There have been many instances of the democratic process

being trampled upon in the rough and tumble of Indian politics. But it is difficult to match the horrors perpetrated by the mob led by elected legislators with the connivance of a political leadership and state administration at the Lucknow state guest house on 2 June 1995. It was a colossal mistake by Mulayam Singh and it helped his opponents to isolate him politically. It also earned sympathy for the BSP in the media, which would otherwise have been far more critical of the political coup and the anointment of so controversial a leader and political novice as Mayawati to the chief ministership of the country's largest state.

As for Mayawati herself, the trauma that she suffered in the ordeal at the state guest house may well have been the final tempering of the steel that would make her the iron lady of Indian politics in the coming years. One can only imagine the outrage and dread, derived from centuries and centuries of torment as both a Dalit and a woman, that Mayawati must have undergone as she heard the filthy abuses and the pounding on the door. Indeed, those who have heard Mayawati describe the nightmare say that her face twists and her voice shakes when she recounts the events—underlining the depth of feeling. As her mentor Kanshi Ram, for once unable to help her from his hospital bed, described it, it was her 'final test of courage'.

# SIX

# Chief Minister Mayawati

'*It* is a miracle of democracy,' was prime minister Narasimha Rao's first reaction when he heard that Mayawati had become chief minister of Uttar Pradesh. The veteran Congress leader was obviously referring to the fact that a Dalit woman had assumed the reins of India's largest state. But it also summed up the amazing—almost miraculous—turn of events that had catapulted a woman still in her thirties, without any administrative experience or political lineage, almost out of nowhere, to such a crucial and exalted post.

The first challenge before Mayawati after Uttar Pradesh governor Moti Lal Vora swore her in on 3 June 1995 was to prove her majority on the floor of the state assembly. Mulayam Singh had clearly burnt his fingers in the ill-conceived attack on Mayawati and her legislators at the state guest house. This had made it easier for the governor, clearly acting on the orders of the Narasimha Rao-led Congress government in New Delhi, to dismiss the Yadav regime and install a minority government led by Mayawati. The wave of condemnation in political and media circles at the scandal enacted at the guest house made it easier for other parties, including the Congress, Janata Dal and smaller parties, to support the new BSP government, which already enjoyed the unconditional support of the BJP.

However, Mulayam Singh still held one trump card. His close

associate, Dhani Ram Verma, was the Speaker of the legislative
assembly. Verma could use his powers to make it difficult for
Mayawati to take the floor test in the House although she had an
assured majority. Indeed, when the assembly met on 19 June,
another dose of political drama turned the proceedings in the
House to a complete farce. First came the extraordinary ruling by
the Speaker declaring the governor's dismissal of the Mulayam
Singh regime, the installation of Mayawati as chief minister, and
the directive for a floor test as 'unconstitutional' and, therefore,
invalid. He then adjourned the House.

If this was in blatant disregard of procedure, the moment the
Speaker and the Samajwadi Party legislators along with the rebel
BSP faction led by Raj Bahadur left the House, the remaining 275
members unanimously elected a new Speaker, BSP legislator
Barkhu Ram Verma. Obviously, the ousted Speaker, the Samajwadi
Party legislators and the BSP rebels were not re-summoned during
this exercise. Apart from the BSP and BJP legislators, those
belonging to the Congress and the Janata Dal, the communist
parties as well as thirteen rebel Samawadi Party legislators who
had formed a separate bloc, also voted in favour of the new
Speaker. The unanimity across such a wide spectrum of parties
against Mulayam Singh underlined his isolation after the guest
house incident and signalled that—for the moment at least—he
had lost the political game in Lucknow.

Not surprisingly, the actual vote of confidence the next day
was a mere formality. But there was interesting episode between
Congress leader Pramod Tiwari and BJP leader Kalyan Singh just
before the confidence vote. Tiwari insisted on a categorical
statement from Singh on the longevity of the current political
arrangement. Kalyan Singh, whose antipathy to the BSP and
Mayawati was well known, and who had been browbeaten by BJP
leaders Atal Bihari Vajpayee and Murli Manohar Joshi into
supporting the minority regime, was clearly reluctant to even
speak on the occasion. Baited by Tiwari on the matter, the BJP
leader first accused the Congress legislator of acting like Shakuni
(the evil uncle in the Mahabharata), and then blustered that
Mayawati would continue in her post till the Congress government
in New Delhi brought her down.

Yet, such minor skirmishes notwithstanding, Mayawati's speech
on the occasion conveyed a significant political message. She

thanked BJP leader Atal Bihari Vajpayee, the prime minister, Narasimha Rao, and the governor. The new chief minister then bitterly attacked her old rival, Dalit leader Ram Vilas Paswan of the Janata Dal. She spent several minutes to express her indignation at Paswan's silence on the guest house incident, even though it involved the honour of a Dalit woman.

The other highlight of her speech was the lengthy emphasis on the BSP's commitment to the security and welfare of the Muslim minority. Clearly aware that there was considerable disquiet among Muslims at the BSP's total dependence on the BJP to stay in power, Mayawati went out of her way to assure the community that she would not compromise her party's commitment to them because of political pressure from her BJP sponsors. She appealed to Muslims not to listen to the propaganda spread by Mulayam Singh that she had sold out to the communal agenda of the BJP, reminding them that the percentage of tickets she had given the minority community far exceeded that by the Samajwadi Party in the 1993 assembly polls. The new chief minister spent a lot of time reeling out facts and figures to prove that it was she—and not her predecessor—who had fought for the welfare of the minority community and that any steps taken on behalf of Muslims during the SP–BSP coalition government were taken at the instigation of the BSP.

Listening to Mayawati make her debut speech as chief minister from the visitors' gallery was her proud mentor, Kanshi Ram, who had by then recuperated sufficiently to travel to Lucknow. There is an evocative photograph of the ailing BSP leader presenting a bouquet of flowers to his protégé after he arrived in Lucknow to give his belated congratulations. Their expressions speak volumes about the intensity of feeling they shared, as well as the overwhelming triumph and achievement of the occasion. Success must have been that much sweeter after so many years of arduous struggle and in the immediate aftermath of the tension and ordeal that accompanied the ascent to power.

Yet, despite the euphoria of the moment, Kanshi Ram showed that he had lost none of his hard-headed pragmatism or political spunk while addressing the media after Mayawati won the confidence vote in the state assembly. Asked by correspondents on how long the minority government would last, the BSP president declared without hesitation, 'It will last as long as the BJP supports the government.' He was then asked about the new government's agenda in the light of its complete dependence on the BJP. 'The agenda will be that of the BSP,' was the short but decisive reply.

The agenda of the BSP turned out to be largely symbolic during Mayawati's first stint in power. Some commentators have rather unfairly described this emphasis on style rather than substance as political showmanship that did little to address the real grievances of the Dalits and other oppressed sections of Uttar Pradesh. In fact, the new chief minister showed great political savvy in making a virtue of a necessity. She had no experience whatsoever of how to operate the levers of administrative power. The minority regime simply did not have the numbers to make substantive policy decisions, and they knew it was just a matter of time before the BJP pulled the plug on the government to unfurl its own saffron banner.

On the other hand this was a golden opportunity, however transient, for Mayawati to demonstrate the distinctive nature of the first ruling dispensation in this country which had a Dalit agenda and not just a few token scheduled caste politicians at the top. Only three Dalit chief ministers, D. Sanjiviah in Andhra Pradesh, Ram Sunder Das in Bihar and Jagannath Pahadiya in Rajasthan had come before her and not one had had the guts to take on the upper-caste establishment that had sponsored them. She seized her chance. Her flamboyant gestures captured the imagination of her core constituency which revelled in Mayawati's audacity. Had she been more tentative and cautious at the beginning, adjusting her agenda to keep her upper caste sponsors happy, the first BSP government may have lasted a few more months. But Mayawati's own stature would have never grown to what it is today, allowing her to make compromises that are now possible because of the brownie points she had collected with her flock right at the start.

The new chief minister began her campaign by launching a massive renaming exercise. Names were plucked out of the Dalit–Bahujan pantheon and arbitrarily pasted on institutions, districts and buildings across Uttar Pradesh. Agra University was renamed Dr Bhimrao Ambedkar University while Kanpur University became Chhatrapati Shahuji Maharaj University. Several districts were reorganized yielding new districts that were named after Ambedkar, Shahuji Maharaj, Mahamaya, the latter after the mother of

Buddha. Even the sports stadium at Agra was renamed after Eklavya, the low-caste archer in the Mahabharata. There was also a concerted drive to build Ambedkar statues all over the state. This was already a popular trend among Dalit masses both in towns and in the countryside. It was pursued with almost religious fervour and had led to violent clashes between Dalits and upper and intermediate caste groups during the SP–BSP coalition government. Now with the BSP controlling administrative power, Dalits could build these memorials to their iconic leader far more freely, as well as have the state fund many of the larger statues. Hundreds of statues mushroomed across Uttar Pradesh.

Mayawati's most ambitious venture was the construction of an enormous twenty-eight-acre Ambedkar Park and Parivarthan Chowk in honour of Dalit–Bahujan leaders right in the heart of the state capital Lucknow. The chief minister announced that the Chowk would display giant statues of the main historical figures who had been in the forefront of anti-brahminical campaigns—Phule, Periyar, Shahuji Maharaj and Ambedkar. Crores of rupees were allocated for the project and work started round the clock to coincide with the first show to be staged at the Chowk. This was to be the Periyar Mela, a festival to celebrate the ideological legacy of the early twentieth-century south Indian iconoclast, E.V. Ramaswamy Naicker, universally known as 'Periyar', who was known for his antipathy towards the brahminical order as well as to orthodox Hinduism. The holding of such a festival was particularly provocative to the BJP with its large band of Lord Rama devotees because of Periyar's controversial book on the Ramayana—an alternative reading that depicted Ram and his consort Sita in what many orthodox Hindus would consider an openly blasphemous manner.

It was clear that much of the symbolism adopted by Mayawati in her first stint in power was deliberately geared to nettle the upper-caste establishment despite her government's dependence on it. This was not out of sheer cussedness but a calculated bid to convince Dalits that it was possible for the lower echelons of Indian society to turn the tables on the upper strata. Even though not much changed in the broad socio-economic equations governing Uttar Pradesh during the first brief BSP regime, it would be unwise to minimize the impact of this practical demonstration by the BSP leadership of what Dalits could do if they had political power and, of course, the courage to use it. This brilliantly audacious strategy to capture the hearts and minds of people who had been subjugated for so many centuries, had the obvious imprint of Kanshi Ram's genius, but it must be said of Mayawati that she implemented her guru's strategy very effectively.

Yet, the BSP regime brought other gains beyond mere symbolic pride for Dalits. A drastic overhaul of the administrative set-up by the new chief minister and the appointment of scheduled caste officers in key posts of both civil and police administrations antagonized the media and other political parties, including the BJP. But these sweeping decisions, often arbitrarily overturning conventional modes of postings, promotions and transfers, sent a loud and clear message to Dalits that for the first time they were stakeholders in the government. For instance, the decision to appoint scheduled caste officers as magistrates in half the districts and put other scheduled caste officers in charge of more than a quarter of UP's police stations, imparted a sense of security to Dalits in the state that they had never felt before.

The chief minister's secretariat was run by a small coterie of scheduled caste officers led by her principal secretary, P.L. Punia. They included Netram, the secretary, and special secretaries Sri Krishna and Aradhana Chowdhury. The only senior non-scheduled caste officer who sat in the chief minister's office on the fifth floor of the secretariat was Jawed Usmani, a secretary-rank official from the Mulayam Singh regime who was retained because Punia wanted his help to run the office. 'Punia's experience as principal secretary during the Mulayam Singh regime and his knowledge of exactly how to operate the levers of power to pursue the Dalit agenda was invaluable to the new chief minister,' said a bureaucrat who worked with Punia in that period. In many cases this agenda was simply to appoint scheduled castes officials arbitrarily to powerful and lucrative posts in the administration. A similar policy was followed by the influential scheduled caste director general of police, Kashmir Singh. All this was, of course, a red rag to the rest of the administration as well as the media. It also was a huge embarrassment for the BJP and other upper caste parties supporting the minority Mayawati regime. But the criticism in the media and grumbling in Lucknow's bureaucratic and political circles only helped to consolidate Maywati's fan following among Dalits who had never imagined that their community would get such royal treatment, and felt a sense of empowerment, whether or not it made a difference to their individual lives.

There were also some economic sops offered by Mayawati to her constituency. She revived the almost defunct Ambedkar Villages Scheme which had been started by Mulayam Singh when he had first come to power in 1990. Mayawati funnelled vast government resources to villages with a scheduled caste population of thirty per cent and in some areas even as little as twenty-two per cent. This represented a dramatic reversal of priorities in resource allocation. Dalit-dominated villages, that had till then been the worst off, were suddenly the most privileged. All of a sudden metal roads, hand pumps, medical clinics and pucca houses came up in areas that had traditionally been starved for funds. In many cases, the road was metalled only in the stretches through Dalit villages, reverting in to pot-holed mud paths as it crossed into territory dominated by other castes. Not surprisingly, the upper and intermediate castes raised a furore, an outcry that was, itself, music to the ears of a community deprived for so long.

Most of the benefits were directed towards the chamars who constituted the core of the BSP's support base. But Mayawati was shrewd enough to woo other sections of the bahujan samaj as well. Generous educational grants were given for the children of the bhangis, the sweeper sub-caste of the scheduled castes, and a rehabilitation programme announced so that the community could be trained for jobs other than their hereditary and widely despised profession of cleaning toilets. Significantly, the bhangis (also called valmikis) were traditional BJP voters. There were also attempts to woo the lower backward castes, for instance, the boatmen and potter communities with special measures tailored to benefit their occupations and skills.

A concerted effort was made to assuage the feelings of the Muslim minority, many of whom felt abandoned by the BSP after it came to power with the help of the hated BJP. Mayawati offered Muslim children the same educational grants as those given to scheduled castes. She also implemented the recommendations of the second UP Backward Classes Commission that had suggested in its 1994 report that lower caste Muslims should benefit from backward caste reservations for posts in the state administration. The previous chief minister Mulayam Singh had resisted the commission's report because of his reluctance to part with the twenty-seven per cent reservation for Hindu backward castes in government jobs that were mostly the monopoly of his core constituency of Yadavs. But Mayawati had no such compunctions and granted 8.44 per cent to Muslims out of the backward-caste quota. An equivalent proportion of eight per cent of police officers' posts was also reserved for Muslims who felt particularly vulnerable during Hindu–Muslim communal riots because of their lack of representation in the police force.

While Muslims appreciated these gestures made by the Mayawati government, what really won their hearts was her defiant resistance in September 1995 to an attempt by the Vishwa Hindu Parishad (VHP) to create another Babri Masjid–Ram Janambhoomi situation in Mathura, a town in western Uttar Pradesh held in reverence by Hindus who believed it to be the birthplace of Lord Krishna. Much like in the case of the Babri Masjid at Ayodhya, the VHP had been agitating for the removal of a mosque adjoining the Krishna temple in Mathura. With a BJP-sponsored government in Lucknow, the Parishad backed by party hardliners decided to use the occasion of Lord Krishna's birthday celebrations in September to mobilize Hindu zealots in a massive congregation and take over the site. The situation was potentially explosive raising fears of another communal conflagration similar to the one witnessed during and after the demolition of the Babri Masjid.

Mayawati met this challenge not only with commendable courage but a fair degree of political savvy. Firstly, she refused to be cowed down by VHP threats despite the dependence of her government on BJP support. Then working along in tandem with Kanshi Ram, she managed to enlist the support of both BJP leader Vajpayee and prime minister Rao in defusing a potentially disastrous situation which would have been a permanent blot on her administrative abilities. The media, usually quite hostile to the chief minister, had to grudgingly appreciate the convincing manner in which she forced the VHP to back down and hold the birthday celebrations of Lord Krishna as far as three kilometres away from the disputed site, completely out of harm's way.

Significantly, even as Mayawati praised prime minister Narasimha Rao for his cooperation in defusing the Mathura crisis, she was openly bitter about the role played by other Congress leaders. 'I want to thank the prime minister for his help.

Unfortunately, I cannot do the same for his Congress party which consistently tried to sabotage an amicable compromise on Mathura and force the downfall of my government so that President's Rule can be declared in Uttar Pradesh. What is even more shameful is that the minister of state for home, Rajesh Pilot, was a ringleader in this conspiracy,' the chief minister alleged in her statement in the Uttar Pradesh Legislative Assembly on 21 August 1995 shortly after the Mathura dispute was resolved peacefully.

Mayawati's firmness in the face of dire threats by the Sangh hardliners, her confident handling of the administration and the triumphant yet restrained speech she made in the state assembly after the crisis blew over, revealed quite another persona to the whimsical power-crazed autocrat portrayed in large sections of the media since she assumed office. Her supporters would cite Mathura time and again in the years to come as proof of her administrative calibre. More importantly, the fact that she so successfully withstood pressure from Hindu fundamentalists to protect Muslim interests considerably enhanced her secular credentials, and this stood her in good stead with the minority community through the BSP's repeated dalliances with the BJP in the future.

Mayawati's moment of glory over Mathura, however, also spelled her doom as chief minister. The local BJP leadership, particularly Kalyan Singh, who had in any case been opposed to propping up the BSP minority government, decided the party could no longer support a leader and a party that was so openly inimical to the interests of the Sangh Parivar. Interestingly, the revolt by BJP leader Shankarsinh Vaghela in Gujarat against the party's central command in October may have played a crucial role in the party's decision to pull the plug on Mayawati. Just five days before the Gujarat revolt, the combined might of the BJP central leadership, including Vajpayee, Advani, Joshi and Sundar Singh Bhandari, had told Uttar Pradesh leaders Kalyan Singh and Kalraj Mishra that it was incumbent on them to support the BSP government till the Lok Sabha polls in 1996. But after Vaghela, the party top brass did not dare risk a similar split in Uttar Pradesh by imposing their diktat. On 18 October 1995, after Mayawati had completed 136 days in power, the BJP withdrew support and ended what most politicians and journalists thought at the time was a brief aberration in Uttar Pradesh politics. Efforts to break the BSP by both the BJP and the Samawadi Party, however, failed to materialize and the assembly was kept in suspended animation under President's Rule.

Giving a long list of reasons for withdrawal of support to the media, Kalraj Mishra, president of the Uttar Pradesh BJP, listed several irregularities in government deals, including the grant of distillery licences, the sale of sugar mills, deliberate insults heaped through the Periyar Mela on Lord Rama—the ruling deity of the party's two successful election campaigns in the past—the confrontation with the Vishwa Hindu Parishad on the Krishna Janambhoomi issue in Mathura, the government's refusal to grant permission to prosecute police personnel involved in the rape of some activists in Uttarakhand, and the brazen transfer and postings of officials in the state. While most of these charges were never proved, there was no denying the BSP's provocative gestures towards some of the BJP's most venerated icons and symbols.

Kanshi Ram scoffed at this litany of complaints. He claimed the underlying reasons were far more mundane as the BJP was hankering after five extra seats in the Uttar Pradesh Legislative Council. The BSP's refusal to accommodate its sponsor had led to the fall of the government. It was characteristic bluster by the BSP president who, many local journalists felt, had overruled Mayawati in her determination to defy the BJP at all costs. There were also rumours that she had desperately tried to negotiate with the BJP behind her mentor's back to save her government but had been thwarted in this aim by Kalyan Singh. But much of the media speculation about a rift between the two was based on mere gossip and was more often a reflection of the media's deep hostility to the ousted chief minister.

Indeed the battle between the media and Mayawati sparked off an unprecedented confrontation soon after she lost power. The media had gloated over her fall and in December, one of her most virulent critics, *Dainik Jagaran*, the largest-circulating daily in Uttar Pradesh, published a story claiming that the BSP leader had a secret—a twelve-year-old daughter.[1] They sourced the story to a former BSP leader who had been thrown out of the party. Not surprisingly, Mayawati was outraged and at a massive public meeting in Lucknow dramatically challenged the newspaper to either produce the daughter or face the consequences. Angry party workers then proceeded to vandalize the *Jagaran* offices in Lucknow although the former chief minister claimed that had they really wanted to attack it 'not a single brick would have remained of the newspaper office' and that 'a mere signal from me can destroy the entire media.' The newspaper owner, Narendra Mohan, known for his proximity to the BJP, refused to publish an apology on the provocative plea: 'Only a medical examination can prove whether Mayawati had a child or not.' The BSP leadership, however, cleverly desisted from inciting its workers to further violent agitations, deciding instead to use the widespread anger among the cadre at the canard against Mayawati to mobilize for the coming elections in 1996. The party issued instructions to all sixty-eight district units in the state to adopt resolutions by 1 January 1996, swearing to sacrifice 'everything to make Mayawati chief minister of the state to ensure that the culprits are brought to book by Behenji's orders'.

Interestingly, nearly a decade later a headline in the same newspaper *Dainik Jagaran* describing Mayawati as a 'chamarin'—a derogatory term used for a woman belonging to the chamar subcaste—provoked yet another attack by BSP workers on the newspaper office.[2] This time Mayawati, with the help of her lawyer-aide, Satish Mishra, slammed a defamation case that demanded 'token compensation of rupees one hundred crores' for the damage caused to her image. The newspaper published an abject apology describing the headline as a typographical mistake.

The hostile relationship that Mayawati and Kanshi Ram had with journalists was one of the main reasons why the BSP's rising political graph was consistently ignored by the media. In 1996, there was the ugly incident of Kanshi Ram and his supporters abusing and assaulting a ZEE TV team at a press conference in his New Delhi residence. This further antagonized the media which began to depict BSP leaders as political cowboys who were completely devoid of a code of conduct. Part of the problem emanated from ordinary bias, particularly in the Hindi-language media, dominated as it was by orthodox upper caste Hindus who were appalled at the rise of the lower castes. In this respect, the BSP leader's constant refrain about a biased manuvadi media was an accurate description.

But the abrasive personal styles of both Mayawati and Kanshi Ram also compounded and deepened the mutual suspicion and hostility. They also made little attempt to network with the media and pander to the giant egos that Indian journalists tend to nurse.

And unlike many other political leaders who backed up sweet talk with some serious sops and junkets to keep the media happy, these were either not forthcoming from Mayawati or too crudely packaged. It was only after she swept to a surprise majority on her own in the 2007 Uttar Pradesh state assembly polls that there were signs that a normal relationship had evolved between the two.

Despite the Lucknow media deriding the Mayawati regime after it fell in October 1995, there were early indications that she had boosted her support at the grassroots level in urban and rural areas during her brief stint in power. The first sign came in the city municipal elections held at the end of 1995 when the BSP managed to capture one city municipal corporation, nine middle-size municipalities and twenty-two small towns. This was a huge improvement from the results of Samajwadi Party-dominated municipal elections held at the beginning of the year when the BSP had been virtually wiped out. It showed that the party had made the correct decision in abandoning the SP–BSP coalition and taking the gamble of running a minority government with the help of the BJP. Clearly, even their short-lived sojourn in power had enhanced the political profile of the party.

The stature of the BSP received an even bigger fillip in the 1996 Lok Sabha polls. It was a period of great political confusion. A fading Congress led by a jaded prime minister P.V. Narasimha Rao was facing a serious challenge from an emerging political power, the BJP. On the eve of the polls, desperate to shore up his flagging political fortunes Rao had unleashed the Hawala money-laundering scandal which implicated some of his Congress rivals and a major BJP leader, Lal Krishna Advani. Nobody quite knew who would win but there was unanimous agreement that no single party could win a majority and smaller regional parties would play a crucial role in the polls. Ultimately, the Congress crashed to its till then worst performance with 140 seats, comfortably beaten by the BJP with 161, but the number was still not enough to sustain the latter's brief stint on the throne of New Delhi because of the party's inability to find allies.

The political impasse was revolved by the installation of a shaky multiparty coalition of regional parties and the Left Front, supported from the outside by the Congress. After days of political drama and indecision on a new prime minister, H.D. Deve Gowda, a Karnataka leader with no national profile, was the compromise candidate. It was an ideal scenario for the BSP, and Kanshi Ram declared that the Bahujan Samaj Party favoured political instability as it helped in its empowerment.

Considering the party was still a political novice and had contested the elections without any allies, the BSP came through the polls with flying colours. It won six seats from Uttar Pradesh—but what is more impressive—captured more than twenty per cent of the vote in the country's largest state. The vote percentage was about the same as that of the Samajwadi Party, a huge achievement, although Mulayam Singh's party got ten more seats because of favourable vote distribution. The BJP got an awesome thirty-three per cent of the vote but a disappointing conversion into fifty-two seats. There was good news for the BSP from two other north Indian states. The party bagged three Lok Sabha seats in Punjab, getting 9.35 per cent of votes and two seats in Madhya Pradesh with 8.8 per cent votes. With eleven seats in the Lok Sabha, over four per cent of the national vote and fast emerging as a dominant force in the largest state, it was a breathtaking leap forward in barely a decade—from 2.4 per cent in 1985 to 20.61 per cent. The BSP had finally arrived.

The first proof of this new brand equity of the BSP came in the shape of an amazing alliance between the party and the Congress that saw the latter swallow the humiliation of accepting the role of a junior partner in the coming state assembly elections in Uttar Pradesh. It was the BSP that got the lion's share of 300 seats and the Congress only 125 of the total 425 assembly seats in the state. Announcing this at a joint press conference Kanshi Ram and Congress president Narasimha Rao, who had just lost his government in the Lok Sabha polls, presented two contrasting images. Boosted by his party's performance in the Lok Sabha polls, Ram oozed self-confidence and appeared to be in charge of the situation. Rao, on the other hand, looked like a defeated politician heading a party that had no sense of direction and just mumbled his lines. When the BSP leader announced that Mayawati would be the chief minister if the alliance won, the Congress president looked surprised—it was obvious that he had not been previously consulted; but just as obviously he felt it wiser not to reveal this before the media.

In many ways the acceptance by the Congress leadership of such a humiliating deal drove the last nail in the party's coffin in the country's largest state. Interestingly, in the assembly polls, on Kanshi Ram's insistence, most of the candidates the Congress fielded were brahmins and virtually none were Dalits. This was supposed to be a ploy to wean away brahmin votes from the BJP, but finished whatever was left of the Congress base among Dalits in the state. Many Congress leaders in Uttar Pradesh privately lamented this abject surrender to the BSP, but they could do little in the face of the complete political paralysis then gripping the party high command in New Delhi.

Kanshi Ram rubbed the point in further during the course of a magazine interview before the polls. Asked by *Outlook* magazine whether he was convinced of the sincerity of the Congress to stick to the terms and conditions of the alliance, he replied, 'I am convinced by their helplessness. They will toe our line.'[3]

BSP leaders also used their new-found clout with the Congress to send tremors through the coalition at the centre. The target was Mulayam Singh Yadav who was now the defence minister in the central cabinet. In fact, the Congress joined the BSP in a walkout in the Lok Sabha, demanding the resignation of Yadav following the publication of the Ramesh Chandra Committee report indicting Yadav for his role in the assault on BSP legislators in the Lucknow state guest house on 2 June 1995. Although Rao stonewalled demands by Kanshi Ram and Mayawati to withdraw his party's support from the Deve Gowda regime unless Mulayam Singh was sacked, the BSP for the first time was flexing its muscles in national politics as well.

The assembly polls in Uttar Pradesh held at the end of September and the first week of October resulted in a political stalemate in the state. The results were, in terms of seats, eerily similar to the previous assembly polls in 1993 and, in terms of vote percentage, reflected the outcome of the recent Lok Sabha polls. The BSP won sixty-seven seats, and along with the Congress tally of thirty-three seats, commanded a bloc of hundred seats in the 425-seat assembly. Mulayam Singh's party had 110 seats, while the BJP once again got the highest number, 180 seats, but still fell short of a clear majority. Since none of the three different political groups had a majority by themselves and nor were they ready to ally with each other, there was no other alternative to another spell of President's Rule for the state.

There were important lessons to be learnt by the BSP leadership from the party's performance in Uttar Pradesh in both the Lok Sabha polls and in the assembly elections. The party had done remarkably well, but this was largely due to the massive consolidation of scheduled caste votes behind the BSP. A Centre for the Study of Developing Societies (CSDS) survey during the 1996 assembly polls revealed that as much as sixty-five per cent of Dalit voters supported the BSP in the elections.

Yet, this overt dependence on the scheduled caste vote also betrayed the weakness of the party and was responsible for the poor seat conversion of its vote percentage linked to the demographic distribution of Dalits across Uttar Pradesh. For instance, with roughly the same percentage of vote, the BSP managed to win six seats compared to the Samajwadi Party's sixteen in the Lok Sabha polls and sixty-seven seats compared to the latter's 110 in the state assembly elections.

It was becoming increasingly clear that if the BSP wanted to get a majority of its own or at least come within striking distance it had to mobilize support beyond its Dalit base. For Kanshi Ram and Mayawati this presented no ideological problems since from the days of BAMCEF, they had made a concerted bid to widen the support base to the entire bahujan samaj of Dalits, backward castes and minorities. As a matter of fact, not only did the BSP distribute election tickets to Dalits, backwards and minorities and even some upper castes, but there was also fair representation of society in the party's sixty-seven winning candidates. There were twenty-six backward castes, twenty Dalits, twelve Muslims and nine upper castes among them. But regardless of the ticket distribution or the caste and community to which the candidates belonged, the reason why they were elected was primarily because of the consolidation of the Dalit vote behind the BSP. What the elections provided was a reality check to the BSP leadership that despite their pleas to the bahujan samaj in general, only the Dalits recognized the special appeal of the party, which while important was not enough to capture power except through the backdoor.

At the same time, the fact that two-thirds of the scheduled castes—who comprised more than a fifth of the population of Uttar Pradesh—had consolidated behind the BSP was a stupendous achievement. It was clear that this was directly linked to the impact made on Dalits by Mayawati's brief stint in power. There was now enough empirical data to suggest that the very notion of their representatives capturing political power was a potent elixir for the Dalit masses. This was particularly true for the numerically dominant chamar community who considered the BSP as its own creature and voted almost en masse for the party. Perhaps, never before had identity politics been distilled in such a pure form in the electoral crucible. The fact that they could count on the unwavering loyalty of Dalit voters in Uttar Pradesh as long as they held out the promise of controlling the administration profoundly influenced the political approach of both Kanshi Ram and Mayawati in the coming years.

SEVEN

# The Second Coming

$\mathcal{T}$he second coming of Mayawati as chief minister of Uttar Pradesh was hatched at the unlikely venue of the wedding ceremony of the daughter of a journalist in Chennai, Tamil Nadu. Noted columnist T. V. R. Shenoy, a friend of Kanshi Ram from the early eighties, had close associations with senior RSS and BJP leaders. It was the last day of February 1997. Ram was invited along with a gamut of BJP luminaries and leaders from other political parties as well. As the celebrity wedding guests exchanged political gossip along with social pleasantries, Jitendra Prasad, Uttar Pradesh Congress chief, suddenly exclaimed, 'Look! Look! There is another marriage taking place!' He was pointing to an intense huddle in one corner between Kanshi Ram and the then BJP president, Lal Krishna Advani. Prasad, with a political instinct as sharp as his wit declared that he was off to Tirupati, the famed Hindu temple in the south, to ask for divine intervention to halt the consummation of what he insisted was the marriage of the BSP and BJP in Uttar Pradesh.

Clearly, the state Congress chief failed to invoke the gods because by the time the wedding celebrations of Shenoy's daughter moved a fortnight later to a reception in New Delhi, the skeleton of a formal agreement had already been worked out for an alliance between the BSP and the BJP in Uttar Pradesh. Shenoy admits that he played a key role in bringing the two parties together, the wedding celebrations of his daughter providing a convenient occasion. But, in fact, he merely helped to clinch a deal that was driven by mutual compulsions.

The political stalemate caused by the fractured mandate in Uttar Pradesh opened the door for Kanshi Ram and Mayawati to renegotiate a fresh bid for the throne in Lucknow. There was pressure from the ruling United Front in New Delhi as well as sections of the Congress on Mayawati to kiss and make up with Mulayam Singh to revive an SP–BSP alliance, thus isolating the BJP. This ran into two problems. Memories of the outrageous assault by Samajwadi Party goons at the Lucknow state guest house were still too fresh for her to forgive and forget. Moreover, Mulayam Singh himself was unwilling to accept the BSP's minimal condition of Mayawati being the chief minister of any SP–BSP coalition that came to power in Uttar Pradesh.

In fact, the Mayawati factor was also the reason why the BSP initially found it difficult to strike a deal with the BJP. Local party boss Kalyan Singh doggedly resisted pressure from national leaders led by Atal Bihari Vajpayee and Murli Manohar Joshi to revive the earlier arrangement between the two parties. Kalyan Singh's antipathy towards Mayawati was so fierce that his supporters manhandled a BJP legislator, Brahm Dutt Dwivedi, a Vajpayee supporter and a strong supporter of Mayawati. After the assembly poll results, Dwivedi had started a campaign within the party to promote her candidacy for the chief minister's post. Dwivedi was gunned down a few months later, possibly the result of a conspiracy said to have been masterminded by local leaders belonging to both the Samajwadi Party and BJP, including some said to be close to Kalyan Singh. Several years later, a Samajwadi Party legislator, Vijay Singh, was sentenced to life imprisonment for his role in the assassination.

Even as this tussle to regain power in Uttar Pradesh continued, Kanshi Ram was shaken by his party's dismal performance in the Punjab assembly polls at the beginning of 1997. The BSP had done well in Ram's home state in the 1996 Lok Sabha polls, winning three seats and nearly ten per cent of the vote. But this had gone to his head: for the assembly elections, he walked out of an alliance with the Congress after the latter refused to accommodate his preposterous demand of forty-five out 117 assembly seats. Ram switched to a last moment tie-up with the former Sikh extremist, Simranjit Singh Mann, who possessed neither an organizational network nor a sufficiently large mass base. Not surprisingly, the BSP slipped by several vote percentage points from its Lok Sabha performance managing to win just a single seat in the assembly. All it managed to do was severely damage the Congress, which crashed to fourteen seats with the newly formed Akali–BJP combine romping home with an unprecedented ninety-three seats in the 117-seat Punjab assembly.

Stung by this electoral rebuff on his home turf, the BSP president may well have been a bit more accommodative when he met Advani at the Chennai wedding. What also made a big difference to the parleys was the personal interest in the deal taken by Advani, who had previously been wary, if not actually hostile, to an alliance with the BSP—a line promoted mainly by his senior party colleagues Vajpayee and Joshi. The change in the BJP president's attitude was clearly linked to a directive by the RSS that had taken a considered decision to support a fresh alliance with the BSP. This was in consonance with the new Sangh strategy of promoting alliances to end its isolation after the Babri Masjid demolition—a policy shift that would earn the party rich political dividends in the coming years. Advani, who had earlier celebrated the BJP's exclusivist agenda by describing it as 'majestic isolation', had little option but to fall in line with orders that came directly from his RSS bosses. He was egged on by his media cheerleaders such as columnist Swapan Dasgupta, who wrote after the formation of the BSP–BJP coalition government in March 1997: 'Advani should take heart from UP. The BJP has lost its innocence; it may gain in maturity. It may even acquire the flexibility to win power.'[1]

Kanshi Ram was quick to recognize the significance of Advani's support for a BSP–BJP alliance. He knew that this, along with the support of Vajpayee and Joshi already in the bag, would be enough to tip the balance in his favour. Despite Kalyan Singh's political clout in Uttar Pradesh, he would not be able to resist the combined might of the big three in the BJP. He was correct in his assessment. Even as the details of the deal were being worked out, Singh was kept in the dark and packed off by his party president to undertake padayatras across Uttar Pradesh. The hapless backward-caste leader was summoned back a day before the deal was announced and it was presented to him as a fait accompli.

The new deal was quite different from the loose and unstructured arrangement that marked the BJP's support to Mayawati during her first stint in power. This time there was a proper memorandum of understanding between the two parties, duly typed out in Advani's Pandara Park residence and then announced to the media at a joint press conference with Kanshi Ram. The salient features of the arrangement worked out between the two parties were:

1. The chief minister's post will be shared on a six-monthly rotational basis by the BSP and BJP with Mayawati getting the first term.
2. Both parties will get equal representation in the ministerial council.
3. The BJP will get the state assembly Speaker's post.
4. A panel consisting of Atal Bihari Vajpayee, Kanshi Ram and Lal Krishna Advani will monitor the coalition.
5. After the completion of one year, the two parties will review the coalition experiment and if satisfied will continue it on the same terms.

Although Kalyan Singh was forced to give his assent to the deal, he did so kicking and screaming. Appearing at an informal press meet with Vajpayee shortly after the coalition government was announced, he walked out rather than answer persistent questions on whether he was upset about the deal, leaving the BJP veteran alone to deal with the media. It took Singh four days after the deal was announced to publicly support it. He had good reason to be annoyed with the humiliating conditions of the deal. Although his party had three times the legislators of the BSP, it was Mayawati who had been chosen to lead the coalition government for the first six-month term. Similarly, despite having a hundred more legislators than the BSP, the number of ministerial posts granted to the BJP was exactly the same as that of the BSP. Kalyan Singh and his supporters saw the political arrangement foisted on them by their national leaders as a complete sell-out of the party's interests in Uttar Pradesh. But, for the moment they had little option but to yield to the BJP bigwigs in New Delhi and to the RSS high priests who were convinced that the immediate advantage of breaking the Congress alliance with the BSP along with the long-term gains from ending the BJP's political isolation far outweighed the momentary heartburn and resentment among local leaders.

It is not that the BSP had its way completely. Kanshi Ram did scale down his demands from his first negotiations with the BJP. He had then insisted on unconditional support from outside for a Mayawati government for a minimum one-year period. The BSP leader had been reluctant to share power with BJP on the plea that it would alienate his party's Muslim supporters. Nor was he particularly keen to give the state assembly Speaker's post to the BJP, knowing the hostile role such a functionary could play in the event of a dispute between the two parties. However, when he found that the national BJP leadership and the RSS were not ready to antagonize Kalyan Singh beyond a point, Kanshi Ram was shrewd enough to accept what was still a very good deal. It achieved his immediate objective—getting Mayawati back into the chief minister's saddle to sustain the political momentum gained during her first stint in power.

There were also other pressing compulsions on the BSP leaders to quickly clinch the deal. Ram and Mayawati were getting jittery about a parallel move by Mulayam Singh Yadav, an increasingly powerful figure because of his position in the central cabinet, to engineer large-scale defections from the BSP and form a government with the help of the Congress. In fact, they were so paranoid about defections from their flock, that shortly after the elections, Mayawati herded BSP legislators into the party headquarters where they were locked up for several weeks and not allowed to meet anyone except close relatives for a brief period every day. BSP leaders were particularly apprehensive about the role played by governor Romesh Bhandari, who was widely perceived as being Mulayam Singh's man.

As speculation about Mayawati's comeback at the helm of a BSP–BJP coalition government grew, there were reports of a secret deal between Mulayam Singh and Kalyan Singh to somehow keep their common enemy out of power. An outrageous move by the governor to install a minority government led by Kalyan Singh, with the tacit support of the Samajwadi Party apparently fell through because Kalyan Singh chickened out at the last moment, fearing the wrath of his RSS bosses. Not surprisingly, the normally suave governor looked palpably ill at ease while swearing in

Mayawati and her council of ministers on 20 March 1997; he stumbled through his ceremonial lines making mistake after mistake.

Although the new government was to be run jointly by the BSP and the BJP, it became clear very soon that the latter had very little role to play in Mayawati's six-month stint in power. The two parties each had eight ministers and twelve ministers of state, but the chief minister bagged virtually all the powerful and lucrative departments. Much like in her first stint in office, she ordered a spate of bureaucratic transfers that, by the time she completed her six-month term, added up to the shifting of as many as 1,350 civil and police officials. The same coterie of Dalit officers appeared around her. Punia returned as principal secretary to the chief minister with Netram and Shri Krishna as secretaries. Mayawati's favourite police officer, Kashmir Singh, was promptly appointed DIG, Lucknow.

In many ways, Maywati approached her second term in office as if she had just been on vacation for the past few months and simply continued with what she had been doing earlier, but with even more gusto. The fact that this time she had a coalition partner to whom she would have to hand over the chief ministerial reins in six months, obviously made little difference. For instance, the creation and renaming of monuments, parks, institutions and districts after iconic Dalit leaders was resumed with great enthusiasm and without much concern about the sensitivities of the BJP.

The ambitious project to create a mammoth twenty-eight-acre Ambedkar Park was swiftly reinstated, negating the governor's move to turn it into a golf course. In fact, the new chief minister more than doubled the budget for the park. Similar official generosity was shown towards Mayawati's other pet project, Parivarthan Chowk. Moreover, within a month of her coming to power, five new districts were created and all of them named after prominent Dalit reformers. Among them was Chitrakoot, associated with the BJP's religious mascot, Lord Ram, and held to be a sacred place by Hindus. Ignoring threats of self-immolation by some Hindu sadhus should the name of Chitrakoot be changed, Mayawati steamrollered through the decision to rename it Shahu Maharajnagar, after the famous Dalit reformer from Maharashtra. The new chief minister also intensified the drive to build Ambedkar statues, so popular with Dalits and hated with equal intensity by upper and intermediate castes across Uttar Pradesh. If her first government funded hundreds of statues, she now installed thousands of them. At least 15,000 statues were installed across the state, including a massive one in the capital, Lucknow, at a cost of nearly Rs 250,000 to the state exchequer.

On the economic front, Mayawati not only revived her Ambedkar Villages Scheme but expanded it further allocating as much as Rs 350 crores for its implementation. It now brought a whole range of infrastructural benefits to millions of Dalits across 11,000 designated villages in Uttar Pradesh. This time a concerted effort was made by her administration to give land to the Dalits, including the distribution of allotted pattas (landownership chits) deliberately held back from genuine Dalit claimants by previous administrations. These alone benefited around 158,000 families who were given 120,000 acres of land. She also announced a fresh campaign to give new pattas to the Dalits, distributing 52,379 acres to 81,500 families. The campaign on land rights included a special drive to stop the eviction of Dalits from village land they had occupied, and this directly benefited 20,000 more Dalit families and involved 15,000 acres of land. This meant that well over 250,000 Dalit families or more than one-and-a-half million Dalits were indebted to Mayawati for the countryside's most precious commodity—agricultural land.

Even more crucial support for Dalits from the new administration came through the stern and widespread implementation of the Scheduled Caste/Scheduled Tribes (Prevention of Atrocities) Act. This particular law, enacted in 1989 with the intention of protecting Dalits from upper-caste oppression, had extensive provisions to actually implement this in practice. For instance, the Mayawati administration used the law to jail those accused of crimes against scheduled castes or tribes and also awarded each victim a sum of six thousand rupees to fight the case in court. This addressed the two main reasons why Dalits rarely took their oppressors to court: they did not file cases of atrocities because of their fear of the perpetrators as well as their inability to pay legal fees. The new chief minister's interpretation of the law, therefore, was hailed by Dalits all over Uttar Pradesh and gave a further boost to her image as a 'messiah' in the community.

Mayawati's zeal to use the law to protect Dalit masses, mostly employed as landless labourers and poor peasants, brought her into direct confrontation with large and medium landowners belonging to the upper, intermediate and even some backward castes. Many were supporters of either the BJP or the Samajwadi Party. The BJP could not afford to be openly critical about these measures because it was supposed to share power with the BSP, but Mulayam Singh saw this as a welcome opportunity to wean away the support base of the hamstrung saffron party. He announced with great fanfare that he would scrap the Scheduled Caste and Scheduled Tribes (Prevention of Atrocities) Act when he came to power. Accusing Mayawati of using the law to launch a vendetta against his party workers, the Samajwadi Party leader submitted a list of those wrongly prosecuted under the act to both the governor and the central home minister, urging them to restrain the chief minister.

It became increasingly clear that the BSP leaders were not particularly concerned with the long term survival of the coalition government. Barely a month after the government was formed, Kanshi Ram declared to the *Asian Age* newspaper, 'I want early elections in Uttar Pradesh.' Describing the coalition as a 'marriage of compulsion', the BSP president maintained that this was 'purely a temporary alliance to teach the Congress and the United Front a lesson. I have told Mayawati to complete six years' work in her six-month term so after that we can go to the people in elections and double our vote percentage.'

A few months later, another interview by Kanshi Ram gave his backers in the BJP the jitters. He declared: 'My aim is that the BSP should move forward. At any given point, I'll enter into a tactical alliance with another party if I feel that it will strengthen the BSP. And it is what I have done in the past. I did not enter into an alliance with the BJP because of any ideological common ground—in fact we are poles apart. ... We entered into an understanding with the BJP to increase the base of the BSP, and when we feel we are not benefiting any longer we'll end it. . . . I'm only looking for a suitable ladder.'[2]

A highlight of Mayawati's second stint in power was her running battle with Governor Romesh Bhandari. Hostilities began from the outset when she made him undergo the humiliation of having to deliver a Governor's Address in front of the entire legislative assembly, which had been written by Mayawati's speechwriters and criticized the mistakes and policy decisions of Bhandari's own rule in previous months. Friendly Samajwadi legislators created such a ruckus that he could stop his speech and was thus saved from the ordeal.

Bhandari hit back soon afterwards by contradictory orders to the administration during violent demonstrations by the Muslim Shia community.[3] The confrontation between the governor and the chief minister reached a crisis point when Bhandari called for the bodies of the Shia youths who had immolated themselves in the agitation to be brought to Lucknow. Denouncing the governor for what she described as 'meddling in the affairs of the state', Mayawati openly accused him at a press conference of being 'an agent of Mulayam Singh Yadav trying to incite a bloodbath in Lucknow'. This was followed by a bitter controversy when the governor refused to nominate a Mayawati favourite, her parliamentary affairs minister, Barkhu Ram Verma, to the Vidhan Parishad. Verma had lost the assembly polls. Unfortunately, nominations to the Parishad rested with the governor, who declared the BSP politician was an unsuitable candidate, much to the annoyance of the chief minister. He further angered her by engaging in a bitter procedural wrangle over a series of ordinances that she wanted him to sign to enable her to implement policy decisions quickly when the assembly was not in session. He returned as many as five ordinances turning a deaf ear to the chief minister's admonitions that he was bound by the government's advice.

The BJP in Uttar Pradesh, in its response to Mayawati's determined bid to push her party's agenda regardless of the cost, was a divided house. One section led by Vajpayee acolytes Kalraj Mishra and Lalji Tandon, were of the opinion that the chief minister should be given complete autonomy during her six-month term and the BJP should wait for its own turn at the helm to play a more proactive role in the administration. On the other hand, Kalyan Singh and his supporters insisted that they could not sit back idly as Mayawati continued to alienate BJP supporters. 'The damage done by Mayawati during her six months can't be repaired by the BJP even if it were to rule the State for the next six years,' a minister close to Singh told a national daily two months after the coalition government was formed.[4]

Kalyan Singh was also getting restless because of the internal politics of the BJP. He feared that the powerful upper-caste lobby in the national party, namely, Atal Bihari Vajpayee and Murli

Manohar Joshi would try to push an upper-caste candidate into the chief minister's seat when the BJP's turn came up. Several names were doing the rounds including that of public works department (PWD) minister Kalraj Mishra, urban development minister Lalji Tandon or state BJP President Raj Nath Singh, all of them upper caste. Ironically, the rationale given for choosing one of them over Kalyan Singh was to mollify upper-caste vote banks which had been antagonized during Mayawati's chief ministership. Alarm bells rang in the Kalyan Singh camp after one of the upper-caste chief ministerial hopefuls was quoted by the media as saying that no final decision had been taken by the BJP on who would replace Mayawati. Singh saw this as a direct violation of the categorical assurance given by both Vajpayee and Advani that he would be the chief minister when Mayawati's six-month term was over. Furious that there were moves to deny him the chief minister's post once again, he is believed to have even threatened to force a fresh election in the state. This was no idle threat, considering that Singh had the support of the bulk of BJP legislators in Uttar Pradesh.

Ultimately, the BJP national leadership decided not to push Kalyan Singh too far and nominated him as chief minister. While this defused tensions within the party, the strains with the BSP heightened as the day approached for Mayawati to hand over charge. The BSP suddenly raised a demand to be given the assembly Speaker's post in lieu of the chief minister's post. The BJP refused, pointing out that there was no mention in the agreement between the two parties of making the Speaker's post rotational like that of the chief minister. This raised a question mark on whether Mayawati would actually hand over power to Kalyan Singh, provoking a fierce controversy that continued for several weeks from the end of August to the middle of September. It took persistent efforts by the triumvirate supervising the coalition, Vajpayee, Kanshi Ram and Advani, to calm things down. On 14 September, the three leaders held a joint press conference to announce that all controversial issues between the two parties including the dispute over who should be the Speaker had been resolved, with the BSP accepting that BJP leader Kesri Nath Tripathi would continue to be in charge of the legislative assembly. This paved the way for Mayawati to step down from her second stint as chief minister of Uttar Pradesh and Kalyan Singh to take over the state administration as scheduled on 21 September.

However, the widening gap between the two parties was evident even at the swearing in ceremony of the new chief minister and his council of ministers held in front of a large audience in a public stadium in Lucknow. Kalyan Singh and the BJP ministers were cheered loudly when they took their oath. But there was pointed silence when the BSP ministers were sworn in. Interestingly, the only BJP ministers who got the silent treatment were Kalraj Mishra and Lalji Tandon, seen as Mayawati supporters and hostile to Kalyan Singh. It was clear that Singh had packed the ceremony with his supporters while the BSP had not bothered to invite its own crowd of cheerleaders, underlining that the party had no stake in the new ministry. Some days later, at his first press conference, the new chief minister dwelt at length in his opening remarks on the 'need to undo a casteist bias in both economic development and the maintenance of law and order'. This was seen as a thinly veiled reference to Mayawati's economic schemes and legal action for the welfare and protection of Dalits. With Singh threatening to dismantle the entire thrust of the BSP agenda, it was just a matter of time before the coalition collapsed.

Trouble erupted within a few days of Kalayan Singh taking over. One of his first actions as chief minister was to visit the site of the demolished Babri Masjid at Ayodhya and pray to the idols of Ram and Sita installed there in a makeshift temple. The BSP deemed this as highly provocative and causing offence to the religious sentiments of the party's Muslim supporters. Shortly after Singh's visit to Ayodhya, a Muslim BSP minister, Buniyad Ansari, declared that he was going to offer prayers at the site of the demolished mosque. Even as local BJP leaders bristled with anger at this ultimatum, Kanshi Ram publicly supported his Muslim minister.

Even stronger hostilities broke out over a controversial government order by the Singh administration on the Scheduled Castes and Scheduled Tribes (Prevention of Atrocities) Act. It diluted the provisions of the law, so that it no longer required the administration to keep the perpetrator of atrocities against scheduled castes and tribes in jail until the case was decided. Nor was the victim any longer assured of the sum of six thousand rupees to pay legal fees. These legal provisions, implemented widely during the Mayawati term, had made her a cult figure among Dalits and a target of hate among upper and intermediate castes. When the

BSP demanded that the government withdraw its order, Kalyan Singh refused point-blank claiming that the objections raised by his coalition partner were unwarranted and that the government order merely sought to ensure justice for all sections of society. He also refused to listen to Vajpayee who admonished the chief minister for not consulting BSP leaders before issuing such a sensitive government order. Singh argued that it would be impossible to engage in such consultations for each and every administrative order. In any case, he pointed out, during Mayawati's term hundreds of government orders were issued without consulting the BJP on a single one of them. Even Vajpayee had no answer to this.

When all attempts by the BJP national leadership failed to persuade Kalyan Singh to withdraw his order on the Scheduled Castes and Tribes (Prevention and Atrocities) Act, Kanshi Ram called for a state-wide agitation by his party cadre against the administration from 15 October. The timing of the agitation was significant since it was two days before Singh appeared before a special court on the pending Babri Masjid demolition case. Obviously, the BSP leadership's calculation was to demand a change of chief minister if the court either indicted Singh or passed strictures against him. This plan had the quiet backing of the upper-caste chief ministerial hopefuls, Kalraj Mishra, Lalji Tandon and Rajnath Singh in the Uttar Pradesh BJP, as well as sections of the national party leadership who were furious about Kalyan Singh's defiance. However, the chief minister managed to get through the court proceedings unscathed, and the BSP had no other option but move to plan B, which was to withdraw support and force yet another state assembly poll.

The Kalyan Singh government did not fall, much to the surprise of Ram and Mayawati. They had calculated that the state BJP was far too divided to save the Kalyan Singh government once the BSP withdrew support. Ram and Mayawati were also convinced that they—not Kalyan Singh—enjoyed the support of Vajpayee, Advani and the RSS. The BSP leadership obviously underestimated Singh's abilities as a no-holds-barred political street fighter. It had also failed to notice the new appetite of the RSS to capture political power in both Uttar Pradesh and in New Delhi by hook or by crook. Thus the BSP leadership, along with many political pundits, was entirely unprepared when Kalyan

Singh turned the tables by engineering defections from a whole range of parties including the BSP, Congress and Janata Dal. He lured away legislators from these parties with ministerial posts in a jumbo ministry that kept on expanding to accommodate anyone willing to save his government. The BSP lost as many as a dozen legislators all of whom were gifted ministerial berths by Kalyan Singh. Significantly, this daring exercise left two of his key local rivals, Kalraj Mishra and Lalji Tandon, stunned. The third rival, state BJP president Rajnath Singh joined forces with Kalyan Singh and used his influence with fellow thakur legislators in other parties to win them over to the government.

None of this could have happened without the sanction of the RSS. The same organization that had promoted an alliance with the BSP to end the political isolation of the BJP, was now being driven by new emerging equations in national politics. By the last quarter of 1997 the United Front, itself a strange mutation spawned by the fractured electoral mandate of 1996, was tottering. Not only was the Front led by the mild and apolitical prime minister, Inder Gujral, its main prop, the Congress, was also in the grip of a severe leadership crisis. The former prime minister Narasimha Rao had been replaced as the Congress party president by the weak and emotional Sitaram Kesri. Kesri was further incapacitated by the mixed signals coming from Rajiv Gandhi's widow, Sonia Gandhi, cloistered behind the walls of 10 Janpath, on whether or not she wished to take the reins of the party. Meanwhile, a growing number of Congress members of the Lok Sabha, along with MPs belonging to smaller parties—including some within the ruling United Front—were looking towards the BJP, as the largest political party, to replace an arrangement whose expiry date appeared to be over. The RSS sensed that this was a golden opportunity for the BJP to sit in the driver's seat of the national engine and it was ready to forget past squeamishness about dirty politics.

It is in this context that the Sangh bosses bought into what was described those days as the 'Kalyan Singh line'. The RSS gave its considered consent to the chief minister's completely unscrupulous policy of buying defectors with ministerial posts, not just to save the BJP regime in Lucknow, but also to send a message to potential defectors in the Lok Sabha at the centre. In sharp contrast to its past espousal of legislative conventions and decorum, the Sangh looked the other way as the state assembly Speaker, Kesri Nath Tripathi, wore his BJP hat while turning down the BSP's justified demand that he declare its defectors as illegitimate since they fell well short of a third of its legislators as required by the anti-defection laws.

Only Vajpayee tried to plead the BSP's case but with little success. He is reported to have reminded his friend, RSS chief Rajendra Singh, of the earlier plan to create a pan-Hindu political identity by bringing back Dalits into the mainstream. But he was met with deafening silence. In any case, Vajpayee himself realized that history beckoned—not just to the party but also him as its foremost leader. As for party president Lal Krishna Advani, always the moralist, he did make a show of expressing concern about the unprecedented size of Kalyan Singh's cabinet. But this was a token gesture to mollify his fans in the urban intelligentsia and among his media cheer leaders, including journalist Swapan Dasgupta who wrote about 'the need to draw a Laxman Rekha' as the Sangh frolicked in the political muck it once despised.[5]

Despite Kalyan Singh's blitzkrieg—the counter-attack against the BSP and the successful poaching of legislators from other political parties—he ran into fierce resistance from Governor Romesh Bhandari, who nursed plans to use the crisis for another stint of President's Rule under his stewardship. Bhandari refused to accept Singh's numbers in the assembly and shot off a report to the Centre recommending President's Rule. For four days there was mounting political crisis as the tussle between the governor and the BJP escalated. It was finally resolved in favour of Kalyan Singh after the intervention of President K.R. Narayanan and central home minister Indrajit Gupta despite strenuous efforts by Mulayam Singh Yadav to get New Delhi to uphold the governor's recommendation.

Bhandari would try to topple the Kalyan Singh government once more a few months later with more spectacular results. On 21 February 1998, barely five months after Kalyan Singh engineered defections from the BSP, Congress and Janata Dal to stay in power, he was paid back in the same coin. The Congress breakaway faction, the Loktantrik Congress, that had been one of the several groups of defectors that had helped to prop up the Singh ministry in return for ministerial posts, suddenly decided to make a bid for power on its own with a little help from the governor. The chief ministerial aspirant, Jagadambika Pal, claimed that he actually had the support of a majority of legislators in the assembly, despite the miniscule nature of his breakaway faction. Considering the dubious nature of his claim, the governor should have asked Kalyan Singh to first prove his majority on the floor of the assembly and only then considered Pal's claim. Instead, Bhandari promptly dismissed Singh and administered the oath of office to Pal giving him three days to prove his majority.

Of all the weird political formations to assume office in Uttar Pradesh since then and afterwards, the Pal micro-minority government is unparalleled. A handful of legislators from a few extremely minor parties and tiny factions were all made ministers on the basis of support from outside given by the Samajwadi Party, BSP, Congress, Janata Dal and a dozen Independents. The swearing in ceremony was attended by a host of Kalyan Singh's political foes—including Mayawati—all delighted that the backward caste leader was being paid back in his own coin. BJP leaders filed petitions in court and led countrywide protest demonstrations including an indefinite fast by Vajpayee in Lucknow. Newspapers wrote anguished editorials about the murder of democracy in Uttar Pradesh. Three days later, the Allahabad High Court declared the dismissal illegal and reinstated Kalyan Singh to the chief ministership. Singh had managed to claw his way back to power for the second time in less than six months.

Singh's return to power left Mayawati and the BSP in tatters. She lost as many as seventeen out of her sixty-seven legislators. A dozen left when Singh first engineered defections to stay in power and five more crossed over to Singh after the Jagadambika Pal fiasco. The collapse of the United Front government at the centre after withdrawal of support by the Congress forced a mid-term general election in the country and the BSP faced the challenge of contesting crucial Lok Sabha polls for which it had no time to prepare.

For once, Kanshi Ram was genuinely perplexed instead of rejoicing—as he usually did—at the twists and turns of politics. He swung from bluster to peevishness. 'I am up for sale,' Ram declared at a tea party on New Year's Day 1998 to celebrate the Election Commission's recognition of the BSP as a national party. Yet he clearly delighted at the number of invitees who turned up as it showed that despite its travails in Uttar Pradesh, the BSP was still in demand. Congress president Sitaram Kesri had sent his seniormost party leaders from Madhya Pradesh, Arjun Singh and Madhavrao Scindia. Former prime minister Chandra Shekhar came with friends, while Devi Lal and Om Prakash Chautala from the Samajwadi Janata Party (SJP) were also present. Bharatiya Kisan Kamgar Party chief Ajit Singh was there. Even caretaker prime minister I.K. Gujral turned up on behalf of the United Front, even though his cabinet colleague, defence minister Mulayam Singh, who was still at daggers drawn with BSP leaders, stayed away. Conspicuous by their absence were BJP leaders, also not on social terms with Kanshi Ram after the confrontation in Uttar Pradesh. A few days later a peevish Kanshi Ram announced he would no longer give tickets to upper-caste candidates since they could not be trusted any more. This was a clear reference to the preponderance of upper castes among the legislators who deserted Mayawati and crossed over to Kalyan Singh in Uttar Pradesh.

A communication gap seemed to be growing between Ram and Mayawati. They conveyed, for instance, conflicting signals on alliances for the coming elections. In mid-December she told journalists that her party no longer believed in pre-poll alliances as it had been established that while the BSP voter base transferred to its allies, the latter were unable to return the favour. The very next day, her mentor announced the BSP's participation in a new secular front comprising Laloo Yadav's Rashtriya Janata Dal (RJD) in Bihar, Chandra Shekhar's Samajwadi Janata Party (SJP) and Ajit Singh's Bharatiya Kisan Kamgar Party (BKKP) in Uttar Pradesh, and Shankarsinh Vaghela's Rashtriya Janata Party (RJP) in Gujarat. Sources close to Kanshi Ram revealed that this provoked a major Mayawati tantrum after which he hastily left out Uttar Pradesh parties from his list of potential alliances.

While in Uttar Pradesh the party contested the elections on its own, Ram decided to forge a full-fledged pact with the Congress in Punjab, a half-baked alliance with Laloo Prasad Yadav in Bihar and a tentative electoral understanding in Madhya Pradesh that did not really work on the ground. The results were disappointing for the BSP. While in Uttar Pradesh the party retained its twenty per cent vote, its winning seats fell from six in the previous 1996 Lok Sabha polls to four including Mayawati's victory from Akbarpur scheduled caste constituency.

What made the Lok Sabha results from Uttar Pradesh seem

worse for the BSP were the impressive performances by both its main political rivals in the state. The BJP got an unprecedented thirty-seven per cent vote with fifty-seven seats, a massive vindication of Kalyan Singh's aggressive brand of politics. Mulayam Singh Yadav also did very well, raising the vote percentage of his Samajwadi Party by eight points to twenty-eight per cent and winning twenty seats—a gain of four seats from the previous parliamentary polls. The Congress was wiped out in Uttar Pradesh, failing to win a single seat with barely six per cent of the vote. This meant that the BJP and the Samajwadi Party between themselves had swept the country's largest state—an ominous signal for the BSP. There was more bad news from other states. The alliance with the Congress in Punjab failed to work and neither party got a single seat in the state, which like the assembly polls was swept by the Akali–BJP combine. This was the second successive blow to Kanshi Ram on his home turf. In Madhya Pradesh too, the BSP failed to win a single seat—a big disappointment in a state that had earlier looked so promising for the party. The only state beyond Uttar Pradesh where the BSP managed to win was Haryana, where it won from Ambala.

Mayawati had good reason to be alarmed by the results from Uttar Pradesh. They showed that the BSP had not only failed to enhance its vote percentage in the state, but the seat conversion rate had further dropped from the previous poll's already disappointing rate. The fact that three out of the four winning candidates were Mayawati herself and two high profile Muslim leaders, Arif Mohammed Khan and Akbar (Dumpy) Ahmed, indicated that even these gains may have had more to do with personal charisma rather than the party's electoral base. Moreover, the party had lost a part of its Muslim support base to Mulayam Singh, who along with Kalyan Singh had also eaten away a sizeable chunk of the BSP's backward caste votes. The only silver lining was the further consolidation of the Dalit vote behind Mayawati, which was responsible for the maintenance of her party's twenty per cent vote in the state. But clearly this was not enough to win seats and that was what mattered in the quest for power.

The 1998 Lok Sabha polls yielded yet another fractured mandate with the BJP bagging its highest ever tally, 182 seats, but still well short of a majority. This time, however, the assiduous efforts by the party leadership—egged on by the RSS—to shed the BJP's exclusivist image over the past year showed results. Vajpayee in his second attempt as prime minister managed to get enough allies to win the confidence vote. Yet, no sooner had he assumed the reins of government, the RSS cut him to size by changing his finance minister from his close associate Jaswant Singh to Yashwant Sinha and seeking to impose a 'Swadeshi' economic agenda that restricted the globalization process of the country's economy. The interference by the Sangh bosses along with the troubles caused by volatile allies like AIADMK supremo Jayalalithaa, chief minister of the southern state of Tamil Nadu, gave the Vajpayee regime a fragile and unstable appearance.

As the BJP-led National Democratic Alliance (NDA) tottered from crisis to crisis, the Congress turned to the BSP to fight a common enemy. The Congress was languishing from its second successive dismal total tally of 140-odd Lok Sabha seats. But the party had at least resolved its leadership crisis with the emergence of Rajiv Gandhi's widow, Sonia, as the latest dynastic avatar to lead the party. While the restlessness amongst party cadre and leaders alike had calmed, there was acute awareness of the vulnerability of the Congress after two electoral debacles, one after the other. For the Congress, which had lost much of its past Dalit vote bank to the BSP in northern India, an alliance with the party was a prime objective. Congress leaders fondly recalled the Congress–BSP alliance for the 1996 Uttar Pradesh assembly polls. Ironically, many of them had been openly critical of the then party president, Narasimha Rao, for giving away too many seats to the BSP when he had crafted the alliance. But the past seemed rosy compared to the present grim scenario. In the 1998 Lok Sabha polls the Congress, fighting alone, had failed to win a single of the eighty-five seats, losing its deposit in seventy of them. On the other hand, the party in alliance with the BSP in the 1996 state assembly polls had won one-third of the 125 seats it contested, not losing its security deposit in even a single one.

The first opportunity for collaboration between the two parties came before the state assembly polls in Madhya Pradesh, Rajasthan and Delhi in the winter of 1998. The BSP had a strong base among Dalits and lower backward castes in Madhya Pradesh, particularly in areas close to the border separating the state from Uttar Pradesh. Clearly, the Congress could gain from an alliance with the BSP. However, with Sonia Gandhi increasingly calling the shots in the Congress, new links were needed to connect with the BSP leadership. Sonia Gandhi's emissaries scurried to cultivate Kanshi Ram, who initially played hard to get. After much difficulty a back channel was established through an income tax officer close to 10 Janpath as well as to aides of the BSP leader.

The officer arranged a secret meeting between Congress representatives and Ram at a private residence in Gulmohar Park in south Delhi. This turned out to be quite a comic episode. Sonia Gandhi sent two of her top aides, Arjun Singh and Manmohan Singh for the rendezvous. While Manmohan Singh arrived quietly, Arjun Singh emerged out of a red Maruti with his head covered with a bright yellow towel—his attempt to be ultra-secretive made him all the more conspicuous, if not hilarious. The two Singhs waited patiently for the BSP leader, but there was no sign of him. Some time later, Ram called the officer to find out whether the Congress leaders had arrived, and when told they had, said that he was not really held up but would deliberately like to keep them waiting for at least one more hour. Indeed, the ludicrous spectacle of two top leaders, one a former distinguished bureaucrat-turned-politician who had heralded historic economic reforms as finance minister in the Narasimha Rao cabinet, and the other a veteran chief minister of Madhya Pradesh and governor of Punjab, waiting patiently for a political maverick like Kanshi Ram, symbolized the shifting power equations in Indian politics.

The BSP leader finally arrived, spent barely half an hour with the Congress duo and then left abruptly. Interestingly, Arjun Singh, the supposedly skilled political negotiator remained silent, while his apolitical colleague Manmohan Singh made a fervent plea for an alliance with the BSP. Although Ram remained brusque and abrasive throughout the meeting, the alliance ultimately materialized and worked with resounding success for the Congress. The party won a second term in Madhya Pradesh—a major achievement—as well as sweeping in Delhi and Rajasthan. While the pact with the BSP in Madhya Pradesh was directly responsible for the Congress victory in the state, even the one in Delhi, facilitated by the anti-incumbency wave against the BJP government fuelled by rising onion prices, was influenced by help from BSP in key constituencies.

Although it was the Congress and Sonia Gandhi—as the new

leader of the party—that were the direct beneficiaries of the resounding victories over the BJP in the three state assembly polls, the BSP drew vicarious pleasure from the discomfiture of the Sangh Parivar in three key northern states. Before the assembly polls, Kanshi Ram had declared that he was helping the Congress in the elections with the sole purpose of defeating the BJP, predicting that this, in turn, would precipitate the collapse of the Vajpayee government at the centre.

Indeed, there was little doubt that the defeat of the BJP in three of its north Indian bastions did aggravate the deepening crisis in the ruling coalition, further eroding the stature of the prime minister, Atal Bihari Vajpayee, and encouraging the party's allies to make more and more outrageous demands. In a matter of months after the polls the NDA was reduced to a minority after the AIADMK, its Tamil Nadu partner, led by the capricious Jayalalithaa, withdrew support. As the BJP's opponents, including the BSP, threatened to topple the government, the besieged prime minister had to use his not inconsiderable personal charm to find allies in the Lok Sabha to save his government. He did manage to enlist the last minute support from two parties hitherto in the enemy camp—the DMK in Tamil Nadu and the Indian National Lok Dal in Haryana. This turnaround in favour of Vajpayee made it a really tight race as the Lok Sabha vote of confidence approached.

Ultimately, the survival of the government boiled down to which way the BSP, with five members in the House, would vote. A day before the vote scheduled for 17 April 1999, Mayawati, who along with Kanshi Ram had been in the forefront of the topple-Vajpayee operation, suddenly announced during the debate on the confidence vote that the BSP would abstain from voting. This immediately improved the BJP-led coalition's chances of survival. In fact, as the prime minister was leaving Parliament on 16 April, Mayawati, standing at the portico, called out to tell him not to worry, as she would save his government. However, the very next evening Mayawati and her MPs voted against the government, which lost the confidence of the Lok Sabha by just one vote.

Both Mayawati and Kanshi Ram declared soon after the vote that they had finally extracted their revenge for Vajpayee's failure to save them from Kalyan Singh's smash-and-grab raids on the

BSP in Uttar Pradesh. There was widespread speculation in political and media circles about why Mayawati first assured Vajpayee she would save his government and then did quite the opposite. Some suggested that she was forced to change her stance by Kanshi Ram who was determined to bring the BJP down. Both BSP leaders strongly denied any difference of opinion on the issue, claiming that the fake assurances to the BJP before the vote was the part of a deliberate strategy. 'Some deceit was required, otherwise they may have split us,' Kanshi Ram explained, clearly referring to the tactics used by Kalyan Singh to split the BSP in Uttar Pradesh barely a year ago. A rift between the two on whether or not to bring the Vajpayee regime down appears unlikely. But it is quite probable that they debated various options on what would benefit the BSP most till the last moment. Backing the Vajpayee regime opened up the possibility of blackmailing the prime minister into sacking Kalyan Singh and putting the BSP back on the road to power in Uttar Pradesh. On the other hand, there was an offer from the Congress to sack Kalyan Singh and put Mayawati in his place with the support of the Samajwadi Party and other constituents of the emerging anti-BJP front. Obviously, the Congress offer—reportedly conveyed to Kanshi Ram by Sharad Pawar—had its problems particularly since it involved the unlikely collaboration between bitter foes, Mayawati and Mulayam Singh. But amidst the political turbulence engulfing the Vajpayee government, it was the Congress and the not the BJP that looked like holding the better cards, and both Kanshi Ram and Mayawati ultimately decided to play along with the Congress.

Much drama intervened between the fall of the Vajpayee government and the 1999 mid-term general elections. First, there was an abortive attempt by Congress and its new leader, Sonia Gandhi, to form an alternative government within the same Lok Sabha. The attempt collapsed along with the anti-BJP front after a series of political blunders that badly dented the image of both Sonia and the Congress party. It also finished Mayawati's hopes of being installed on the throne of Lucknow with the help of a Congress-led coalition front in New Delhi.

This political theatre in the national capital was followed by the sudden Kargil invasion by Pakistan. This first threatened to overwhelm the caretaker Vajpayee government, but then as Indian troops bravely pushed back the infiltrators across the border, it boosted support for a prime minister, seen to be fighting to save the nation at a time when he was beleaguered by his political foes.

The BJP bagged exactly the same number of seats, 182, as in the elections of 1998. But the distribution of seats across India was different with the party doing far better in the states of Maharashtra, Rajasthan and Andhra Pradesh but sharply declining in Uttar Pradesh. Significantly, the BJP's allies also did well giving the NDA a comfortable majority. This meant that it was no longer vulnerable to collapse—unlike after the last general elections—if one big party in the coalition withdrew support. It was a disastrous election for the Congress that saw the once predominant political force in India slump to as low as 116 seats, suffering a series of losses even in its former citadel of southern India.

For the BSP, the results meant a huge boost to Mayawati and a moral victory for her over Kanshi Ram. There were reported differences over poll strategy between the two before the mid-term elections. Ram felt that with the NDA looking stronger than before, it was necessary to ally with its opponents wherever possible, including Uttar Pradesh. Mayawati was not concerned with Kanshi Ram's strategies in other states, but she was absolutely adamant about going it alone on her home turf of Uttar Pradesh. The results vindicated her position. The BSP not only enhanced its vote percentage in Uttar Pradesh by a couple of percentile points, but it dramatically increased its seats from four to fourteen. This was clearly a far better conversion rate of seats to vote percentage than ever before—the result of systematic and painstaking labour before the polls at the constituency level under the guidance of Mayawati.

Ram, on the other hand, gained little from his political perambulations with other parties in different states. The BSP drew a blank in the rest of the country, including potential bases in Punjab and Madhya Pradesh. In Punjab this was the third time in rapid succession that Ram's party had failed to make any electoral headway and effectively finished his political ambitions in his home state. Negotiations between the Congress and BSP for an alliance in Madhya Pradesh on the lines of the successful pact in the 1998 state assembly polls had been sabotaged at the last moment by the state chief minister, Digvijay Singh. Although he had been the chief beneficiary of the 1998 pact, a second term in office had obviously gone to his head. He felt that accommodating the BSP in the state would ultimately boomerang on the Congress, which he was confident would do well on its own. He had to eat his words after the polls because the Congress managed to win only eleven out of forty seats in the state, losing several seats because of the BSP factor. However, the BSP also suffered without an alliance, not only failing to win a single seat but also losing in vote percentage.

The victory of the Mayawati line in the 1999 Lok Sabha polls did subtly change the equation between mentor and protégé—the roles no longer as sharply defined as before. From now on, the BSP would increasingly focus on consolidating its hold in Uttar Pradesh, even though the party continued to contest both assembly and parliamentary polls from across the country. The BSP's shrinking political profile in other northern states, particularly his home state of Punjab, diminished Ram's own stature. In any case his failing health severely curtailed his travels and also reduced his confabulations with politicians and journalists. By the time the new millennium began, it was Mayawati who was calling the shots in the BSP and her unwavering mission was to get back on that throne in Lucknow that she had occupied twice in succession, albeit briefly.

Uttar Pradesh after the 1999 Lok Sabha polls presented a fast changing political scenario. The Congress, wiped out in the previous parliamentary elections had managed a revival of sorts though it was still far from becoming a major political force. This was largely due to a return of the Muslim vote, encouraged by a Gandhi once again leading the party. The minority community had lost confidence in the Congress after prime minister Narasimha Rao failed to save the Babri Masjid in 1992. The Sonia-led Congress had made inroads among the upper castes, particularly the brahmins, who were disenchanted with the BJP under Kalyan Singh's leadership. The new enthusiasm for the Congress among Muslims and brahmins helped raise the party's vote percentage from six to fifteen per cent and the number of seats from none to ten in just one year.

The increased Muslim vote for the Congress mainly hurt Mulayam Singh's Samajwadi Party, its vote dipping by four percentile points, although the Yadav leader's clever electoral management remarkably managed to add six seats to his previous tally of twenty. But the real surprise package of the 1999 Lok

Sabha polls that otherwise proved so favourable to the BJP and its prime minister Vajpayee, was the sharp decline of the party in Uttar Pradesh both in terms of vote percentage and seats. In an incredible slump, the BJP lost a good ten per cent of the thirty-seven per cent vote it had won in the 1998 Lok Sabha polls from the state. The drop in seats was even sharper—from fifty-seven to twenty-nine seats. This marked a turning point for the party in Uttar Pradesh.

The decline of the BJP in Uttar Pradesh which began from the 1999 Lok Sabha polls is important to examine in some detail. It vacated a vital political space—much like the Congress had done before—for Mayawati to steadily move towards a dominant position in the state. It also halted the BJP's rising national curve that was heavily dependent on its electoral predominance in the country's largest state.

Rampant factionalism within the BJP was compounded by the dogged refusal of the upper-caste lobby in the state unit as well as among national leadership of the party to accept a backward-caste leader. Clearly, the rough-and-ready methods used by Kalyan Singh in late 1997 and early 1998, while ensuring the survival of his government earned him many enemies. For instance, the RSS, which had earlier sanctioned Singh's smash-and-grab tactics, felt uncomfortable when dealing with him over the long term. So when the 1999 polls came, the chief minister, accustomed to getting his own way in the election-ticket distribution, found that he had virtually no say in the selection of candidates. Even a request that his son, Rajveer Singh, and close associate, Urmila Rajput, be given tickets, was flatly turned down.

He was particularly offended after a direct order from prime minister Vajpayee in New Delhi cancelled the election ticket of Sakshi Maharaj, the sitting MP from Farukhabad, who belonged to Singh's Lodh Rajput sub-caste and was closely identified with him. The controversial MP had been linked to the murder of Brahm Dutt Diwedi, a Vajpayee acolyte and although the charges had not been proved, the denial of a ticket was widely believed to be his punishment from the top. Stung by this humiliation, the chief minister retaliated by making a not so secret deal with Mulayam Singh Yadav against particular BJP candidates he wanted to defeat. The fact that the party's own chief minister was sabotaging its prospects in the polls further damaged the BJP's poll prospects.

Blamed for the BJP's dismal performance in the polls, Kalyan Singh's position as chief minister became untenable. Shortly afterwards, Vajpayee had him removed from the chief minister's post. It did not take long for the ousted leader to rebel openly and thus provoke expulsion from the party. In an effort to keep all warring factions within the state unit happy, the national leadership replaced Singh with a pleasant but quite ineffective seventy-six-year-old leader, Ram Prakash Gupta, known for his embarrassing memory lapses.

Not surprisingly, the party declined further, as the 2002 assembly polls loomed nearer. In less than a year, the BJP once again changed its chief minister in Uttar Pradesh. Gupta was replaced with Rajnath Singh, reputed to be a dynamic organization man, in the hope he would revitalize the party in time for the elections. But it was far too late to reverse the party's downward slide. To make matters worse, the factional wars that had subsided during Gupta's reign, flared up once again with Singh, a thakur by caste, becoming a target of the brahmin lobby headed by Kalraj Mishra.

Meanwhile, Kanshi Ram gave a formal seal of approval to Mayawati's complete control of the party in December 2001. There was no immediate particular catalyst, but it was rather the steady evolution of a partnership that led to the emergence of Mayawati as Kanshi Ram's successor. Addressing a massive rally at the Laxman Mela ground in Lucknow, the ailing founding father of the bahujan samaj movement named his young protégé as his political inheritor. After two decades of relentless struggle with her rivals in the party, many of them more senior and experienced, Mayawati had finally achieved her objective. There were hardly any veterans or heavyweights left in the BSP. She had managed to get rid of them one by one, each time persuading Kanshi Ram to take her side in factional squabbles. Now, once she no longer had to fight these internal battles, she could concentrate on the larger objective of capturing political power.

Armed with her new authority, Mayawati prepared for the 2002 elections with characteristic zeal and innovation. She had already been preparing to widen the party's social base. In July 2001, the BSP leader had created a stir by sacking three of the party's senior most leaders, Barkhu Ram Verma, R.K. Chaudhury and Krishnapal Singh. Two of them, Verma and Chaudhury, were loyal old soldiers and were with her in suites1–2 during the terrible Lucknow guest house ordeal. But they had committed the blunder of not being on the same page over a new proposal by the BJP government to give special benefits to the most deprived sections of Dalits and backward castes. Although initially critical of the policy, Mayawati later declared her support for the quota within quota policy. The senior BSP leaders, however, continued with their attack on the policy that threatened to dilute the privileges monopolized so far by the dominant scheduled sub-caste of the chamars, who constituted the core support base of the party. The sacking of the old guard was decried by the media as the latest proof of Mayawati's autocratic style of functioning, but there was strong electoral logic behind the move. Confident of her hold on the chamars, the BSP leader wanted to expand her voter pool by making a special gesture to the poorer Dalits, particularly the Valmikis who traditionally voted for the BJP.

Similarly, Mayawati tried to cultivate the lower rungs of the backward castes among both Hindus and Muslims. She knew that of the backward castes who comprised over half of the state's population, more than a third belonged to the most backward category. These communities were almost as badly deprived and oppressed as the Dalits. She was convinced that a coalition of Dalits and poorer backward castes would be both a feasible and potent combine.

In another interesting gamble, she gave tickets to upper- and intermediate-caste candidates who had a strong personal following in their caste group. This was a novel strategy that pooled the candidate's own kinship support base with the transferable Dalit and poorer backward caste base of the BSP making him a formidable contestant in an electoral contest. She and her aides spent hours and hours, day after day, pouring over the demographic profile of constituencies, statistics on past elections and the caste and community distribution in different regions, to hone the best possible poll strategy. The list of BSP candidates for the polls was based on a meticulously worked out formula based on a clear understanding of social engineering, giving an indication that the party hoped to reach out to a wide section of people. The largest chunk, 126 tickets, went to backward castes, many of them belonging to the most backward castes, while as many as ninety-one were given to upper-caste candidates. Dalits were given ninety-seven tickets and Muslims eighty-six. Even her opponents conceded that Mayawati's list of candidates appeared to be representative of the entire social spectrum.

The fruits of Mayawati's labours were impressive. The BSP captured ninety-eight seats in the 2002 assembly polls in Uttar Pradesh with twenty-three per cent of the vote. This time the party had jumped ahead—in terms of both seats and vote percentage—of the BJP, which slumped further to eighty-eight seats and twenty per cent of the vote. The Samajwadi Party had also done very well moving to the top of the table with 143 seats and twenty-five per cent of the vote. But the BSP was the real winner in the 2002 assembly polls, far exceeding the predictions made by opinion and exit polls that had tilted towards the BJP and the Samajwadi Party. It had moved ahead of the BJP and was in striking distance of the Samajwadi Party. With Kanshi Ram more or less out of the picture in Uttar Pradesh, Mayawati had achieved this single-handedly from conceptualizing the poll strategy to its execution. The BSP was still nowhere near capturing power by itself. But with Mulayam Singh well short of a majority and in no position to form a government, she knew it was just a matter of waiting for her 'eternal admirers', the jaded, faded brahmins of BJP to come wooing her once more.

# EIGHT

# Third Time Unlucky

 $\mathcal{T}$ he third dalliance between Mayawati and the BJP began against the backdrop of the horrendous communal bloodbath in Gujarat in 2002. It remains the only serious blot on her secular credentials that have survived remarkably well despite so many cohabitations with the BJP. Her stints in power with the help of the BJP in 1995 and 1997 adequately proved the BSP leader's autonomy from the saffron agenda. In fact, despite being dependent on a political entity so hated by Muslims, she had earned their trust in two successive terms as chief minister by protecting the lives, properties and shrines of the minority community, along with promoting welfare schemes for its poor and deprived.

Despite her past record, Mayawati's overtures to the BJP when its leaders and activists were running amuck against Muslims in Gujarat, offended the sensibilities of even those who believe that no party can be regarded as a political untouchable. But during those days of bloody pogroms which were orchestrated by Narendra Modi, a BJP chief minister himself, the party had become untouchable. Mayawati's acquiescence in the Gujarat tragedy was evident by her deafening silence when the entire Opposition demanded a ban on Sangh organizations including the Bajrang Dal and the VHP, the resignation of home minister L.K. Advani and the dismissal of Gujarat chief minister Narendra Modi. Even the Telegu Desam, Trinamul Congress and the DMK—all BJP allies—

were increasingly restless, demanding action to stop the madness in the riot-torn state.

Clearly for Mayawati and her mentor, Kanshi Ram, nothing mattered except the emerging prospect of ruling the country's largest state once again. Ram rubbed this point in amidst speculation in media and political circles that some NDA allies could withdraw support in protest against Gujarat and thus jeopardize the ruling coalition. He unapologetically offered to support the Vajpayee regime if the BJP supported Mayawati as chief minister of Uttar Pradesh in return. The fact that Mayawati campaigned in Gujarat on behalf of the BJP before the state assembly polls later in the year, only compounded her dubious role during a period of grievous communal strife.

Her apologists maintain that the BSP leader's refusal to condemn Hindutva's war dance in Gujarat was not out of ideological affinity, but dictated solely by power equations of the day. After all, she was scrupulously fair and protective towards Muslims during her third tenure as chief minister which came after her tango with Modi. They also point out that for all the surface angst over Gujarat by the supposedly secular allies of the BJP, such as the DMK, Telegu Dasam and Trinamul Congress, none of them actually withdrew support from the ruling coalition. Nevertheless, the manner in which Mayawati pushed the communal flames of Gujarat out of her vision to single-mindedly pursue power is chilling.

It has to be said that the stakes were extremely high. This was by far the best of the three deals offered to Mayawati by the BJP since 1995. The first time she did get unqualified support from the BJP and some other parties, but it was widely known that this was just a temporary ploy to get rid of Mulayam Singh Yadav. In 1997 she was given only a six-month term in an untenable rotational arrangement with her inveterate foe, Kalyan Singh. The 2002 alliance arrived at after a series of meetings between Mayawati and Kanshi Ram with prime minister Vajpayee and home minister Advani, unconditionally granted her the right to rule Uttar Pradesh for a full five-year term. This undertaking, not only from her old well-wisher Vajpayee but also Advani, made the deal look that much more solid and secure, coming as it did with the support of the two people who really mattered in the BJP. Indeed, this was the period when the Big Two in the BJP were briefly on the same page and working in close coordination. Advani was shortly afterwards made deputy prime minister by Vajpayee.

The blessings of the prime minister and his second-in-command did not mean that Mayawati's return to power for the third time with BJP support was welcomed by local party leaders. Her old enemy, Kalyan Singh, had been thrown out of the party for his unconcealed hostility towards several national leaders, most notably the prime minister. But Kalyan Singh's successor and former chief minister, Rajnath Singh, too, bitterly opposed the deal with Mayawati. He and other senior local leaders, including Kalraj Mishra and state BJP chief Katiyar publicly expressed their grave misgivings about a third marriage with a partner who had proved so capricious twice before.

However, the electoral debacle had considerably weakened local BJP leaders. For instance, the BJP had fewer legislators in the assembly than the BSP. Thus, unlike in their past alliances with the BSP, the BJP could no longer protest about the tail wagging the dog. The BSP now could legitimately claim to be the senior partner, however much local BJP leaders and cadre grumbled.

In any case, well before Mayawati was ultimately sworn in as chief minister, the prime minister himself signalled that he would brook no opposition from within the party to the deal. Delivering his valedictory address at the national executive in Goa in April, Vajpayee lambasted those who sought to sabotage the emerging alliance between the BJP and the BSP in Uttar Pradesh. When reports reached him that Rajnath Singh was still sulking even after Mayawati had been sworn in as chief minister, the BJP patriarch picked up the phone and read the riot act to the hapless thakur leader, who then hastily issued a press statement hailing the alliance as the 'ultimate symbol of nationalist and Dalit awakening'.

Mayawati was sworn in on 3 May and was asked by the governor to prove her majority within three weeks. The House had an effective strength of 399 and she needed the support of at least 200 MLAs. On 17 May, she won the trial of strength in the assembly by thirty-seven votes, with 217 members voting in favour of the motion of confidence moved by the government, and 180 voting against. There had been no doubt that she would win the vote; what came as a surprise was the margin of victory. The additional support for Mayawati came from the Janata Dal (U) and the Loktantrik Congress, which had two members each; one MLA from the Lok Janshakti Party (LJP) of Ram Vilas Paswan, and one independent. Interestingly, the list she had submitted to Governor Vishnu Kant Shastri on 29 April while staking her claim to form the government, had only 211 names. The voting, which took place after a seven-hour debate, was taken up thrice: by voice vote, by the raising of hands, and finally, on the Opposition's insistence, by a lobby division. Interestingly, in the show of hands the count showed 216 supporters, but the number went up in the lobby division. The verdict underlined that the MLAs, cutting across party lines, did not want another round of assembly elections in the state any time soon.

Mayawati's comfortable victory also belied sustained speculation in political and media circles that the BSP's fourteen Muslim MLAs would desert her at the time of voting in view of her liaison with the BJP after Gujarat. These rumours grew particularly after Arif Khan, the BSP's most senior Muslim leader, quit the party, making Gujarat an issue. Many felt that Muslim legislators would at least abstain from the vote, which could have made the floor test much closer. But as it turned out, the legislators stayed with Mayawati, partly no doubt lured by the promise of ministerial berths and other favours, but also because they still trusted her in Uttar Pradesh regardless of her stance on Gujarat. As for Arif Khan, he made a mockery of his stance on the Gujarat riots by joining the BJP less than two years later.

Mayawati was acutely conscious of the disquiet with which the minority community regarded her alliance with the BJP in the aftermath of the Gujarat carnage. She knew that Mulayam Singh was assiduously spreading rumours that the BJP was planning similar Gujarat-style pogroms in Uttar Pradesh to fuel these fears. Participating in the debate preceding the confidence vote, she appealed to her Muslim supporters to remember her record of protecting their lives, and went out of her way to give a cast iron guarantee that her administration would do so once again. The BSP leader shrewdly played on the insecurity prevailing among Muslims in the state, pointing out that since Mulayam Singh had left the Muslims in the lurch by failing to form the government, it was left to her to take up reins of power and ensure that the minority community did not suffer.

The first indication that she would keep her promise came in the way she dismissed attempts by the BJP to foist a common minimum programme on her. The move was made under the instructions of the RSS to ensure the BJP did not lose out on pushing its own agenda as it had done during its past two collaborations with the BSP leader. But Mayawati was far too smart to fall into this trap and sidestepped the BJP demand saying that the only programme of her government was 'pro-people and pro-Dalit', which she insisted was the common agenda of both coalition partners. While the BJP and the RSS had no answers to this piece of filibustering, the Muslim minority of Uttar Pradesh breathed a collective sigh of relief that Behenji was still following her own agenda.

At the same time, in sharp contrast to her earlier stints as chief minister, Mayawati made a genuine attempt not to openly provoke her ally. For instance, she took a conciliatory stand when state BJP chief Vinay Katiyar, known for his antipathy to the BSP leader, vehemently opposed a move to install Periyar's statue at the Ambedkar Udayan in Lucknow. She quickly backed off saying that since the Dalit social reformer was more popular in the south, it would be better to install his statue there.

The chief minister also sought to allay fears of upper castes in the BJP about the indiscriminate use of the Schedule Castes and Tribes (Prevention of Atrocities) Act. In the past Mayawati had consolidated her hold on the Dalit masses by using this law not just to punish those who committed atrocities against them, but also sometimes to intimidate upper-caste landowners. As a matter of fact, the dilution of the Act by Kalyan Singh during his term as chief minister had been cited as the reason for the BSP withdrawing support from his government. But this time Mayawati herself amended the Act to prosecute only those who were accused of rape and murder against Dalits.

As a sop to orthodox Hindus and pandering to a major fetish of the Sangh Parivar, she went to the extent of amending the provisions of the UP Prevention of the Cow Slaughter Act to facilitate a more effective ban on the slaughter of cows. Even state BJP chief Vinay Katiyar, usually implacably opposed to her, applauded the move.

Most importantly, the chief minister who had so far been protected by Vajpayee, made a deliberate effort to cultivate Advani, the other centre of power in the national party and government. In an unusual gesture, she invited him to speak at a

BSP rally. Mayawati also obliged the home minister by refraining from issuing a fresh notification in the Babri Masjid demolition case in which he was accused. Instead, she did him a big favour by allowing the case to be transferred to the session's court in Rae Bareilly. Political opponents suspected that a separate trial for Advani and a few select BJP leaders in the Rae Bareilly court, under a separate charge sheet from the rest of the accused in the Ayodhya case which was being heard by the Lucknow Bench of the Allahabad High Court, meant the leaders might get off lightly.

In another major departure from previous coalition experiments with the BJP, this time the BSP leadership appeared ready for a long-term commitment. Unlike in the past, Mayawati and Kanshi Ram no longer constantly spoke of a divorce even before the marriage had time to settle down. In fact, Maywati thrilled the leadership of the Sangh Parivar by promising to remain faithful not just in Uttar Pradesh, but to take the relationship to a higher level with a full-fledged national alliance in the 2004 Lok Sabha polls.

In return for Mayawati's new, accommodating approach to sensitive political and social issues concerning the BJP, the party agreed to look the other way as the BSP leader sought with characteristic bluster to turn the state bureaucracy upside down. Within minutes of taking oath, Mayawati rushed to get a coterie of favourite officials around her. Her favourite, P.L. Punia, headed the list and was back as principal secretary to the chief minister. On the same day, the chief minister also ordered the appointment of three more secretaries under Punia and five special secretaries to handle the chief minister's office. Soon the total number of officials in the chief minister's secretariat reached thirteen, a record high for the state. These included Mayawati's long-time favourite police officer, Kashmir Singh, who was now accommodated in her personal secretariat, a move bitterly criticized by the IAS but popular in the police service.

However, some changes in Mayawati's approach to administration were evident during her third term in office. While the bulk of her favourite officers remained Dalits, the most notable being Punia, officers belonging to upper castes also started acquiring prominence. The most significant of them was Shashank Shekhar Singh, a former pilot belonging to the jat community, who had acquired the reputation of being a bureaucrat for all seasons, having been the key administrative aide of a whole range of rulers in the state, including Mulayam Singh Yadav and Romesh Bhandari. Singh was appointed to the key post of industrial development commissioner. With his winning ways with politicians, he became an immediate rival to Punia who boasted a similar profile. The tussle between the two on who was closer to the chief minister provided an undercurrent of tension and intrigue in the corridors of power throughout her third stint in power. Yet the fact that Mayawati was no longer playing the Dalit card so openly while dealing with the administration and had almost stopped mentioning her favourite M-word—manuvadi—provided considerable relief to the BJP, which had feared another fusillade of upper-caste baiting on the lines of her earlier stints in power.

Mayawati now reserved her choicest abuses for Mulayam Singh. The mud slinging between the two old rivals was actually institutionalized by their parties: the BSP organized *dhikkar* (taunting) meetings and the Samajwadi Party retaliated with *thoo-thoo* (spitting) rallies, and both became unique mechanisms to showcase their mutual antipathy. For instance, Mulayam Singh described the chief minister's pet project, the Ambedkar Park as a 'den of vice', provoking the BSP to organize a special dhikkar rally to respond in kind. Addressing thousands of party cadres who attended the rally, Kanshi Ram asked them to hound the Yadav leader out of the state. Mayawati added her bit by predicting that his declining political graph would soon force him back to his ancestral occupation of grazing buffalos.

Mayawati also took on the Gandhi dynasty and the Congress. In November 2002, Sonia Gandhi's daughter, Priyanka Vadra, had intervened in the Gandhi 'family constituency' of Amethi on behalf of a Dalit supporter who had complained that local thakurs had razed his house to the ground. Priyanka, who looked after the constituency on behalf of her mother, accompanied the aggrieved Dalit to the police station and lodged a first information report (FIR) against the accused and announced that local Youth Congress workers would organize a *shramdaan* (labour camp) to rebuild the house of the victim.

Annoyed that a member of the Gandhi dynasty and the Congress party had muscled in on her turf, the chief minister hit back. She swiftly imposed Section 144 in the constituency, banning the assembly of more than four persons at the same place,

Mayawati (second right) with her parents, Prabhu Das Dayal and Ramrati Devi (second and third left), and five of her seven siblings in the 1960s. (*UP Government Information Office, New Delhi*)

Mayawati receiving a bouquet from her mentor, Kanshi Ram (right), in 1995. *(UP Government Information Office, New Delhi)*

Mayawati with Kanshi Ram in 1996; her close aide, P L Punia, stands just behind. *(UP Government Information Office, New Delhi)*

On her forty-seventh birthday, Mayawati stands with Kanshi Ram (right) next to the birthday cake. *(UP Government Information Office, New Delhi)*

Mayawati: the quiet school teacher who became a powerful national leader. *(UP Government Information Office, New Delhi)*

Mayawati in her twenties: a statue of B L Ambedkar, the architect of the Indian Constitution, is in the background. *(UP Government Information Office, New Delhi)*

Mayawati in her first stint as chief minister of Uttar Pradesh, being sworn in by Moti Lal Vora in 1995. *(UP Government Information Office, New Delhi)*

Chief Minister for the second time: Uttar Pradesh Governor Romesh Bhandari administering the oath of office to Mayawati in 1997. *(UP Government Information Office, New Delhi)*

Uttar Pradesh Governor Vishnukant Shashtri swears-in Mayawati for her third stint as chief minister in 2002. *(UP Government Information Office, New Delhi)*

Chief Minister for the fourth time: Mayawati takes the oath of office from Uttar Pradesh Governer T V Rajeshwer in 2007. *(UP Government Information Office, New Delhi)*

Congress chief Sonia Gandhi meets Mayawati after the latter becomes chief minister of Uttar Pradesh for the fourth time. *(UP Government Information Office, New Delhi)*

Mayawati meeeting BJP chief A B Vajpayee during her third term as UP chief minister. *(UP Government Information Office, New Delhi)*

Prime Minister Manmohan Singh greets Mayawati after she becomes chief minister of Uttar Pradesh for the fourth time. *(UP Government Information Office, New Delhi)*

Close aide Satish Mishra (right) accompanies Mayawati to her meeting with PM Manmohan Singh after her victory in 2007. *(UP Government Information Office, New Delhi)*

Mayawati with her two top advisors: Satish Mishra (left) and Sasank
Sekhar Singh (right). *(UP Government Information Office, New Delhi)*

Chief Minister Mayawati with long-time aide P L Punia in the
background. *(UP Government Information Office, New Delhi)*

on the plea that the Youth Congress programme threatened public peace. While this effectively disrupted the proposed shramdaan, local Congress workers still managed to rebuild the house of the Dalit supporter and some weeks later Sonia Gandhi came to her constituency and formally handed over possession to him.

Fuming at what she saw as meddling by the Gandhis with her caste and in her state, Mayawati publicly denounced Sonia for 'creating caste tension in the region'. She even vowed to get the Congress leader defeated from Amethi in the next Lok Sabha polls. Interestingly, some weeks later, the BSP leader broke the state Congress party, managing to lure away eight legislators with the promise of ministerial berths. Her ferocious response to a token gesture by the Gandhis in their family constituency was yet another example of her fierce possessiveness about her flock and territory.

These proprietary instincts about her Dalit constituency sparked off Mayawati's troubles with the BJP after a relatively amicable relationship during her first few months as chief minister. Not surprisingly, the provocation came from an old adversary—backward-caste leader and state BJP chief Vinay Katiyar. The local BJP boss ruffled BSP feathers with a tour across Uttar Pradesh in December 2002, ostensibly to mobilize Dalits with a new political interpretation of Ambedkar, their most revered icon. He did not even bother to consult the BSP leadership before embarking on his tour and compounded his sins by quoting Ambedkar out of context to portray him as hostile to Muslims.

Both Mayawati and Kanshi Ram were furious at this attempt by Katiyar to give their beloved idol a saffron hue. Apart from their outrage at the local BJP chief twisting the facts of history, they were nervous about the damage this kind of communal propaganda could do to the BSP's Muslim support base that was already apprehensive about the party's alliance with the BJP. Katiyar's attempt to indoctrinate Dalits was also viewed as flagrant poaching of Mayawati's captive vote bank. The BSP leaders rushed to New Delhi to lodge a strong protest with Vajpayee, who—helpful as always—temporarily bought peace by getting Katiyar to cancel his tour programme. The Uttar Pradesh BJP chief was, however, allowed to resume his tour after hectic lobbying with Advani, who advised him to be extra careful about what he said about Ambedkar, Dalits or Muslims.

Despite a tentative truce between Mayawati and Katiyar on his controversial tour, the cracks in the alliance were already visible by the beginning of 2003. This became evident at Mayawati's forty-seventh birthday celebrations in mid-January that year. While the birthday bash was mired in huge public controversy because of the ostentatious display of Bollywood-style sets, a skyscraper birthday cake and glittering diamonds, not many heeded the ringing political alarm bells. For instance, few senior BJP leaders attended the massive birthday party in Lucknow except Mayawati's rakhi bhai and neighbour, Lalji Tandon, who was on the stage with Kanshi Ram when she cut the cake. Significantly, the BSP chief minister had not issued a personal invitation to the local BJP leadership, who received cards from the chief secretary informing them of the birthday party.

When a second Mayawati birthday bash was celebrated at the Talkatora Stadium in New Delhi later in the evening on 15 January, the storm signals became even clearer. While several BJP leaders attended the celebrations in the capital, they shifted uneasily in their seats as Kanshi Ram made a highly provocative speech. After pointing out that in the current hierarchy of political parties, the number one spot was occupied by the BJP with the Congress in second place and the BSP third, Ram declared with characteristic candour that it was his aim to unseat the BJP from its perch. Significantly, Mayawati had declared her lavish birthday celebrations as 'Self-respect Day' for Dalits. This was not merely to justify the vast expense by the state exchequer and funds collected, but also to send a message to the entire political class that she regarded the Dalits as her very own constituency and would not tolerate anybody hijacking it.

Throughout her life, whenever Mayawati sensed danger, she went on the offensive. In a personal tribute written in 2001 Kanshi Ram described this rare form of courage as her 'supreme quality'. Her battle and ultimate triumph over notorious thakur don, Raja Bhaiya, is a classic example. Despite state BJP chief Katiyar's constant pinpricks, the chief minister knew that the more potent threat came from the former chief minister, Rajnath Singh. The prime minister had given him a central cabinet post, deliberately shifting him out of Uttar Pradesh, to prevent a possible confrontation between Singh and Mayawati.

Unfazed by this Vajpayee manoeuvre, Singh had decided to

make his moves against the chief minister through his henchmen and thakur kinsman, Raghuraj Pratap Singh, nicknamed Raja Bhaiya, a feudal lord turned politician infamous for his muscle and money power. He belonged to a fast proliferating breed of criminal politicians or political criminals in many states of India particularly prevalent in the backward cow belt of Uttar Pradesh and Bihar. Although Raja Bhaiya remained an independent legislator, he ensured his own victory at successive polls and also wielded enormous clout with political leaders of various mainstream parties. He did so through a lethal combination of terror tactics and financial patronage. When his cavalcade full of gunmen roared through the countryside, everybody stopped and stood on the roadside with folded hands. A scooterist, who did not and was silly enough to try and overtake the cavalcade, wound up dead. So did a witness who was supposed to give vital evidence in the case accusing the don and his father for the murder of the scooterist. Raja Bhaiya or Chhote Raja—by whichever of his two nicknames you called him, had an unsurpassed reputation as a legendary bad guy and nobody tangled with him.

He was a colourful character who inspired much press coverage. 'There's an old cow belt saying—*Jiski lathi uski bhains* (might is right)—that sums up the power structure in Uttar Pradesh. Traditionally, it is the mighty Thakurs who have wielded the stick here. And independent MLA Raghuraj Pratap Singh alias Raja Bhaiya has always been the epitome of Thakur might. A minor "raja" of Pratapgarh district, he was till recently the very picture of feudal power with all the trappings of Hindi films: guns, horses, henchmen and prostrating villagers.'[1]

He first shot into the limelight during the high political drama in Lucknow after the BSP withdrew support from the Kalyan Singh government in 1997. In a muscular defence of Kalyan Singh, Raja Bhaiya led a group of rowdy independent MLAs to ensure that the former had a smooth passage proving his numbers in the legislative assembly. Since Singh was completely dependent on defectors whose loyalties were still wavering, it was the thakur strongman who forced the issue through his rough and ready ways that involved, among other things, throwing mike handles at Opposition legislators. Photographs of Raja Bhaiya persuading legislators in his own unique manner were splashed across morning papers in Lucknow next day. He was rewarded for his labours with a ministerial berth in the Kalyan Singh government and also accommodated in the Rajnath Singh cabinet when the latter became chief minister. Subsequently, the two became very close.

Having got used to ministerial perks, Raja Bhaiya was extremely peeved that he did not find a ministerial berth in the Mayawati-led BSP–BJP coalition government. He sent several messages to her suggesting that she accommodate him. After the new chief minister persistently ignored his overtures for several months, the don decided that it was time to teach her a lesson. In October 2002 Raja Bhaiya led a group of independent legislators to the governor to announce the withdrawal of their support to her government. This sparked off a minor revo't in the local BJP, with some of the rebel legislators approaching the governor to inform him that they too had 'lost faith' in the Mayawati administration and demanding a special assembly session to test the strength of the government. Obviously, the plan was to get a special session convened and allow Raja Bhaiya to once again display his persuasive skills with legislators. However, the combined support of Vajpayee and Advani saw Mayawati through the crisis.

Not long afterwards, the chief minister struck back using the Prevention of Terrorism Act (POTA). The innovative use of this draconian anti-terrorist law that gave sweeping powers to the police to raid, search and arrest suspects, took everyone by surprise—most of all the BJP, which associated POTA with punishing Muslim extremists. Party leaders, most notably Rajnath Singh, were flabbergasted that Mayawati had interpreted the provisions of the concerned law to counter terror tactics adopted by criminal politicians.

In fact, Raja Bhaiya was initially picked up for 'terrorizing' a BJP rebel into giving statements against the chief minister. After arresting the thakur don as well as his father under POTA, she proceeded to reopen other pending criminal cases against him under various sections of the Indian Penal Code. Various properties owned by his family were seized, the educational institutions run by them taken over, and every other source of income sealed on the plea that they were all illegally acquired. And in a final blow to Raja Bhaiya's pride, the huge pond in his palace in Bainti was declared a reserved bird sanctuary, named after B.R. Ambedkar and handed over to the forest department.

There is little doubt that the chief minister bent the rules quite a bit in her relentless assault on Raja Bhaiya and his family. But she silenced her detractors by pointing out that her administration was putting away one she called a dangerous terrorist. After all, she pointed out, the raids on the estates and mansions of the family in Bainti and Bhadri had led to the recovery of a staggering cache of arms and ammunition, besides a rich haul of jewellery and silver utensils. The seized weaponry included two rifles with telescopic sights, 250 cartridges, twelve guns, two pistols, one Springfield rifle, an AK-56 and thirty-six swords. Mayawati claimed the son and the father may well have had links with Pakistan's Inter Services Intelligence (ISI) agency and that intelligence reports indicated they were planning to assassinate her during the Republic Day celebrations.

By daring to take the proverbial bull by the horns and wrestling him to the ground in such a comprehensive manner, Mayawati added several notches to her already larger than life reputation as a gutsy leader. The bureaucracy—particularly the police force—looked at her with new respect. In the past their political masters had prevented them from prosecuting dons of the ilk of Raja Bhaiya, and the fact that a lady chief minister had displayed the guts to act otherwise, showed what could be done provided there was political will. Even the media, normally hostile to Mayawati, grudgingly accepted that it was no mean achievement to put Raja Bhaiya behind bars.

But the real impact of the Hollywood Western-style gunfight at O.K. Corral from which Mayawati emerged so victoriously, was evident among Dalits and poorer backward castes who were simply overwhelmed by the enormity of the deed. The spectacle of a 'Dalit ki Beti' making a thakur goon bite the dust reversed centuries and centuries of rapine, murder and loot by marauding landlords of the upper caste, quite a lot of them thakurs. She became the stuff of folklore in Dalit villages and ghettos, acquiring an aura that would remain a great political asset in the future.

The *Outlook* article concluded:

Mayawati has earned the wrath of the Thakurs, but she doesn't appear to be bothered. For among the oppressed, her stock has only gone soaring since she had Raja Bhaiya arrested. This is because it is not just his feudal antecedents that made Raja Bhaiya a feared figure in Pratapgarh; he had several cases lodged against him over the years ranging from kidnappings, dacoities, robberies and extortion. He was the archetypal Hindi film villain come to life: a gun-toting fiend riding roughshod over the poor villager. Such figures only get vanquished in reel-life Bollywood blockbusters. By defeating the marauding Thakur in real life, Mayawati has lent it her own twist.

Significantly, her triumph over Raja Bhaiya also impressed certain upper castes, the brahmins and banias in particular, who were increasingly at the receiving end of the crude oppression of the aggressive landowning castes. They drew vicarious pleasure at the plight of an overbearing thakur goon subdued by an untouchable woman. For at least a section of the brahmins and banias, it provided the first glimmer of a solution to how they could cope in a jungle raj where their professional or financial skills were not enough to protect them.

Mayawati had made very powerful enemies because of her savage attack on Raja Bhaiya and his father. For the feudal thakurs, it was a fate worse than death to have been humiliated so publicly by a woman belonging to the lowly chamar caste. Indeed, when he first started his campaign to topple Mayawati, Raja Bhaiya is believed to have boasted to his compatriots that he would teach a lesson to the 'chamarin', a derogatory term for a woman belonging to the chamar caste. It was devastating for the thakurs that it was the 'chamarin' who had taught their man a lesson.

The same message had gone out loud and clear to other macho landed feudals belonging to upper, intermediate and backward castes, including the yadavs, kurmis and lodh rajputs. All of them had powerful political lobbies and leaders and quite a few were her old enemies. They included Kalyan Singh, now heading his own backward caste party, while Mulayam Singh and his thakur associate, Amar Singh, represented another battlefront. Finally, there was the BJP, where both Rajnath Singh and Vinay Katiyar unanimously condemned the use of POTA against Raja Bhaiya and his father. She had stirred up a political storm in Uttar Pradesh and would have to pay the price.

For the moment, however, Mayawati's triumph seemed complete. She had powerful friends in the prime minister and deputy prime minister who turned a deaf ear to the long litany of complaints against her from BJP leaders in Uttar Pradesh. A delegation of state leaders and legislators who came to the capital desperately pleading with the national leadership to curb Mayawati before she destroyed the BJP in Uttar Pradesh, got little cheer from the Big Two in the party. Advani actually lost his temper with the delegation, scolding them for allowing petty local agendas to obscure the larger national picture despite the coming general elections. Vajpayee was more polite; he gave the delegation high tea during which he proceeded to lecture them on the nuances of coalition politics. The message from the two main national leaders of the BJP was clear: with a nationwide alliance with the BSP in the coming general elections on the anvil, they were not going to allow local leaders to disturb the political status quo in Lucknow whatever be the provocation. Advani even made a statement in the Rajya Sabha giving a clean chit to the chief minister for taking action against Raja Bhaiya and his father under POTA, much to the embarrassment of BJP leaders in Uttar Pradesh who had been arguing exactly the opposite.

Unlike the BJP leaders, Mulayam Singh had nobody to restrain him from going after Mayawati. Having organized thoo-thoo rallies across the state in the last quarter of 2002 to abuse the chief minister, he stepped up his campaign in 2003 by attempting to link her to a series of financial scams. The Samajwadi Party leader first raised a hue and cry over the vast sums of government money and collected funds spent on her forty-seventh birthday celebrations. Mulayam Singh produced coupons that he said were specially printed by Mayawati to blatantly demand money from her ministers, legislators, MPs and government officials in the form of a 'birthday gift' for herself. He alleged that she had collected several hundred crore rupees using political and government channels and demanded a Central Bureau of Invesigation (CBI) enquiry into the 'birthday gift scam'.

Hardly had the furore over the chief minister's birthday celebrations died down, when Mulayam Singh hit her with another scandal. This time he produced a videotape that he presented to Governor Vishnu Kant Shastri. The tape purported to show Mayawati asking her party legislators for donations from the area development funds—an allocated sum given by the state exchequer to both parliamentarians and legislators for development initiatives and projects in their respective constituencies.

Describing the allegations as 'false and fabricated', Mayawati's retaliated by accusing Mulayam of accepting crores of rupees from the MLAs' fund for a school named after his father. She alleged that Samajwadi Party MPs and MLAs had given large sums of money from their funds to institutions run by Mulayam's relatives and for his personal needs. Not only that, the chief minister promptly ordered the chief secretary, D.S. Bagga, to conduct a probe into the misuse of discretionary funds during Mulayam's regime which had provisions to prosecute for criminal offence.

Mulayam and his men were not going to sit back and wait for Mayawati to hit them in the way she had hit Raja Bhaiya. To pre-empt legal and police action, the Samajwadi Party leader quickly moved a no-confidence motion against the government in the state assembly. Sensing trouble, the Speaker, Kesri Nath Tripathi of the BJP, stayed away from the assembly, leaving the proceedings of the vote in the House under the supervision of a presiding officer. The latter was quite incapable of controlling the mayhem that erupted amidst scenes reminiscent of the unruly vote that Kalyan Singh had won in 1997. The portable mikes used by Singh's supporters led by Raja Bhaiya were missing, having been replaced with fixed mikes; so was the thakur don himself, now incarcerated in a maximum-security cell. But the antagonists in the assembly fought each other undaunted, flinging paper missiles, food packets and virtually anything they could lay their hands on. Samajwadi Party legislators screaming '*Gali gali mein shor hain, Mayawati chor hain*' (in the lanes and bylanes eveyone is shouting that Mayawati is a thief), came to blows with their BSP counterparts. This time the BSP legislators managed to give as good as they got, and despite the best efforts of the Samajwadi Party, Mayawati managed to survive the day through a voice vote after a six-hour-long pandemonium in the House.

The mud-slinging between Mayawati and Mulayam Singh put the BJP in an extremely awkward position. Many state party leaders secretly sided with the Samajwadi Party leader, and were convinced that the charges against Mayawati were far more serious than the ones against Mulayam. Most of them were resentful that for no fault of their own, the BJP had been dragged into a sordid financial scam because of its association with the chief minister. The fact that party leaders were forced to keep mum about the scandal to keep Mayawati happy, appalled the BJP's base in the urban intelligentsia. 'The alliance with the BSP is the biggest mistake that the party has made in Uttar Pradesh', a senior BJP leader complained.[2]

In a further loss of face for the Sangh Parivar, a fresh expose on the controversial videotape alleged that Mayawati had been recorded on tape making some highly derogatory remarks about Hindu gods and goddesses. She was shown to say: '*Gaon mein to kutta bhi devata hota hai. Woh pehle ja ke gangajal chadhata hai aur phir devata ka prasad khata hai. Jo devata apni raksha nahin kar sakta, woh aapko kya dega?*' (In our villages even dogs are gods. They too make offerings of holy water and eat up the offerings. When these gods can't even protect themselves, what can they do for you?) While Vajpayee and Advani hemmed and hawed about the new revelations, the RSS and affiliated bodies like the VHP and Bajrang Dal were furious at what they perceived as a public insult to the Hindu faith. All the previous fears and prejudices about Mayawati and the BSP's ideology started resurfacing within the Sangh Parivar, now under the leadership of K. Sudarshan, who had his own doubts about the importance given by the prime minister and his deputy to an alliance with the BSP in Uttar Pradesh and elsewhere for the coming general elections. The mood against Mayawati was steadily building up in the Sangh.

Yet, despite these storm signals, everyone was astonished when the alliance between the BSP and the BJP did blow up, sparked off by the most unlikely catalyst—the seventh wonder of the world, the Taj Mahal. A newspaper story in the third week of June about an illegal corridor being constructed on the Yamuna riverbed behind the world famous heritage monument, provoked the central culture and tourism minister, Jagmohan, to ask the Uttar Pradesh government to immediately stop the construction. The next day Mayawati announced at a press conference that work on the corridor had been halted. 'I have no differences with honourable Jagmohanji on the issue of preserving the beauty and dignity of the Taj. The Taj Mahal is our national heritage and I'll not allow any activity which would detract from the beauty of this monument,' she told the media. The chief minister followed this up by ordering the transfer and then suspension of the principal secretary (environment), R.K. Sharma, for sanctioning thirty-seven crore rupees for the Taj Corridor scheme.

Less than a month later, however, Mayawati went ballistic

against central minister Jagmohan's stand on the Taj Corridor. In a press conference on 28 July, the chief minister sent ripples through both the state government and the ruling NDA coalition in New Delhi by declaring, 'It is obvious that Mr Jagmohan knew everything that was happening in the Taj Corridor project, and once it got highlighted in the media, he is trying to shift the blame on to Uttar Pradesh officials. . . . Mr Jagmohan should be immediately asked for a clarification on his complicity in the Taj Corridor scandal and dismissed from the council of ministers without further delay; otherwise our party (the BSP) will raise the issue in Parliament and expose Mr Jagmohan.'

Mayawati's outburst against Jagmohan appeared to be linked to a Supreme Court order asking the CBI to enquire into the alleged illegality and irregularities by the government in Uttar Pradesh in the construction of the Taj Corridor project at Agra. It had asked the investigative agency to treat the court order on a most urgent basis and submit a report within two months. There was little doubt that the chief minister suspected that a serious conspiracy against her was afoot, and that the time had come for her to go on the offensive before matters got out of hand. On her orders, BSP members of Parliament created bedlam in both Houses, forcing the adjournment of the Lok Sabha.

But in a significant turnaround, these aggressive tactics seemed to alienate the Big Two in the BJP, Vajpayee and Advani, who had been protecting the chief minister so far from her political opponents. The prime minister summarily rejected the demand for Jagmohan's dismissal; the latter had, he said, his 'full confidence'. Lashing out at BSP MPs for stalling parliamentary proceedings, the BJP veteran declared that he was not ready to put up with such arm-twisting tactics and if Mayawati did not mend her ways, 'withdrawal of support (in Uttar Pradesh) was also an option.' Simultaneously, the BJP president, M. Venkaiah Naidu, known to be close to Advani, convened a press conference at the party headquarters and disclosed that twenty BJP MPs had met the prime minister and demanded the withdrawal of support to the Mayawati government.

Besides these public warnings, Mayawati also had to face some tough talk in private from both Vajpayee and Advani, who were believed to have told her in no uncertain terms that they would no longer support her if she did not back off. On the face of it, the belligerence by her chief sponsors in the BJP appeared to work. The chief minister momentarily retreated, withdrawing her demand for Jagmohan's dismissal and claiming that differences between her party and the BJP were being sorted out. But she was seething inside at being scolded like an errant schoolgirl by the prime minister and his deputy. After returning from the capital to Lucknow, Mayawati is believed to have said tersely to her close party leaders just one sentence: 'Be ready for polls.'

By the third week of August, the Supreme Court started pushing the pedal on the Taj Corridor scandal. In response to the interim report filed by the CBI, the court asked the investigative agency to get a move on and start questioning those implicated in the Taj scam. On 24 August, the CBI grilled officials involved in the funding of the Corridor project and the next day started questioning the environment minister, Nasimuddin Siddique, known to be close to the chief minister. She could feel the noose tightening around her neck. Mayawati's instincts as a natural fighter made her go into attack mode again. On 25 August, even as CBI investigators moved to cross-examine her minister of environment, the chief minister pulled the plug on her own government, taking the BJP leadership completely by surprise.

Although the night before she had announced to the media to be prepared for some 'spicy news' the next day, everyone was taken aback at Mayawati's dramatic decision to sever ties with the BJP and simultaneously recommend to the state governor to dissolve the assembly and hold fresh elections. The BSP leader also released a rambling thirty-page letter addressed to the prime minister that sought to explain the reason for her course of action. 'I have come to know through reliable sources that the BJP is planning to pressure me in the Taj Corridor controversy in order to make me surrender the maximum number of seats in the Lok Sabha elections. This behaviour is immoral,' she wrote.

Mayawati's bold move was based not just on bravado, but also on hard-headed calculation. She had genuinely believed that the BJP, in its desperation to contest the Lok Sabha elections in alliance with the BSP, would agree to the imposition of President's Rule in the state and simultaneous Lok Sabha and assembly elections. Mayawati also felt that with elections around the corner, the Taj controversy was bound to be put on the back burner, and that even the courts and CBI would wait for an electoral verdict. As far as the polls were concerned, the BSP leader was supremely confident of doing better than ever before in the state assembly as well as the Lok Sabha.

However, the BJP leadership, after being initially stunned by the Mayawati bombshell on 25 August, managed to recover its wits and take her by surprise. To her utter astonishment, the BJP decided that instead of being blackmailed and humiliated by the BSP leader, it would allow an alternative government to be formed by the only person capable of doing so, Mulayam Singh Yadav. The power equations in the state swiftly changed with the governor being quietly asked by the central BJP leadership to go along with the political games played by the Samajwadi Party leader.

First, leaders of the three main political groups, former chief minister and Rashtriya Kranti Party (RKP) leader, Kalyan Singh; Rashtriya Lok Dal (RLD) leader, Ajit Singh; and Uttar Pradesh Congress Committee president, Jagdambika Pal, met the governor separately and expressed support for an alternative government led by Mulayam Singh. By late evening on 26 August, Mulayam Singh met the governor and staked his claim to form the government on the basis of being the largest party in the assembly and pressed for a trial of strength on the floor of the House. However, a problem arose when the governor asked him to provide a list of supporting legislators since he was still short of a majority with the BJP not willing to openly support the government.

The Samajwadi Party leader with his phenomenal skills at breaking parties, had the option of making up the numbers through defectors from the BJP. He chose not to do so, underlining his secret pact with the Sangh. Instead he rustled up the required numbers with fourteen defectors from the BSP and armed with a list of 210 supporting legislators, staked his claim again. Yet, even this claim should not have been entertained, since the support of fourteen BSP defectors was actually invalid because they did not constitute one-third of their parent legislative party as required by the anti-defection rules. It is here that the governor, ignoring the legitimate protests of the BSP, invited Mulayam Singh to take the oath as chief minister on 28 August. Once he acquired power, it did not take long for the Yadav strongman to engineer a fresh flow of defections from the BSP and by the first week of September he had collected as many as thirty-seven legislators from Mayawat's flock, completely outmanoeuvring the BSP leader.

For Mulayam Singh it was a moment of triumph as well as irony. All the main players who had helped him ascend the throne of Lucknow for the third time had been his bitterest foes in the past. Kalyan Singh used to call him the 'Ravana' and held him responsible for the massacre of Ram devotees in the Samajwadi Party leader's first stint in power. Ajit Singh had fought a relentless battle with him for nearly two decades on whether he or Mulayam Singh should inherit the mantle of the former's father, peasant patriarch Charan Singh. Even Sonia Gandhi, who was denied power at the centre in 1999 by the recalcitrant Yadav leader questioning her leadership credentials as a 'foreigner', lent her hand to his coronation.

As for the Sangh Parivar's amazing turnaround on Mulayam Singh, it was indeed a seminal moment in its political quest. BJP propaganda mills had worked for over a decade to demonize him as 'Mullah Mulayam', depicting the Samajwadi Party leader as the most visible symbol of Muslim appeasement by the political class. In fact, the party leadership had justified its repeated dubious dalliances with Mayawati on the plea of keeping the greater evil of Mulayam Singh out of power. At least while propping her up, the Sangh could claim to have been working for a larger mission of pan-Hindu unity to bring estranged Dalits back to the faith. In the case of its tacit support for Mulayam Singh, there was no such sense of ideological purpose, only a petty power game that exposed the BJP's dwindling stature as an independent political force in Uttar Pradesh.

Clearly, a long list of Mayawati baiters in the party's state unit spearheaded by Rajnath Singh facilitated the deal. But this would have been impossible without the sanction of the big two in the BJP or the blessings of the RSS. Vajpayee, who was the oldest and strongest advocate in the party of an alliance with the BSP, appeared to have been misled by the then rising BJP political star, the late Pramod Mahajan, who had moved close to the prime minister. Mahajan convinced him that propping up Mulayam Singh in Uttar Pradesh would kill three birds with one stone. Firstly, it would allow the BJP to punish Mayawati by proxy without directly antagonizing the Dalits; secondly, it allowed the party to revive the Ayodhya issue sitting in the Opposition benches without any administrative responsibility; and finally, it would avoid the anti-incumbency factor that was plaguing the party while in coalition with the BSP.

As for the loss of BSP support in the coming general elections, Mahajan insisted that the prime minister's personal stock was so high at the moment that he would get a second term regardless of who supported him. To some extent it was Vajpayee's self-conceit that bought into the tactical shift on Uttar Pradesh being sold by Mahajan. The latter subsequently went on to coin the politically naïve slogans of 'India Shining' and 'Feel Good Factor' before the Lok Sabha polls. At the same time, there was also a mysterious parallel game afoot in the Sangh Parivar from the middle of 2003 that precipitated their parting from two of the BJP's major political alliances. These were with Mayawati in Uttar Pradesh and with DMK supremo Karunanidhi in Tamil Nadu. Together the divorces ultimately cost Vajpayee a second term. Both leaders were known for their proximity to Vajpayee, and their sudden departure from the NDA fold may well have something to do with a reported plan by the RSS sarsangchalak (chief), K. Sudarshan himself, to change the prime minister after the general elections.

Advani's exact role during this period is not very clear. The deputy prime minister was vaguely aware that something strange was afoot, but he wanted to be on the right side of it and, therefore, went along without sticking his neck out. Whatever the compulsions and conspiracies that drove the BJP to the deal with Mulayam, it severely dented the party's performance in Uttar Pradesh in the 2004 Lok Sabha polls and continued to haunt the party till the 2007 state assembly polls where the association did it even more grievous harm. There is little doubt that the deal was the biggest in a series of blunders that drastically diminished the BJP's electoral prospects in the country's largest state, which really meant bidding goodbye to the party's ambition of being the main pole in national politics.

Yet, these represented long term political trends that would unfold in the future. For the moment it was Mayawati who looked like the biggest loser. She was totally isolated in Uttar Pradesh with every major political party ganging up against her and propping up the Mulayam Singh government. Her own party was in tatters, having lost thirty-seven legislators, most of them upper castes, yadavs or Muslims, to the Samajwadi Party. She was like a cornered rat encircled by her political foes: Rajnath Singh, Kalyan Singh, Vinay Katiyar and, of course, Mulayam Singh, all of whom were rubbing their hands in glee at the prospect of finishing her while she was down.

There was physical danger as well with the release of the thakur don Raja Bhaiya in September, one of the first administrative decisions taken by Mulayam Singh after coming to power and it won applause from local BJP leaders. Although the political gangster declared contemptuously after his release, 'Why should I dirty my hands by touching her?' there was constant speculation in the media about a vendetta by upper-caste robber barons against the Dalit woman who dared to humiliate them. Partly to avoid the taunts of her political opponents and perhaps also conscious of the risk of an attack, Mayawati resigned from the assembly and spent most of her time behind the heavily guarded walls of her Lucknow residence.

The biggest threat, however, came from a proactive Supreme Court that relentlessly goaded the CBI to hunt down those responsible for the Taj Corridor scam. She was grilled by the investigative agency less than a week after she quit as chief minister, and a month later the CBI conducted day-long raids on her residences in New Delhi, Lucknow and some other towns in Uttar Pradesh. The investigations would soon be enlarged by the Supreme Court to inquire into the various properties, jewellery and other assets she and her family owned, how they were acquired and whether the requisite taxes were paid on them. In short, the Supreme Court and the CBI had put Mayawati under a magnifying glass—not a pleasant prospect for any political leader with even a slightly successful career graph.

To complicate matters further, there were disturbing reports that two of her most trusted aides, principal secretary P.L. Punia and chief secretary G.S. Bagga, had kept her in the dark on quite a few vital aspects of the Taj Corridor project. There was also growing speculation that the officials could put the blame on their former chief minister to satisfy powerful political lobbies of the day. Aggravating this sea of troubles was her worry about her mentor, Kanshi Ram, who had been crippled by a devastating stroke. Not only was he in no condition to give her advice on the crisis, but she also stood in danger of losing forever the person she cared for most of all.

A more faint-hearted woman would have crumbled under this grim predicament; a lesser leader besieged on so many fronts might have surrendered to her foes. Certainly, most politicians faced by such formidable challenges, would have kept a very low profile.

But Mayawati belongs to a different species altogether. She came out of her corner punching furiously. Interestingly, her rage seemed to be directed at some of her old benefactors, the prime minister, Vajpayee, and her old rakhi bhai and neighbour, Lalji Tandon. Speaking to the media in the first week of September, the BSP leader blamed the internal battles of the BJP for the break-up of the alliance. 'I was betrayed by the pro-Vajpayee group within the BJP. Even though Vajpayee wanted my government to complete its term, he was forced by the members of his group. Those who pressured him into toppling my government are Rajnath Singh, Pramod Mahajan, Lalji Tandon and NDA convener George Fernandes,' she declared at a press conference in Lucknow.

After the CBI raided her residences in October, a livid Mayawati shrieked imprecations at the prime minister as well as at his foster daughter and son-in-law, who lived with him. Alleging that Vajpayee's foster family had amassed vast illegal fortunes, she demanded that the prime minister first ask the CBI to conduct an enquiry in his own home. In an emotional outburst to the media, the BSP leader lamented what she saw as unfair discrimination from Vajpayee, who she claimed once called her his other adopted daughter.

These high-octane statements were partly reflective of a genuine sense of grievance and insecurity in a leader who felt betrayed by those to whom she had looked for support in the past. It is also possible that Mayawati was deliberately misinformed about the prime minister's role in the CBI investigations against her, by Vajpayee's enemies in the party. Curiously, she did not make a single statement criticizing Advani during this period. But this war of words unleashed by the BSP leader was also designed to keep her own morale up, as well as warn enemies that she was not going to go quietly.

Her bluster also contained thinly veiled political messages. For instance, while Mayawati lashed out at BJP bigwigs for not even bothering to enquire about the ailing Kanshi Ram's health, she praised the contrasting approach of Congress president Sonia Gandhi, who had been anxiously enquiring about the invalid leader and even wanted to visit him. 'She has fully learnt about our Indian culture,' declared Mayawati. The plaudits for the Gandhi widow came barely a few weeks before the BSP and Congress announced a tentative understanding for the state assembly polls in Delhi, Madhya Pradesh, Chhattisgarh and Rajasthan in the winter of 2003.

Yet, her rhetorical fusillades were only a part of her battle to stay alive. After all, Mayawati was not just spunky, she was also a survivor. She had to fight a complicated political and legal battle that required a clever and systematic approach. Two key aides helped the BSP leader to craft a survival strategy in this period of struggle. Neither of them were Dalits. Ironically, they belonged to castes that are normally associated with the oppression and discrimination against Dalits. One was a jat, a community notorious for its tyranny over scheduled castes in the villages of western Uttar Pradesh. The other was a brahmin, the highest in the caste system and bearing the moral responsibility for its inequities.

We have already met Shashank Shekhar Singh, the jat pilot turned bureaucrat earlier on in this chapter; the other aide, Satish Mishra, a brahmin lawyer and son of a widely respected judge, was appointed in 2002 as the state's advocate general on the advice of Arun Jaitley, the union law minister, who had been impressed by his legal acumen. A polling agent of the legendary Congress leader H.N. Bahuguna in the seventies and close to a top BJP leader like Jaitley, the brahmin advocate general had no particular political affiliations, but had a good network among the Uttar Pradesh elite partly because of his family lineage, but also because of his own skills at making friends and influencing people.

Shekhar Singh advised Mayawati on how to escape the noose that Mulayam Singh sought to put around her neck. Having been a close aide of both Mulayam Singh in his first stint as chief minister, and of his henchman Romesh Bhandari, when the latter was state governor, the bureaucrat was well placed to counter the administration's moves to implicate the BSP leader. Mishra held out legal hope to her after combing through voluminous documents of past court cases. He would prove to be an able legal brain who would help her win a decisive concession from the judiciary—an order from the Lucknow Bench of the Allahabad High Court restraining the police from arresting her until investigations into the Taj Corridor affair were completed.

Both Singh and Mishra had to initially pay a heavy price for supporting the beleaguered leader. Singh was hounded by chief minister Mulayam Singh after he doggedly refused all kinds of bribes to turn against Mayawati. He was given a punishment posting and spent most of his office hours languishing at his residence in Lucknow. Mishra, the advocate general, resigned from his post after taking up legal cudgels on behalf of the BSP leader. Their dedicated support to her also went against advice from their family and friends who were appalled at their support for what at that time appeared to be a lost cause and a controversial Dalit leader. Clearly, the two were struck by a quality in Mayawati so rare that it persuaded them against all odds to hitch their wagons to her star. The fact that the gamble has paid off with such a massive bonanza today is a telling commentary on the foresight of the two aides, as well as the brand equity of their investment.

With the threat of imminent arrest receding from the horizon, Mayawati could turn back in 2003 to the political battlefront. Declaring the BJP as her enemy number one, the BSP leader plunged into the state assembly elections for Madhya Pradesh, Chhattisgarh, Rajasthan and Delhi in the winter of 2003 with a single mission: she wanted to somehow defeat the BJP in the polls that were widely billed as the semi-final of the general elections of 2004. Although there was no formal electoral pact with the BJP's main political opponent in these states, the Congress, Mayawati instructed her partymen in the four states to contest the polls in a manner that ensured the defeat of BJP candidates.

This was really good news for the Congress, which ruled all the four states and feared a serious anti-incumbency backlash against its government. The growing bonhomie between Mayawati and Sonia Gandhi, first signalled by the former's praise for the latter's concern about Kanshi Ram's health, was consolidated further. On the other hand, there was perceptible nervousness in the BJP about the possible implications of this emerging alliance which the Sangh Parivar had repeatedly tried to scupper in the past. There was intense speculation in the media on the impact of this deal on the coming 2004 general elections and although the main protagonists in both the state and parliamentary polls were the BJP and the Congress, the performance of the BSP suddenly became crucial in deciding the battle either way.

The party suffered a setback in Madhya Pradesh before the polls when the state unit of the BSP split over an electoral understanding with the Congress. State party chief Phool Singh Baraiya, an old associate of Kanshi Ram, walked out with his followers in protest against the deal with the Congress in a state where the BSP had for more than a decade shown immense promise that had not been realized. The departure of such an experienced local leader so close to the elections, no doubt, affected the party's performance. When the results of the four state assembly polls were announced, it signalled both good and bad news for the BSP.

In terms of vote share, the party had improved its position in all four states, which was a remarkable achievement considering the woes of Mayawati in Uttar Pradesh, the illness of Kanshi Ram and the split in Madhya Pradesh. On the other hand, the conversion of votes into seats was dismal in all four states. This was most evident in Madhya Pradesh and Chhattisgarh where the BSP got a combined 7.6 per cent of the vote share compared to 6.3 per cent in the then undivided state in the 1998 state elections. But it could wrest only two seats each in Madhya Pradesh and Chhattisgarh, as against eleven in the previous election in the undivided state. In Rajasthan, the party got two seats in both the 2003 and 1998 state elections, although its vote share rose from 2.17 to 3.97 per cent. In Delhi, the BSP still failed to open its account despite its vote share rising sharply from 3.09 to 5.7 per cent.

Apart from getting very few seats of its own, the BSP also failed to tilt the balance against the BJP in its fight with the Congress. The BJP scored comprehensive victories in Madhya Pradesh, Chhattisgarh and Rajasthan, but lost in Delhi where the Congress continued its fabulous run, winning a second term in office. Pramod Mahajan who played a key role in managing the state elections was ecstatic at the BSP's inability to seriously harm the BJP. It vindicated his line of casting aside Mayawati and propping up the Mulayam Singh government in Uttar Pradesh.

In another move to isolate the BSP leader and shore up its own backward caste vote, the BJP invited her old enemy Kalayan Singh back to the party's fold, forgiving Singh's past misdemeanours and criticism of Vajpayee. With virtually the entire media seeing the BJP success in the assembly polls as a precursor to a triumph in the general elections, the party leadership, prime minister included, was in high spirits. The optimism about the BJP's electoral prospects sold by Mahajan and the media had been infectious. Quite contrary to his basically cautious nature, Vajpayee agreed to set forward the general elections to the summer of 2004.

As the BJP camp dreamt of a famous victory in the Lok Sabha polls, Sonia Gandhi nursed her defeated forces. She had been badly stung by the humiliating losses in three northern states, with the victory in Delhi hardly any consolation. It was a turning point in her politics and that of the Congress. She became the first member of the Gandhi dynasty to seek out allies for a national coalition, a move unimaginable in the past for this once predominant political force.

As the elections drew nearer, Sonia Gandhi showed uncharacteristic humility as she personally pleaded with potential allies, one by one, to join hands with her against the BJP. For instance, she actually walked across the road from her house on 10 Janpath to the nearby residence of NDA rebel leader, Ram Vilas Paswan, to craft an alliance with him and with Laloo Prasad Yadav of the Rashtriya Janata Dal, to bring together on the same electoral platform Dalits, Muslim, yadavs and the remnants of the Congress upper caste base in Bihar. In the south, the Congress president offered an olive branch to M. Karunanidhi of the DMK, a target of hostility so far because of the alleged links between his party and the assassins of Rajiv Gandhi. Along with Paswan's party, the DMK, too, had left the NDA not so long ago, making way for its traditional rival, the AIADMK. In the western state of Maharashtra, Sonia Gandhi made peace with the veteran leader, Sharad Pawar, of the Congress rebel faction, the Nationalist Congress Party (NCP), which shared power with the Congress in the state, but was constantly fighting with them. She told her partymen to back off and magnanimously allowed Pawar to take charge of the electoral strategy and seat distribution for the Lok Sabha polls in the state.

As for Mayawati, Sonia Gandhi had already been in touch with her while negotiating an electoral understanding for the assembly polls in the four northern states. Despite the failure of the alliance to stop the BJP from winning the state polls, the relationship between the two leaders continued to grow closer. In a surprise gesture, Sonia Gandhi attended the birthday celebrations of Mayawati at her house on 15 January 2004. Photographs of the two smiling ladies happily posing with each other in next morning's dailies sent out a loud political message. Technically, the Congress was still supporting the Mulayam Singh government in Lucknow, while the BJP sat in the Opposition. But Sonia's display of public bonhomie with Mayawati made it clear that she was closer to the latter than to the Uttar Pradesh chief minister. This in turn pointed a finger at the quiet deal on the opposite side between the BJP and the Mulayam Singh regime.

The dramatic fall of the NDA regime in the 2004 elections and the return of the Congress at the head of a coalition government in New Delhi were like a political fairy tale come true. It vindicated Sonia Gandhi's new-found faith in alliance politics and set India firmly in the mould of coalition rule. On the other hand, the results clearly punctured the bloated visions of BJP leaders, including Pramod Mahajan, and the pre-poll media hype that had all but conceded the elections to the ruling party. And nowhere had the BJP's denouement been so sweeping than in the state that first pitchforked the party to political limelight.

In Uttar Pradesh the BJP had crashed to a mere eleven seats, just one more than the ten seats that the Congress had won. This drop from the twenty-seven seats it won in the last general elections was no doubt an exaggerated reflection of the drop in its actual vote share from 28.62 per cent to twenty-three per cent. But this only underlined the woeful poll management by the party. In sharp contrast, Mulayam Singh Yadav had once again displayed his superb organizational skills winning a massive thirty-six seats, an improvement of ten seats from his tally in the previous parliamentary polls despite only a modest 1.5 per cent increase in vote share. The BSP continued its upward curve increasing its vote share by two percentile points to 24.67 per cent, but although this was quite close to that of the Samajwadi Party, the party won only nineteen seats. This along with the fact that the party failed to win seats from any other state, meant that it still had a lot of work to do to convert its growing number of votes into seats.

Still it was an impressive march forward for the BSP in Uttar Pradesh, having left the two national parties—the Congress and the BJP—well behind and inching towards overtaking Mulayam Singh. Most importantly, Mayawati had the satisfaction of playing a key role—just as she had promised before—in toppling the Vajpayee regime at the centre, thus creating a whole, new political field for herself.

# NINE

# A Historic Triumph

*H*aving achieved her goal of destroying the BJP-led central government in the 2004 general elections, Mayawati turned to tackle her other political enemy, Mulayam Singh Yadav, who still stood between her and the throne in Lucknow. Fortunately for her, she found a fellow Mulayam-hater in Sonia Gandhi, the new queen bee calling the shots in national politics after her Congress party formed the United Progressive Alliance (UPA), the ruling alliance at the centre. Sonia Gandhi regarded the Yadav leader with almost as much animosity and suspicion as Mayawati. It was because of the Congress president's aversion to Mulayam Singh and to his chief lieutenant, Amar Singh, that they were—much to their chagrin—shut out from any role in central politics despite the Samajwadi Party's superb performance in the Lok Sabha polls.

In a humiliating rebuff, Sonia Gandhi spurned a tentative offer of support from them as she set about forming the UPA government with her allies. To add insult to injury, Amar Singh was actually asked to leave a dinner party held by the Congress and its allies when he sought with characteristic bluster to gatecrash the event. This crushing snub set the tone for the openly hostile relationship between the Congress and the Samajwadi Party that continues till today.

Over the next few years the UPA government and the Congress party would seek to harass Mulayam Singh and his friends on an almost monthly basis. Initially, efforts were made to topple his government by weaning away one of his allies, Ajit Singh and his Rashtriya Lok Dal, with offers of ministerial berths at the centre. But the chief minister was far too clever and resourceful to be toppled. Besides, the local BJP leadership led by Rajnath Singh and Kalyan Singh stood quietly but solidly behind the Samajwadi Party leader, so the numbers never really added up. However, there were concerted efforts to pester him as well as his associates, who included celebrity film stars and businessmen. A favourite target was Amar Singh, whose telephones were tapped to embroil him in an unseemly tape scandal that rocked both Houses of Parliament. Mulayam Singh himself was arbitrarily evicted from his government bungalow in New Delhi.

The Congress-led government may have been harsher still on the Yadav leader had he not been protected by a key prop of the UPA government, the Left Front, which counted the Samajwadi Party among its political allies. Mulayam Singh and Amar Singh responded to this ceaseless hostility by criticizing Sonia Gandhi and the Congress on every possible public occasion. They also constantly schemed to find strategies to destabilize the UPA regime.

Their common enmity to Mulayam Singh formed a bond between Mayawati and Sonia Gandhi. The BSP had offered support to the UPA government from the very first day, but did not join the government, nor, unlike the Left Front, was it involved in guiding the government from outside. Despite the lack of a formal pact between their parties, however, the personal chemistry between the two ladies was good and this was evident from the easy familiarity between the two whenever they did meet.

Mayawati and Sonia also shared the bond of being women in a world of politics so totally dominated by men. 'It is interesting to watch them together, whether in Parliament or travelling by chance together in a plane. They often go in a huddle and speak intensely to each other,' observed a politician. The shared political goals with the Congress, along with the good personal equation Mayawati had with Sonia Gandhi eased the tension of the pending Taj Corridor case that still hung like a Damocles Sword over her. However, with her enemies in the BJP defeated and Mulayam Singh and his cronies implicated in myriad scandals, the likelihood of a witch hunt against Mayawati receded. Guided by the sound counsel of Satish Mishra, the BSP leader steadily loosened the legal tangle around her. Nonetheless, there were some setbacks: she was put on the defensive by damaging comments from the chief vigilance commissioner who called for her prosecution even after the attorney general had given her a clean chit. But slowly, the dark clouds that had at one point threatened to put her behind bars, melted away.

Reassured that there was no imminent threat from the courts or the CBI investigators, Mayawati turned her attention outside Uttar Pradesh. She decided that her party would contest the state assembly polls in the western state of Maharashtra where the ruling Congress–NCP alliance was fighting the BJP–Shiv Sena combine. Maharashtra had symbolic value for the BSP since it was Ambedkar's birthplace and the launching pad of Kanshi Ram and his movement. Several decades ago, the sizeable scheduled caste population in the state, under the leadership of the Republican Party of India (RPI) and later the Dalit Panthers, had been more organized and combative than in any other state of the country. But over the years this sense of direction was lost; Dalits were let down by both moderates and militants.

Mayawati decided that the time had come for the BSP to make a serious play in the state, particularly since the party's Dalit base had ensured the defeat of at least eight Congress–NCP candidates in the 2004 Lok Sabha polls, most of them in the Vidarbha region that had a large scheduled caste population. An alliance with the Congress was not possible because its main partner, the NCP, insisted that they were better off in collaboration with the RPI faction led by Ramdas Athawale. So the BSP decided to contest nearly all—272 seats out of a total of 288—independently in the assembly polls, despite knowing that this would harm the Congress–NCP alliance rather than the opposing BJP–Shiv Sena combine. This underlined an important aspect of the BSP's relationship with the Congress—despite the good personal chemistry between their leaders, they were still locked in fierce political competition to capture electoral turf. Not surprisingly, the BJP and the Sena were delighted, hoping that the transfer of Dalit votes from the Congress-led alliance to the BSP would help them—theBJP–Shiv Sena combine—come back to power in the state.

Although the BSP did stop the Congress–NCP alliance from

winning in fourteen of the sixty-six constituencies in Vidarbha, the latter still managed to win enough seats for a second successive term in office. In a major loss of face, the BSP failed to win a single seat, getting a little less than four per cent of the vote. This did not mean that the party had no potential in Maharashtra, since many of its candidates came close to winning in Vidarbha. But the elections once again proved that the distribution and management of votes, constituency by constituency, were key elements determining the conversion of electoral potential into actual seats.

Having failed to make much political headway from her foray into Maharashtra at the end of 2004, Mayawati decided to concentrate all her efforts on the most crucial electoral event of all—the state assembly polls in Uttar Pradesh scheduled for the summer of 2007. Although the state elections were two-and-a-half years away, the BSP leader sat down with her aides in real earnest to plan both tactics and strategy for coming electoral challenge. It is at this stage that Satish Mishra, who was till then her legal counsel, started playing a key role in the BSP leader's political strategizing as well.

This was a bold move, overturning decades of anti-brahminical positions held by the party and its leaders. Some saw it as a reversal of the movement started by Kanshi Ram to overthrow the topmost rung of the caste system. However, Mayawati was convinced this was a logical leap forward from the kind of overtures that the party had been making for a number of years to the upper castes. She had—with wholehearted support from Kanshi Ram—started giving an increasing percentage of tickets for both state assembly as well as parliamentary elections to a variety of upper castes from as early as the mid-nineties.

However, there was a vital difference between the past overtures to brahmins and Mishra's new plan. The electoral dealings with the upper castes so far had been mere transactions with individual candidates in specific constituencies. They had sought to add the candidate's financial clout and personal caste base to the BSP's captive Dalit vote bank to make a winning combine. This strategy had a high success rate in elections. The only problem was that these party legislators and parliamentarians were the most liable to defect from the party in times of adversity, having no ideological or political stakes in the BSP.

Mishra's suggestion to Mayawati in the beginning of 2005 took social engineering to a different plane. He pointed to the mounting insecurity in the once predominant brahmin community and the challenge it faced from the rising economic and political clout of the intermediate castes, the yadavs and jats in particular. When some intermediate castes joined hands with aggressive, landowning upper castes, for instance the thakurs, cutting across party lines—as exemplified by the pact between Mulayam Singh and Rajnath Singh—the brahmins felt even more insecure. Despite their high social perch, the brahmins of Uttar Pradesh neither owned enough land nor were aggressive enough to match the might of the landed barons who routinely zoomed through the countryside on motorcycles brandishing pistols as an assertion of their power. The brahmins had also been politically orphaned by the changing contours of the two parties that had claimed to represent their interests.

The Congress party was the first to collapse after losing its Dalit and Muslim base. This forced the brahmins to shift their allegiance to the BJP. Unfortunately, the BJP was overrun by backward caste leaders, Kalyan Singh and Vinay Katiyar for instance, as well as thakur bosses such as Rajnath Singh, who were unconcerned with the plight of brahmins. Atal Bihari Vajpayee, the last brahmin hope, faded out of the picture after his government's ouster in the 2004 Lok Sabha polls, leaving the community feeling politically vulnerable.

Satish Mishra who had wide network of contacts across the community was only too aware of the alienation of brahmins. He proposed the revival of the old Congress alliance between the top and the bottom rungs of the caste ladder, but this time in reverse order. In the past a brahmin-run Congress extended patronage to scheduled castes promising them protection and prosperity; now a party ruled by a Dalit's daughter could offer similar sanctuary to brahmins looking for a political patron.

Mishra convinced Mayawati that if the alliance with brahmins could be made to work, it would be of enormous advantage to the BSP. Not only would it mean support from brahmins who constituted nearly ten per cent of the electorate, but was also likely to influence the bania community, who, too, were oppressed by the landed mafia. Since many banias were local traders and shopkeepers, they felt even more vulnerable to kidnappings and extortions. The need for a protector among the brahmins and banias was particularly acute in the last few years of Mulayam Singh's rule when regional warlords, many of them belonging to the yadav, thakur or kurmi communities, had imposed what was described by the media, as 'Jungle Raj'.

Displaying a capacity for sustained hard work as well as great innovation, Mishra criss-crossed Uttar Pradesh organizing brahmin sammelans. The campaign ended with a maha sammelan (grand meeting) in the state capital Lucknow on 9 June. Even hardbitten journalists came away from these meetings awestruck at the unprecedented scenes of social transformation. Rows and rows of brahmins, many with trademark pigtails and red tilaks smeared on their foreheads, bent down to touch the feet of the daughter of an untouchable with the cry, *'Behenji, bachao* (Behenji, save us)!'

Newspaper reports reflected the new mood among the brahmins as well as the media:

> ... brahmin participants who thronged the venue of the mega sammelan on Thursday amidst Opposition's speculation and sniggers about will they, wont they, looked a trifle self-conscious, sheepish and even diffident but equally determined to join Behenji's bandwagon to hitch a comfortable ride after fourteen years of inertia in the state politics. The gathering seemed a motley mix of all age(s) and class(es). The trishul-wielding, shloka-spouting class shared the pandal with the young and old neo-converts who seriously discussed the changing socio-political dynamics and the possible impact of the new combo on wider national canvas. ... So if Mayawati greeted her new friends with a brand new slogan *'Hathi nahi Ganesh hai'* (the BSP elephant represents Lord Ganesh)', the recipients responded with befitting *'Brahmanon ki yahi pukar, Mayawati chauthi bar'* (Brahmins want Mayawati as CM for the fourth time).[1]

These unique meetings where brahmins paid homage to Mayawati and she in turn assured them of protection, were not just token shows of political gimmickry. They were followed up by coordination mechanisms in every village called 'bhaichara samitis' or brotherhood organizations that were jointly manned by Dalits and brahmins. A similar initiative was also launched later involving banias, under the stewardship of another BSP leader, Sudhir Goel, an old associate of Kanshi Ram, who belonged to that community.

When Mishra started his novel experiment, there were many who scoffed at his seemingly impossible mission of getting brahmins to accept a Dalit leader. However, as the brahmin sammelans became increasingly popular, there was palpable nervousness in both the Congress and the BJP at the prospect of their electoral bases shrinking further.

'If she loved brahmins so much, why did she bring down the government of Atal Bihari Vajpayee?' fumed BJP president Kesri Nath Tripathi a few days after the mega brahmin sammelan in Lucknow. There were also rumblings from some Dalit leaders, especially among those cast out from the BSP into the political wilderness by Mayawati. They condemned the rise of Satish Mishra and the overtures to the brahmins by the BSP as a grand betrayal of Kanshi Ram's vision of the bahujan samaj movement. 'The brahmin sammelans are a big farce and both Dalits and brahmins will soon realize they are being exploited by Mayawati for her personal ends,' declared rival Dalit leader Udit Raj, president of the Indian Justice Party.

Significantly, apart from the BSP's rejects, an overwhelming majority of the community enthusiastically supported the move to have an alliance with the brahmins. Many felt thrilled that the party had grown so strong that it was in a position to provide shelter under its wings to the highest caste. Indeed, Mishra's enterprise as it picked up momentum had a ripple effect across civil society in Uttar Pradesh on a whole range of castes. The Muslim community, too, were more and more curious about this unprecedented attempt to reverse the social pyramid. If nothing else, it certainly raised the stock of the BSP in virtually every village, further consolidating vote banks that were already with the party and attracting new voters from castes and communities that had traditionally not been part of the BSP's constituency.

Mayawati's intensive preparation for the Uttar Pradesh assembly polls in the summer of 2007 was temporarily disrupted in October 2006 by the sad demise of her beloved guru, Kanshi Ram. He had been in a virtually vegetative state for the past two years, unable to speak and even think clearly. It was a miserable end for such an original politician, whose intellectual audacity was matched by his indefatigable energy for action at the grassroots level. Once upon a time, he had been the sun, moon and the stars for Mayawati, but as his body turned frail and his mental faculties faded with advancing years, she had slowly outgrown him. Since his crippling stroke in 2003 confined him to his bed, she had tried her best to make him as comfortable as possible, ignoring the wild allegations by some members of his family about forcible confinement and ill-treatment—allegations obviously made at the behest of her political enemies. Considering his disabled state, his death was perhaps a relief for him and his loved ones. Yet, it seemed a great shame that the man who diverted a young Dalit schoolteacher from the path of bureaucracy to that of politics, would not be there to observe her reaching for higher and higher political goals.

Mayawati herself looked sad but composed at her New Delhi residence while performing the final rites of her mentor in accordance with Buddhist ritual. Forty-two monks had come from different corners of the country to help her conduct the funeral. Neither she nor Kanshi Ram had converted to Buddhism, but he had left categorical instructions for a Buddhist funeral. 'He wanted his last rites to be observed according to the Buddhist rituals,' she told newspersons, with Kashi Ram's photograph and the five candles placed before it providing the backdrop. In keeping with the Buddhist tradition that celebrates the freedom of the soul, the white canopy on the lawn where the press conference was held, was bedecked with strings of marigolds and bunches of roses, while the strains of Buddhist chants floated in the air. She admitted that both had considered conversion, but like everything else in their lives, even this was linked to a larger political purpose. 'We had decided that we will embrace Buddhism along with millions of Dalits once we get an absolute majority on our own at the centre and in several states,' she said, asserting that political power was the 'master key' for effecting social transformation. She pointed out that Ashoka could successfully promote Buddhism only because he was an emperor. Asked as to how long it would take to rule at the centre, Mayawati smiled mysteriously, declaring, 'not too long'.

The first opportunity to test the electoral waters with the new brahmin alliance came in November 2005, six months before Uttar Pradesh went to polls to elect a new government. These were elections to the three-tier panchayati raj institutions, which consisted of a dozen Nagar Nigams (municipal corporations), 191

Nagar Parishads (town municipalities) and 414 Nagar Panchayats (rural municipalities). But in a decision that surprised everyone, the BSP cried off the Nagar elections announcing that it would instead back independent candidates. The official explanation by the party leadership was that they did not want to expend their energies and resources on civic elections with a state assembly poll around the corner. While a lot of independent candidates did win in the polls, it was difficult to make out who was backed by whom, with the Samajwadi Party, too, claiming that it had sponsored several independents.

In the end, everyone declared that they had gained from the polls. The BJP swept the Nagar Nigams, winning eight mayoral posts, while the Congress won three and the Samajwadi Party one. On the other hand, it was the Samajwadi Party, followed closely by Independents, that won the majority of the Nagar Nigams and Nagar Panchayats, leaving the BJP and Congress far behind. The BSP, of course, insisted that all the winning Independents won with the support of the party. Yet since it had no way of proving its claim, confusion prevailed over the real political clout of the BSP.

Mayawati's own brash statements in the wake of the municipal elections did not help much and were seen as a case of nerves brought about by the impending state assembly polls barely a few months away. She quite needlessly made off-the-cuff remarks just after the polls that offended sections of both the bania and Muslim communities. Her public annoyance at Muslim support for Samajwadi Party-supported candidates, many of them fundamentalists, led her to blame the minority community for being swayed by religious extremism, and created quite a stir in political and media circles. She was clearly miffed that even after she had proved her secular credentials to the Muslims of Uttar Pradesh, a large section of the community, particularly those influenced by clerical edicts, continued to support Mulayam Singh. Thrilled at this gaffe, Mulayam Singh furiously spread rumours that Mayawati was preparing the ground for another alliance with the BJP by this criticism of the Muslim community. Although the BSP leader quickly clarified her comments and reiterated her secular credentials, a question mark had been raised in her Muslim voter base on the eve of the polls. Similar indiscreet remarks about the banias also raised doubts about support from a community that was believed to be tilting towards the BSP for the first time.

According to an article in the magazine, *Frontline*: 'The former Chief Minister seemed flustered in her post-poll interactions with the media. First, Mayawati advanced the argument that she had instructed her cadre to transfer votes to the BJP and the Congress in order to defeat the SP. Later, she said that a section of Dalits, unhappy with Muslim fundamentalism, voted for the BJP. In the course of these arguments she used derogatory Hindi slang to describe the trader (Vaishya[bania]) community in a bid to win back her core Dalit constituency. Her statements, however, have evoked strong reactions from both the Muslim and Vaishya communities and generated a new controversy. Mayawati was forced to retract these statements, but the resentment has persisted in both communities.'[2]

The BSP was discomfited again just a few months before the Uttar Pradesh polls. In March 2007 the party performed dismally in the assembly polls held in Punjab where its downward slide continued. A decade before, Punjab was thought to be the most promising state after Uttar Pradesh for the BSP, since apart from being Kanshi Ram's home state it also had one of the highest scheduled caste populations in the country. But instead of making headway after a promising start in the late eighties and early nineties, the party had been losing ground steadily and the assembly polls in 2007 marked a further slump with the BSP losing even the third largest party position it had held for a number of years. While the decline in Punjab compared to the success in Uttar Pradesh underlined the importance of a charismatic leader like Mayawati, it also meant that the BSP's growth in the country's largest state was not being replicated anywhere else.

While the Akali–BJP combine comfortably regained power in Punjab, the real success story of the polls appeared to be the BJP, which increased its tally from three seats in the last state elections to as many as nineteen. The party, despite being knocked out of power at the centre, had clearly recaptured its urban Hindu base from the Congress in the state. Always prone to get carried away by their own propaganda, the BJP and its cheerleaders added up this limited success in Punjab along with a parallel poll victory in the tiny hill state of Uttarakhand as well as the sweep of mayoral elections in Uttar Pradesh, to conclude rather prematurely that it was on the road back to power. Indeed, all it needed was a revival in the country's largest state for the BJP to conjure up visions of political grandeur.

Most party leaders were convinced that even the worst-case scenario for the BJP in the 2007 Uttar Pradesh elections would be a win–win situation or, as described by the unforgettable one-liner of the ever smug BJP diva Sushma Swaraj, '*Hamein to dono hath mein laddoo.*' (We have laddoos in both hands.) In the specific context of Uttar Pradesh this meant that even if the BJP did not get a majority or come first in the polls, it was bound to get enough seats to decide whether Mulayam Singh or Mayawati formed the government. Significantly, the RSS leadership, which supposedly did not fully support the BJP effort in the 2004 polls because it wanted to cut Vajpayee to size, was clearly behind the party this time since the prestige of its own appointee at the helm, BJP president Rajnath Singh, was at stake in the elections. The 2007 state elections, therefore, became a crucial make-or-break test for the BJP as well as its parent body, on whether they were moving forward or back.

Petrified at the prospect of a Sangh Parivar revival, the Congress hastily turned to its own holy family. Rahul Gandhi, the young scion of the Gandhi dynasty, was unleashed in the Uttar Pradesh election campaign. He proved to be an instant hit—much like his father—drawing huge audiences at a series of road shows across the state. With television cameras recording virtually every move of the young Gandhi in the campaign, there was a carefully orchestrated campaign by the mainstream media to interpret the large crowds at his meetings to mean that the Congress was on to a good thing. Nobody, of course bothered to find out whether the crowds were turning up out of sheer curiosity or genuine intent to vote for the Congress. The party leadership certainly was not objecting to the media hype. It calculated that at the very least the Congress would improve on its paltry tally of twenty-five seats in the last state elections, which could then be credited to Rahul Gandhi.

Unfortunately for the political debutant, the constant presence of television cameras meant that his every fumble and faux pas was telecast live, including a comical claim that his family had orchestrated the break-up of Pakistan in 1971. 'You know that when my family decides to do anything, it does it. Be it the freedom struggle, the division of Pakistan or taking India to the twenty-first century,' he said at an election rally in Badaun. This farcical interlude in the poll campaign became funnier still because Rahul Gandhi's boast about dismembering Pakistan momentarily stunned the Sangh, leaving it undecided on whether to criticize the offensive gaffe about a neighbouring country with which the UPA government was conducting delicate negotiations, or keep quiet about any statement that put down the enemy. After all, no one in the Sangh wanted to repeat Advani's rhetorical blunder on Jinnah and be seen as a Pakistan lover.

Meanwhile, Mulayam Singh was twisting and turning like a cornered snake. He was not concerned about the posturings of the two rival Parivars—the Sangh or the Gandhi. The canny yadav leader knew that the real danger came from an old opponent in the electoral ring that he had often wounded in the past but never managed to subdue. And much to his dismay Mayawati and her party had just kept on growing larger and deadlier every year, and had now assumed proportions that threatened to overwhelm him instead. Nothing better illustrated the widening gap between the two main political rivals in the state than their sharply contrasting reactions as the electoral process, spread over a month and a half, unfolded. The beleaguered chief minister bitterly complained about 'strong-arm tactics' by Election Commission officials scaring away voters. Mayawati, on the other hand, was openly congratulating the same officials for providing enough security for voters, particularly Dalits, to caste their vote.

The crucial role played by the Election Commission's insistence on conducting a fair poll was not in doubt. Indeed, the unprecedented security arrangements were especially effective because the polls were spread out over seven phases. It severely maimed the Samajwadi Party's capacity to influence the elections through muscle power. With massive security arrangements now possible with enough police and paramilitary forces available for all polling centres, dominant castes, such as the yadavs, gujjars and jats, were not able to intimidate voters from poor and oppressed communities. This allowed BSP storm troopers to freely mobilize both their traditional Dalit vote bank as well as newly acquired allies among upper castes. It also emboldened the many enemies of the chief minister, including the kurmi leader, Beni Prasad Verma, to pull him down from his pedestal without fear of retribution. There were even reports that Mulayam Singh Yadav was himself getting nervous over whether he would win both the assembly seats he was contesting.

The stakes for Mulayam Singh and his friends went well beyond just winning or losing elections. They were absolutely petrified at the prospect of a BSP government formed in Lucknow with the help of the Congress. The chief minister and his main lieutenant, Amar Singh, feared that Mayawati and Sonia Gandhi together would carry out a relentless witch hunt against them. As a matter of fact, when his election managers told him after a few rounds of polling that the party was not doing well and—more alarmingly—that the BSP was steaming ahead, Mulayam Singh is believed to have even considered pushing captive yadav votes towards BJP candidates in constituencies where Samajwadi Party's prospects appeared hopeless. This was in the hope that if the BJP remained an important political player in the state, his friends in the party, Rajnath Singh and Kalyan Singh, for instance, would be able to save him from the two ladies. However, better sense prevailed and the yadav leader abandoned these devious plans which were reportedly the brainchild of an increasingly panicky Amar Singh. Instead, in one final superhuman effort, the battle-scarred veteran of many an electoral battle rallied his forces to try and improve his party's performance in the last few rounds. When the results came out, they showed that Mulayam Singh's last-ditch efforts had borne some fruit.

As for Mayawati's own campaign, journalists travelling with her were astonished at her relaxed self-assurance before such a crucial poll. One would have expected the Dalit firebrand to be a bit more frenzied as she fought the most important electoral battle in her life. Yet, even as the BSP juggernaut overtook all others in the arena with every passing day; there was no shrill honking of horns or changing of gears; just the quiet purr of a well-oiled machine. Amazingly, in an election split into seven different phases Mayawati was at least two phases ahead of her rivals on the campaign trail. She obviously felt no need for last-minute histrionics to woo voters on the eve of the polls. Her party had been the first to announce its election candidates and they filed their nomination papers well before the others. Having prepared for the polls so long in advance, she could afford to set a relatively easy pace of two to three public meetings in a day, compared to the frantic schedules of her rivals.

Interestingly, resources seemed no problem for a party that had been starved of money not so long ago The plentiful funds now available were being used with maximum efficacy and not frittered away in cosmetic showmanship. For instance, Mayawati had not only hired a chopper for herself but also provided one each to party general secretaries, Satish Mishra and Nasimuddin Siddique, so that they too could campaign far and wide. Indeed, this strictly pragmatic approach to the use of resources for the election campaign, exploded certain myths about a leader supposedly suffering from megalomania.

The most impressive aspect of the BSP's campaign in 2007 was its organizational infrastructure—elaborate yet meticulously efficient. It was directed by coordinators each in charge of five districts, which in turn were headed by district presidents supervising those in charge of specific assembly segments. Assembly segment leaders were backed up by a lower ring of cadre who controlled clusters of booths, each of which was the responsibility of an individual BSP worker, who brought up the bottom-most rung of this formidable chain of electoral command. Mayawati herself dealt directly with the coordinators and the district presidents, while they were responsible for the lower rungs of the organizational infrastructure. The organizational muscle of the BSP was also evident in the management of its election rallies where the police appeared as mere spectators. It was the BSP volunteer force, not the police, that took charge of the vast crowds who assembled in urban and rural centres to hear Mayawati and other BSP leaders. The uniformed volunteers—men dressed in white shirts, dark blue trousers, and the women in dark blue saris and salwar suits—were ranked army-style in a star system. They were palpably more effective in maintaining peace and order at the meetings than the local constabulary.

'We find it so much easier to handle these BSP meetings than the chaos we have to cope with at meetings organized by other political parties. These fellows do it all on their own making it really a cushy job for us,' said a senior police officer with a satisfied smirk as the dark blue line of BSP volunteers kept the crowds peaceful and in order in well-manned enclosures.

The other remarkable feature of Mayawati's campaign meetings for the Uttar Pradesh assembly polls of 2007 was the lack of hysteria and hype that normally accompany election fever. In marked contrast to the angry and confrontationist outbursts on display at rallies organized by the BSP in the past and even more so by its earlier avatar DS4—there was no longer an overbearing sense of lower-caste grievance against upper-caste oppression. Instead, there was just a quiet buzz of self-confidence among the Dalit audience who were seen brushing shoulders quite easily in the same enclosure with a whole assortment of brahmins, banias and other upper castes who had flocked to the BSP camp. Mayawati's own speeches were conspicuously devoid of caste hatred. In fact, she did not even indulge in oratorical flourishes. Instead the former schoolteacher was back in the classroom lecturing her audience about how to win the elections for themselves. For instance, she would go through patiently, if boringly, an endless list of the dos and don'ts required from each and every BSP supporter on voting day. And at every meeting Mayawati would make it a point to read out a detailed break-up of the various castes and communities to which her party candidates belonged.

'Her new message of cooperation instead of confrontation between the lower and upper castes has unquestionably been a very positive development in Uttar Pradesh politics and society. A lot of upper castes like brahmins, banias and kayasthas, who were feeling quite apprehensive about the boiling caste cauldron, now feel far more reassured. This sense of appreciation from the upper castes could give Mayawati a crucial advantage in the coming months,' said a newspaper editor in Lucknow.

The change in upper-caste attitudes was remarkable in the context of prejudices nursed against Dalits for so many centuries. This shift was palpable—and not just among a section of impoverished rural brahmins who had turned in desperation to Mayawati for protection from yadav and thakur mafia muscle in the countryside. Even well-heeled, educated, urban upper castes were reviewing their political options. For instance, at a Mayawati rally in Sitapur, two young local brahmin doctors, Dr Umesh Mishra and Dr Manju Shukla happily sat along with the unwashed masses, many of them Dalits. The two were new supporters of the BSP and were backing the local party candidate who happened to be a Dalit. This represented a significant change from the past when upper castes would support BSP candidates from their own communities, but not from the lower castes.

'We admit that our support is on a trial basis and whether we continue with it or not depends on what happens in the future. But there is no reason why we should not try out something that seems so promising,' declared the two doctors almost as if they were investing in new company stock. They were aware of the risks but still ready to take a calculated gamble. Both stressed that what they really liked about Mayawati was her blunt and no-nonsense style that they felt would make her just the kind of tough administrator a lawless, chaotic state like Uttar Pradesh needed.

Significantly, Muslims, too, were inclined to believe that Mayawati would run a far better administration than the 'jungle raj' presided over by Mulayam Singh. 'Who said Mulayam has the Muslim vote in his pocket? There is a wave building for the BSP and Muslims are as much a part of it as any other community or caste,' asserted Mohammed Issar Ansari of Leharpur village in central Uttar Pradesh. Indeed the collapse of law and order with gangsters and criminals ruling the roost, was even more of an issue with the minority community that felt particularly vulnerable. Muslims across the state were not really all that bothered by controversies over fundamentalism, communalism and the US war on Iraq—issues that agitate their supporters in the seminar circuit of New Delhi. Most of the concerns listed by the minority community were surprisingly similar to other sections of society: rising crime, unemployment and the absence of basic facilities. Significantly, a majority of Muslims felt no longer particularly threatened by the BJP and Sangh affiliates like the Bajrang Dal and VHP, which they felt had lost both their popularity among Hindus and the administrative clout to do the minority community serious harm.

Dalits, the BSP's core constituency, seemed to be floating on a cloud during the election campaign. Most of them smirked when asked whether the overtures by Mayawati to the upper castes meant a betrayal of the Dalit cause. They obviously did not believe this to be true. As one of them asked quite matter-of-factly, 'How can Behenji betray us? After all she is one of us.' Having built up her credentials for so many years among the Dalit masses of the state, Mayawati stood in no danger of being mistaken for the Uncle Tom Dalits of the past, who had sold out their community for personal benefits. As a matter of fact, the entry of upper castes into the BSP fold and Maywati increasingly speaking in tones of the sarvajana samaj (society for every community), instead of just bahujan samaj, made many Dalits feel several inches taller. They were not at all worried about the disappearance of the old provocative election slogans like the notorious '*Tilak, Tarazu, Talwar*' that had preached caste conflict; in fact they actually welcomed the newer ones, for instance, '*Hathi nahin, Ganesh hain, Brahma, Vishnu , Mahesh hain* (It is not just an elephant, it is Lord Ganesh, it is Lord Brahma, Lord Vishnu and Lord Mahesh),' and '*Brahmin sankh bajaegi, Hathi dilli jaegi*' (the brahmin will blow the conch shell and the elephant will march to Delhi),' that appealed to Hindu religious sentiments, pandering in particular to brahmin religious sensibilities.

Dalits were able to accept Mayawati's sudden decision to offer an olive branch to upper castes that had earlier been reviled as enemies because she did so from a position of overwhelming strength, and not weakness. The fact that a Dalit leader was now capable of attracting upper-caste votes on her own terms, further consolidated her Dalit base swelling her traditional vote bank of chamars with large inflows from other lowest caste sub-groups, including the pasis, koris and even a section of the hitherto hostile valmikis. Dalits were overwhelmed by the sight of upper castes paying homage to the daughter of an untouchable. This added to Mayawati's aura among her people. The Dalit leader herself seemed acutely aware of the impact that the alliance with brahmins and some other upper castes had made on her own flock. Asked as the elections drew to an end on whether her new upper caste supporters would bring her back to power, she remarked with a broad grin, 'Why only upper castes, even the Bahujan Samaj is turning up in much larger numbers.'[3]

Even as the long electoral process drew to a close, a parallel battle of the polls was raging. Indeed this was almost a parallel universe in which various television channels predicted with complete authority which party would get how many seats in the Uttar Pradesh polls. All of them based their results on exit polls that were based on supposedly widespread interviews with voters after they had cast their ballot. All of them claimed to have highly scientific methods of data selection. And all of them turned out wrong.

One television channel, for instance, actually predicted a dead heat between the BSP, the SP and the BJP (117–27 seats for the BSP; 113–23 seats for the SP; 108–18 seats for the BJP). Another channel tried to be more balanced in its forecast (152–68 seats for the BSP; 99–111 seats for the SP; 80–90 for the BJP), but still managed to be quite off the mark. The average seat range culled from all the different sets of polls stood thus: the BSP between 116 and 168; the SP between 96 and 123; and the BJP between 80 and 124. Within just a few hours after counting started in the morning, the pollsters were eating their own predictions because the actual tally read thus: 206 seats to the BSP, 97 seats to the SP and 50 seats to the BJP.

Once again the BJP had been the biggest loser in the Uttar Pradesh polls, suffering one more killer blow to its chances of revival. The electoral outcome clearly established that voters in the country's largest state that had, in the early nineties, pitchforked the BJP to national prominence, were pushing the party back to the ground with equal velocity in the new millennium. The BJP electoral graph in the state had slid alarmingly over the past few elections. It had won 174 seats in 1996, eighty-eight in 2002 and was reduced to fifty in 2007. The vote share, too, plummeted correspondingly from 32.52 per cent in 1996 to 20.08 per cent in 2002 and just seventeen per cent in 2007. It now seemed to be just a matter of time before the BJP in Uttar Pradesh took on the political-fossil status of the Congress, which had incredibly dipped to less than even its pathetic past score of twenty-five seats that it had been so sure of improving. Desperate to divert attention from this cruel expose of the Gandhi scion's failure in the polls, Congress leaders and spokespersons appearing on post-poll television analysis programmes determinedly celebrated the spectacular downfall of the BJP in the hope of diverting public attention from the near demise of the party in the ancestral home of the Nehru–Gandhi clan.

For Mulayam Singh the polls conveyed a mixed message. By scrambling his forces together in the last few rounds, he had managed to retain his vote percentage, in fact even improving it by a few decimal points to twenty-six per cent. But he had been bested at his own game of electoral management that had so far always given him the best conversion ratio of vote percentage into seats. While his party had managed to win 143 seats in the last elections, it had slumped to ninety-seven in 2007, despite slightly improving its vote percentage. This was because of a combination of different factors—Mulayam Singh's crumbling image and organization, the Election Commission's measures to stop vote manipulation and perhaps, most importantly, the surge in the BSP vote share as well as the latter's improved election management. The yadav leader's worst nightmare had come true. Mayawati was firmly ensconced on the throne of Lucknow even as Sonia Gandhi continued to call the shots in New Delhi. He and his associate Amar Singh had little option but to wait and see what fiendish tortures the two ladies had in store for him.

'The Elephant marched on to victory kicking the Cycle out of the way, trampling the Lotus under its feet and wiping out of existence the Hand that tried to stop it.' This evocative ditty sung to a Bollywood tune was on the lips of many BSP workers a day after Mayawati's historic triumph. It showed a keen awareness of the political ramifications of her achievement. Drawing its imagery from election symbols of the four main protagonists of the 2007 polls, the song pointed out that the BSP's elephant had pushed aside the Samajwadi cycle, while crushing the BJP lotus and obliterating the Congress hand. Despite the poetic licence, the lyrics were a remarkably accurate depiction of the actual electoral outcome.

Mayawati has had her share of spectacular successes in the past, as we have noted earlier. But she had never before been the recipient of such universal acclaim as after being anointed the chief minister of Uttar Pradesh for an incredible fourth time. The fact that this time the BSP leader enjoyed a full majority gave her a political halo that went well beyond the afterglow of an electoral victory. Her feat was all the more creditable in a state where no party had won on its own for over one-and-a-half decades and which was accustomed to repeated political crises leading to frequent periods of President's Rule. She also got kudos for succeeding in a daring social engineering gamble that had come up trumps. Significantly, the winning BSP candidates reflected her success across the social spectrum. Out of the party's tally of 206 seats, sixty-two were Dalits, fifty-one brahmins, fifty-one OBCs (other backward castes), twenty-four Muslims and eighteen thakurs. It was also a triumph for her chief lieutenant Satish Mishra, who had delivered big time with his electoral strategy. Significantly, she demonstrated her appreciation by having him appear constantly by her side after her victory. It was almost as if Mishra had assumed the role of political advisor that Kanshi Ram used to play in the past although the relationship between Mayawati and the brahmin lawyer was obviously vastly different to her relationship with late mentor and guru.

As soon as it became certain that the BSP would have a full majority on its own, Mayawati emerged in her victory outfit of pink chiffon salwar kameez to hold a press conference in front of the statues of her most revered icons, Babasaheb Ambedkar, her late guru Kanshi Ram, and herself at the Bahujan Prerna Kendra in Lucknow. She began by dedicating the victory to the entire Dalit pantheon—Phule, Shahuji Maharaj, Periyar, Narayana Guru, Ambedkar and Kanshi Ram—but then quickly turned to establish her new credentials as leader of the sarvajana samaj. She did not have to say very much. Her close political aides who flanked the BSP leader on either side on the dais—Satish Mishra, a brahmin, Nasimuddin Siddique, a Muslim and Babu Singh Kushwaha, a member of the backward caste—were a conspicuous illustration of the multi-tiered social coalition that had swept Mayawati to a landmark victory.

The novel emphasis on social balance was reflected in the caste composition of her new council of ministers as well. The list of cabinet ministers included eight Dalits, four brahmins, four OBCs and one each from the Muslim, baniya, thakur and bhumihar communities. The ministers of state with independent charge included eleven Dalits, seven OBC members and four each from the brahmin, thakur and Muslim communities. Live television images of the swearing-in ceremony beamed across the country conveyed powerful messages. As her ministers, regardless of caste or community, bent down one by one to pay homage to Mayawati, some touching her feet, others folding their hands in namaste, it was difficult not to be carried away by this public repudiation of the deep caste and communal divisions that had been the hallmark of the state's politics for so long. The fact that these unprecedented scenes of bonhomie were being presided over by the leader of a party that had chanted social conflict as its mantra for so many years, made the occasion appear even more surreal.

There was also a marked difference in the bureaucratic team chosen by Mayawati in her fourth term as chief minister, compared to her earlier stints in power. We did note earlier that even in

2002, she was moving away from her earlier obsession of creating a coterie of Dalit officers around her. One of the key upper-caste officers she had appointed in her third term was the jat pilot turned bureaucrat, Shashank Shekhar Singh. He now became her super bureaucrat posted in a specially created state designation of cabinet secretary and given the rank of a cabinet minister. More importantly, the chief minister gave him full authority to choose the right people for the right posts regardless of their caste or community. This was a huge leap forward for Mayawati, not just in terms of looking beyond Dalit officials, but more crucially in delegating such sweeping powers that she would previously clutch to herself. This more than anything else underlined how much self-confidence she had acquired from winning a full majority.

The other big change in the BSP leader appeared to be her new, rather patronizing approach to the media with whom she always had an uneasy, if not openly hostile, relationship. Having completely miscalculated before the polls about her rising political curve, the media went to the opposite extreme after the results surprised them. They jostled with each other to shout hosannas for Mayawati, even speculating on her prospects of being the next prime minister. Her first press conference in New Delhi, therefore, attracted a mad rush of journalists and television cameras. It was an amazing turnaround for a tribe that had all along quite openly despised the BSP leader. One could almost sense the same sentiments go through Mayawati's mind as she surveyed the excited buzz of the vast media contingent assembled in a banquet hall of a five star hotel.

The following observations of a newspaper columnist described the scene eloquently: 'Mayawati began her press conference in the Capital with an uncharacteristic giggle. Victory is sweet but sweeter still was the sight of a fawning media, packed to standing-room-only capacity in the plush ballroom of a five star hotel to listen to the woman it once reviled as boorish and uncouth. There were at least 1,000 journos, including the chief editor, in coat and tie, of a leading daily. The giggle escaped involuntarily, betraying the thrill coursing through Mayawati as she surveyed the hack pack she has always seen as her tormentors.

'The tables were turned. She mocked them ("At least do some introspection NOW!"), laughed at them (as they fought for the privilege of getting her attention) and upbraided them ("You don't know how to ask a question"). The journos lapped it up. So witty, they gushed. A charm offensive, they raved. And when she wound up the press conference with a peremptory order ("Go and eat. Your food is getting cold. There's chicken for you."), they went obediently, their roar tamed to a purr. Nothing succeeds like success.'[4]

Her first visit to the capital after ascending the throne in Lucknow for the fourth time was also quite a political triumph. She was entertained by none other than UPA chairperson, Sonia Gandhi, who laid on the charm at a private tête-à-tête over tea that went on for one-and-a-half hours. Mayawati arrived at 10 Janpath, the Gandhi residence in a cavalcade that included a car full of orchids for her hostess. Her cavalcade was allowed to drive straight up to the portico of the Gandhi house, a privilege so far granted only to members of the family and the prime minister. It symbolized the BSP leader's new status in the corridors of national power. She also met the prime minister, Dr Manmohan Singh, for what she said were preliminary discussions towards a more substantive meeting on the kind of financial resources her state needed from the central government. The prime minister, she said, was most kind. Almost overnight, Mayawati had become extremely relevant in a whole range of national issues starting with the presidential and vice-presidential elections that took place shortly after the assembly polls in Uttar Pradesh. She graciously agreed to support the candidates chosen by the UPA and its allies, instantly sparking off speculation in political and media circles on the BSP joining the ruling coalition, with some pundits even suggesting that Sonia Gandhi and Mayawati had already decided to walk hand in hand towards the next general elections.

It did not take long for Mayawati to show her claws. Two months later, the chief minister was back with her little list of demands for Uttar Pradesh from the prime minister. This time Dr Singh almost fell off his chair. She wanted the astronomical sum of eighty thousand crore rupees for various projects in her state, many of which she claimed could barely wait. Still playing the upper-caste card, she also urged the government to take an initiative in Parliament to amend the laws to facilitate reservations for economically deprived sections of the upper castes in education and jobs similar to that given to scheduled and backward castes. Already under pressure from various backward- and lower-caste social groups for privilege quotas, Dr Singh groaned at this fresh demand for reservations on behalf of the upper castes by a Dalit leader. The prime minister was used to stonewalling on demands made by various state chief ministers, although none had been quite so demanding in so short a period. He put Mayawati's demands in the drawer and went back to push the nuclear deal with the United States hoping that she would get more real about her demands. A few months later, while campaigning for assembly by-elections in Uttar Pradesh in August 2007, the chief minister erupted against the UPA government at the centre upbraiding the prime minister taking so long to respond to her demands. 'I had met prime minister Manmohan Singh seeking a special economic package for the backward regions of Purvanchal and Bundelkhand, but sadly he has not cared to even send a reply so far. Apparently, the Congress party is bothered only about the interest of corporate houses and not the poor and the downtrodden,' Mayawati declared at one election meeting. In another speech she even threatened to unseat the Congress-led coalition. 'Very soon you will see our party establishing itself in a big way in several other states and the day is not far when we will take over Delhi. It will then be too late for the Congress to realize its mistake of ignoring us.' The honeymoon between Mayawati and New Delhi was over even before it really began.

Back in the saddle for the fourth time, the BSP leader quickly proved that she had not lost her abilities to stir things up. Typically, both sides of her Dr Jekyll and Mr Hyde personality marked her first few months as chief minister. She tweaked the ears of errant officials to justify her nickname 'Iron Lady', even as she displayed complete disdain for public opinion. Swift punishment was meted out to a district magistrate who had in a shocking display of communal bias, forced a Muslim family to undergo family planning in return for a gun licence. Similarly, an order from the chief minister's office saved three women human rights activists fighting for the rights of labourers in a remote district, from the clutches of police officials in cahoots with local landlords. At the same time, angry sports lovers shrieked at her for planning to demolish a popular sports stadium in the heart of Lucknow just to expand her pet project, the Ambedkar Park complex standing next door. Mayawati also baited the media and urban middle class opinion by razing a row of bungalows near her private residence on the posh Mall Avenue in Lucknow, on the plea that she needed more security.

On the economic front the new Mayawati regime sent some self-contradictory signals in the first few months. Her government began with a bang announcing contract farming and the setting up of retail outlets by big corporates, which was wildly cheered by the chattering classes and the pink papers. In a few weeks, however, these policies were suddenly reversed ostensibly on the plea that they would have antagonized farmers and local traders. Considering that the contract farm policy was initially justified by the same government for getting a better price for agricultural produce to farmers from big private players who would buy directly from them cutting out the middlemen, the rather lame explanation that intelligence reports suggested that this would be unpopular in the countryside did not have many takers. Similarly, it is difficult to believe that a tough administrator like Mayawati would back off from the not-so-menacing threat of agitating local traders. Both decisions and their reversals appeared to reflect on the still tentative and emerging process of policy making by a fourth-time chief minister who was still trying to come to terms with the novel prospect of an assured full five-year term in office for the first time in her career.

Mayawati's first political test in her fourth stint in power came shortly after she celebrated one hundred days in office. These were three assembly by-elections: in Swarn Tanda, Gunnaur and Farukkhabad. These were important not just as the first popular feedback to the BSP government, but also because of their specific backgrounds. All the three assembly constituencies had been won by the Samajwadi Party in the April–May 2007 polls but had to go to the hustings again because the candidates resigned. The Swarn Tanda candidate, Kazim Ali Khan, Nawab of Rampur, resigned from the Samajwadi Party when he resigned his assembly seat and crossed over to the BSP after it came to power. He was given the BSP ticket for the by-poll and the Muslim aristocrat's contest against the Samajwadi Party candidate became a prestigious tussle between the two parties which would signify who had more clout with the minority community. The fact that the Nawab's mother, Begum Noor Bano, former Member of Parliament from the region, was also an important Muslim leader of the Congress, added a further political twist. Khan comfortably won the by-poll for the BSP by nearly 50,000 votes, far more than his victory margin on the Samajwadi Party ticket. However, the Samajwadi Party supremo, Mulayam Singh, saved his prestige by getting his party candidate to win from Gunnaur, one of the two seats he had himself won in the assembly polls and had resigned. Although the BSP put up a hard fight, drastically reducing the margin of the Samajwadi Party in this yadav-dominated constituency, the former chief minister proved that his caste brethren were still with him even after losing power.

Farukkhabad was the most interesting by-poll of all, not least because it became a test of Mayawati's own political clout. The fascinating tale of the elections needs to be told in detail and placed in its historical context. The Samajwadi Party candidate, Vijay Singh, who had won the seat in the assembly polls, had a chequered past. A powerful local gangster, he had been accused of murdering the local BJP legislator, Brahm Dutt Dwivedi. Singh had been very close to Mayawati from the mid-nineties and had mobilized support in his party for her to be the chief minister. The powerful political bloc that backed Singh, on the other hand, were the BSP leader's implacable foes—Mulayam Singh and Kalyan Singh. With their support and his local connections, Singh defeated the slain BJP legislator's widow, Prabha Dwivedi, from Farukkhabad in the 2002 polls. Although, the next year he was found guilty by a CBI court and sentenced to life imprisonment, Singh managed to get bail and contest once again in the 2007 state elections from the same constituency on a Samajwadi Party ticket. He won again, this time defeating Dwivedi's son, Major Sunil Dutt Dwivedi.

After Mayawati swept to power, Singh, in a bid to align himself to the winning horse, announced that he was joining the BSP, dramatically resigning from the Samajwadi Party and his assembly seat. His strategy backfired. He was plainly expecting to be given a ticket by the BSP from Farukkhabad, from where he was confident of being re-elected through his own clout aided by the BSP tailwind. But Singh's schemes were rudely shattered after Mayawati refused to accept him, saying that she did not do business with murderers and that, too, of old friends. The Farukkhabad strongman was in a fix. He could not go back to the Samjawadi Party, nor would the BJP accommodate someone who had been sentenced for murdering a party legislator. Curiously, the Congress came to his rescue and nominated Singh as its candidate for the Farukkhabad by-polls. Mayawati took this as a personal affront from a party which she had recently supported in the presidential and vice-presidential polls at the centre. She added yet another dimension to the polls by nominating Satish Mishra's nephew, Anant Mishra, to be the BSP candidate from Farukkhabad. He had earlier been appointed state minister for health despite having lost in the assembly polls.

It turned out to be a fiercely contested by-poll. Vijay Singh was a formidable candidate whose personal influence in the constituency was further enhanced by the combined backing— openly or tacitly—of all the other three big parties, Congress, Samajwadi Party and BJP, who were determined to use this opportunity to embarrass the new chief minister. Sensing the crucial importance of the by-poll, Mayawati rallied all her forces pushing in a dozen ministers into the campaign and going to the trouble of personally addressing an election meeting in Farukkhabad. Ultimately, the BSP leader did triumph with her candidate Misra romping home by a margin of 14,500 votes. She had passed one more political test with flying colours.

As we leave Mayawati at this new career peak, this is clearly not the end of her amazing saga. Nor was there any question of the chief minister resting on her laurels. There were both huge challenges and opportunities ahead. A spate of riots in Agra and Allahabad as she completed a hundred days in power showed that there were forces at work to blot her copybook on law and order. Mysteriously, the riots were provoked by Muslim mobs and the administration had to pull out the stops in both cities to prevent the violence snowballing into a communal conflagration. Although vanquished for the moment, Mulayam Singh, her only remaining serious opponent at the state level, was definitely not going to roll over and die—as he proved by clinging on to Gunnaur. She would have to sustain and expand the social alliance that had swept her into office to counter the powerful landlord lobbies that were bound to rally around the yadav leader.

A much larger national role beckons as the run up to the run up to the next general elections starts. The tentative on-and-off relationship with the Congress and its leader, Sonia Gandhi, is one of many imponderables the BSP leader would have to negotiate in the future. She always tended to move forward in the fear that otherwise she would slide back. Having achieved phenomenal success, Mayawati is now poised like a coiled spring ready to leap into a larger political orbit. Only time will tell whether she will fall on her face or reach new heights.

# Section Two

*The evolution of an obscure Dalit schoolteacher into one of the most powerful political figures of modern India as described in the previous section is a fascinating story. Yet, amazing as this chronological narrative may be, there is need to examine in more detail some of the more crucial and unique aspects of Mayawati and her politics. Indeed, there is perhaps no other political leader in this county so far who has generated so much debate and raised so many questions.*

*There are six key questions that have come to the fore in the ongoing debate across the country on Mayawati and what she means for Indian democracy. Can she provide good administration and how important is this for her politics? Is the BSP different from all other parties? Can her attempts to join the bottom and top rungs of the caste ladder work? Is she the Dalit messiah or a pretender? How much wealth has she accumulated and can it get her into trouble? Finally, will she, in the foreseeable future, become the country's prime minister?*

*In this section, I attempt to answer these questions. It is meant to be a Mayawati guide that puts under the magnifying glass both her strengths and weaknesses to achieve a better understanding of her rise so far as well as her future trajectory.*

# TEN

## *Iron Lady Versus Transfer Rani*

$\mathcal{M}$ayawati's administrative record at the helm of government adds up to less than three years despite becoming chief minister of Uttar Pradesh as many as four times. This is simply because her previous three stints at the top did not last very long. Yet, even in a relatively brief duration in power her sweeping style of governance has left a vivid impression on the public mind. Her detractors point to the frequent and arbitrary transfers of officials as only one of the many deficiencies of her administration. On the other hand, there are those who see her as a tough no-nonsense 'Iron Lady' who keeps the bureaucracy on its toes. These sharply differing perceptions of the same person—and perhaps the same set of decisions—make it all the more necessary to examine her chief ministerial record in the context of the social and political environment in which she has operated.

It is also important to trace whether she has evolved as leader and manager over the past dozen years, starting from the time in the mid-nineties when she was quite miraculously pitchforked, young and inexperienced, into the driver's seat of India's largest and possibly most chaotic state. Political and media circles are abuzz today over Mayawati's political future, though many pundits have predicted that much would depend on the quality of governance of her present term in office. Is this, in fact, the case? Indeed, is this distinction drawn between a good administrator and a successful politician valid?

The most common charge levelled against Mayawati is that she shifts officials at her whim and fancy. Indeed the sheer volume of bureaucratic transfers during her various stints in power seem overwhelming at first glance. After one month of her third stint in power, a newsmagazine published some astonishing facts and figures of transfers and postings, including those effected during Mayawati's two previous stints as chief minister.[1] In her first innings as chief minister from June 1995 to October 1995, she ordered 386 transfers. In 1997, as many as 470 officers were shifted during her six-month term. And the 'transfer toll' less than a month after she became chief minister for the third time in 2002 was 305, including eighty-five IAS and fifty IPS officers spread across thirty-two districts. Some of the specific cases from her first month in office in 2002 involving individual officers who were tossed around like salad can be quite shocking as illustrated by two examples cited in the same article.

- N.R. Srivastava, deputy inspector general of police (Anti-corruption) was transferred to DIG (Intelligence) for a day. He was then directed to take over as DIG (Railway Police). He lasted in this post for a few hours before he was ordered to take over as DIG, Chitrakoot Dham, a Hindu pilgrimage town. He had not even reached the town when he was transferred as DIG (Security), only to be posted back again as DIG (Railway Police). Five transfers in six days.

- Ramlal Ram, inspector general of police, Gorakhpur, was posted as IG, Provincial Armed Constabulary (PAC). Before he could begin his new assignment, he was sent off as IG (Power Corporation). However, before he could take over his new post, this was pre-empted by a transfer order appointing him IG (Administration) in Lucknow. Four transfers in six days.

Despite these horror stories, the record of other chief ministers in the state is similar. Published figures reveal that Mayawati's two immediate predecessors, Mulayam Singh Yadav and Kalyan Singh, were equally guilty of constantly pressing the transfer button.[2] Mulayam Singh in his first term—between December 1989 and

June 1991—transferred 419 IAS and 228 IPS officers. His successor Kalyan Singh shifted 460 IAS and 319 IPS officers between June 1991 and December 1992. Yadav in his second stint in power from December 1993 to June 1995 kept up the spate of transfers, shunting out as many as 321 IAS and 493 IPS officers.

It is not only chief ministers who sent officials scurrying from post to post. Even when the state was under President's Rule, governors, unburdened by pressures politicians face to keep their constituents happy, have also behaved in the same irresponsible manner. Uttar Pradesh Governor Romesh Bhandari, during President's Rule from July 1996 to March 1997, transferred an incredible 344 IAS and 380 IPS officers. Mayawati thus merely followed the established pattern of frequent and arbitrary transfers set by other rulers of the state. It may even be argued that she had little choice but to undo all the transfers and posting of her predecessor, which automatically started the game of musical chairs with officials all over again.

Widespread allegations of cronyism, nepotism and, of course, casteism have also been levelled against Mayawati during her chief ministership. Her first two stints in office and, to a lesser extent, the third term were marked by a complete disregard for both administrative propriety and procedure. Rules and regulations were openly flouted as the chief minister took the administration by the scruff of its neck and sought to do with it what she wanted. Seniority was more often than not bypassed and confidential records were not worth the paper they were written on. In her second term she was reported to be considering a novel change in government service rules which would enable local BSP leaders to write the confidential records of district magistrates and superintendents of police, instead of the official they reported to, as was normally the case.

Clearly, corruption was not held against bureaucrats when deciding postings or promotions. Lucknow newspapers raised a stink in 2002 after the chief minister rehabilitated Ram Kumar, an officer who was compulsorily retired on corruption charges after he managed to get the courts to stay his retirement. Despite the pending charges, he was made principal secretary of four supposedly lucrative departments—minor irrigation, mahila kalyan, bal vikas and rural engineering services. The media also smelt a rat when Net Ram, a favourite Dalit officer and a fixture in the chief minister's secretariat for her first three terms, was given additional charge of the basic shiksha department that had a whopping budget of 1,500 crore rupees. Even the relatives of favourite bureaucrats were obliged with official positions. Sri Krishna, another chief ministerial favourite and close aide for her first three terms, managed to have his brother appointed as head of the state human rights commission, bypassing many distinguished retired civil servants. Indira Punia, wife of Mayawati's three-time principal secretary P.L. Punia, was appointed chairperson of the state women's commission with a rank equal to that of a minister. Giving details of the various postings, a national daily commented, 'As there is no probity in public life, no transparency and no accountability, what one desperately misses is judicial activism.'[3]

However, Mayawati was certainly not the first or only chief minister in the state to manipulate the administration for her own ends. The rule book has been trampled on by every ruler of Uttar Pradesh at least over the past three decades, if not from earlier. The BSP leader's theatrical excesses while riding roughshod over personnel and institutions caught public attention and created media headlines. But many of her political peers got away with far worse abuse of the administration because they used more insidious methods.

Several factors need to be considered while judging Mayawati's administrative shortcomings. When first made chief minister, she had no governmental experience and perhaps had never inspected an official file. In her first term, she was so afraid of being misled by bureaucrats that she insisted on scrutinizing and signing virtually every official document. This meant incredibly long hours of work that stretched to late at night. Officials lined up with files outside her private quarters on occasion. Many of them were stunned when she emerged in what looked suspiciously like a nightdress, to hold meetings and sign files.

Her naiveté and insecurity made Mayawati appreciate the loyalty of an officer rather than his efficiency or integrity. There is a hilarious but illustrative anecdote of her attempts to reward an upper-caste officer who had saved her in the Lucknow guest house incident. The new chief minister repeatedly summoned him to her private chambers so that he could ask for a favour. Unfortunately, the officer belonged to the rare minority of bureaucrats who did not want or know how to curry political favour. Baffled at the officer's pointed silence and monosyllabic answers each time he came before her, the chief minister kept on calling the officer assuming he was simply raising the stakes. This farcical tug of war between the chief minister wanting to reward the officer and the officer desperate to get her off his back, continued for a few days till the officer realized what was happening. He swiftly ended his ordeal by demanding the most lucrative post in Lucknow. A relieved Mayawati while denying him that post, (which had already been booked for a close favourite), assigned the officer a reasonable department.

Mayawati's Dalit agenda created a lot of heartburn in the bureaucracy. The large pool of Dalit officers in Uttar Pradesh made Mayawati's casteist bias all the more glaring. In her first two stints scheduled caste officers bagged virtually every key post. Some appointments that sought to post scheduled caste officers in sensitive field posts across the state were justified. The CM wanted to ensure that policies guaranteeing security and land rights for Dalits were implemented. But other postings merely created personal fiefdoms for the BSP leader, vitiating the bureaucratic atmosphere.

In a state where caste and community had already erected so many barriers, the emergence of a charmed circle of Dalit officers who were said to have the chief minister's blessings, spread resentment in the service. This arose partly out of the inability of other castes particularly upper castes to appreciate the intrinsic solidarity among scheduled caste officers. Rajiv Verma, the Lucknow district magistrate who had firmly intervened in the Lucknow guest house and stopped the attack on Mayawati, was taken aback when scheduled caste officers of his cadre came to thank him 'for saving our leader's honour'. Verma would recall many years later, 'Only then I realized how important Mayawati was to these officers and how pleasantly surprised they were that I protected her despite my upper-caste background.' The BSP's political agenda actively encouraged scheduled caste officers to wear their caste as an identity badge and Mayawati accordingly played the caste card.

The same political agenda motivated the other controversial highlight of Mayawati's previous regimes—the creation of new districts, the construction of monuments, buildings and parks, and a major renaming drive to promote the Dalit cause. The cost of this sustained and vast exercise was exorbitant as we can judge by the escalating price tag of the Ambedkar Park: up from 500 million rupees to two billion rupees and still rising. The new districts created by the chief minister in honour of various Dalit leaders of the past, made a gaping hole in the state exchequer. After she announced the formation of six new districts during her second term in 1997, a national daily calculated the cost of each district to be between 125 crore to 150 crore rupees.[4]

Mayawati has faced a lot of flak for spending these resources on political propaganda instead of on the economic welfare of Uttar Pradesh which, her critics say, would have far better served the interests of the backward state, including its poorest and most deprived social segments. But from the BSP leader's viewpoint, conventional economic welfare schemes were mostly lengthy projects that soaked up funds and took a long time to be effective. Her brand of identity politics required instant graphic symbols to project political messages and she used the resources at her command for this purpose.

We need to remember that all her three previous terms were unstable and temporary in nature. This denied her the opportunity to do any long-term planning. To her credit, the BSP leader did introduce some economic welfare and developmental schemes as, for instance, the Ambedkar Villages programme as well as special educational grants for the poor and backward social groups, even though their implementation was haphazard and incomplete. The fact that even the little she did on the economic and developmental front for the wretched of Uttar Pradesh earned her their loyalty in subsequent elections underlines the absence of any effort by other, supposedly more politically correct, chief ministers of the state. Most of them had more stable majorities and longer stints in office.

Mayawati has been portrayed by sections of the media as a despot who enjoyed humiliating bureaucrats. Surprisingly, a large number of bureaucrats who worked with her vehemently deny this charge. They avow that while the lady is extraordinarily demanding, she is rarely nasty or offensive. 'I have never heard her be personally offensive to bureaucrats, although we all knew that there would be hell to pay if we did not carry out her orders. This is different from other chief ministers who took pleasure in insulting bureaucrats in public but were far less demanding,' said a bureaucrat who had worked with Mayawati and at least two other chief ministers in Uttar Pradesh. Officers were transferred, suspended or sacked at short notice for genuine or spurious reasons. But the chief minister rarely harassed officials who ran foul of her. This is in sharp contrast to the witch hunts launched by Kalyan Singh, Mulayam Singh and Rajnath Singh against bureaucrats they considered foes. For instance, Mulayam Singh, when he took over as chief minister after Mayawati's government collapsed in August 2004, went out of his way to hound bureaucrats close to her—Shashank Shekhar Singh and Rohit Nandan, for instance. Singh was not given a charge and was reduced to staying at home. Nandan, who was not even a bureaucratic heavyweight like Singh, and had held the post of Mayawati's director of information, was banished to the department of handicapped. Even when he managed to get a posting on deputation to the central government, the Mulayam Singh government refused to relieve him from his posting in the state.

Several officials praised Mayawati for her direct and transparent style of functioning and said they preferred it to the insidious and opaque ways of other chief ministers. She did startle officers during her first term by being unaware of basic chief ministerial protocol as illustrated, for instance, by her signing files while clad in a nightdress. But despite their embarrassment, the officers appreciated her innocence and her enthusiasm for the job. It was a refreshing change from the jaded netas they were used to as political masters. Amazingly, for a leader who demanded total loyalty and had megalomaniac ambitions, she hardly encouraged sycophancy otherwise so prevalent in the still feudal political and bureaucratic culture of Uttar Pradesh. This meant that while she was uninterested in courtiers bowing, scraping and chanting *jee huzoor*s, she expected her subordinates in government and the party to unquestioningly carry out her bidding.

Mayawati has also been known to be quite charming in the most unexpected situations. Shortly after assuming office in 2002, the new chief minister bowled over senior bureaucrat Ajay Prakash Verma, even as she removed him from the chief secretary's post to accommodate Kanshi Ram's favourite, D. S. Bagga, who superseded half a dozen senior officials. Much to Verma's astonishment Mayawati was completely honest with him. She apologized for removing him from his post, confessing she could not say no to her guru, Kanshi Ram, who had insisted on Bagga as chief secretary. 'She was so nice and frank about the whole thing, I did not feel bad at all at being sacked as chief secretary,' recalled Verma.

Mayawati's apologetic explanation to the ousted chief secretary also reflects her personal unease at some of the bureaucratic appointments she had to make under pressure from her mentor. A bureaucrat who has worked closely with her for a number of years revealed that once Kanshi Ram became too ill to interfere in administrative matters, there was a big improvement in her style of functioning. Most neutral observers of the bureaucratic scene in Uttar Pradesh agree that it was Kanshi Ram, far more than Mayawati, who was prone to nepotism, favouritism and the tendency to disregard the political consequences of poor administration. They feel that it is quite possible some of the worst excesses in bureaucratic transfers and postings, particularly in the first two stints of her chief ministership, may have been avoided if she had not been compelled to accommodate Kanshi Ram's constant demands to favour his candidates, many of them scheduled caste officers who had helped Kanshi Ram during the initial stages of the bahujan samaj movement. The accuracy of this analysis is borne out by the much tighter and more efficient administration run by Mayawati in her fourth stint in power, although there is little doubt that the stability and security brought by an absolute majority has also contributed to a more sober and performance-oriented approach to administration.

The other interesting point made by a key bureaucratic aide in Mayawati's defence against allegations of administrative bungling and abuse, particularly in her initial stints as chief minister, is that the senior bureaucracy itself was partly responsible. 'She was without any administrative experience and she could be misled by senior officials who either had their own agendas or were incompetent. As she gathered experience and knowledge about the bureaucratic system, she herself realized what was happening. I can tell you from personal experience of working with several chief ministers, she is one of the few who were ready to change her own decision if you managed to convince her that it was wrong,' the aide asserted.

Along with the brickbats, Mayawati has also received several bouquets for her administration. The BSP leader's biggest plus point has been her firm and capable handling of law and order.

People first glimpsed her administrative steel when as a debutante chief minister in 1995 she refused to back down from a menacing Vishwa Hindu Parishad threatening to provoke a communal conflagration by planning a religious function next to a disputed shrine in the holy city of Mathura. She impressed everyone by combining courage with pragmatism; using administrative and political methods in tandem to defuse a potentially explosive situation. This was in sharp contrast to Mulayam Singh, who as chief minister in 1991 had also taken a tough stance with the Parishad while protecting the Babri Masjid at Ayodhya. But he had made an absolute mess using excessive force on agitating Hindu zealots that resulted in the death of several—including some sadhus—in police firing. The fierce backlash by the Hindu majority community against the yadav leader not only decimated him in the state elections the following year, it also boosted Hindu fundamentalism in the country.

The other feather in Mayawati's cap is her intrepid pursuit of gangsters, brigands and Mafiosi. These are three different types of criminals that proliferate in Uttar Pradesh. Gangsters are small groups of local hoodlums in towns and villages; brigands are mainly dacoits operating in rural areas and Mafiosi are big-time criminals whose bases are in cities or towns. We examined in an earlier chapter her epic victory over the thakur don, Raja Bhaiya, during her third stint as chief minister. More recently, within a few months of her assuming charge of the state for the fourth time, her police force hunted down and shot dead the dreaded bandit, Dadua, who had terrorized large parts of Uttar Pradesh for many years. This was possible because the Special Task Force, responsible for putting down Dadua under the leadership of crack police officer Amitabh Yash, were given a carte blanche to go after the big gangs without fear and with extreme prejudice. The fact that in her fourth term the chief minister appointed one of the most decorated police officers in the country, Vikram Singh, as her director general of police indicates her determination to restore law and order after several years of 'Jungle Raj' under Mulayam Singh Yadav.

Mayawati's war on crime does not mean that she has not taken the help of criminals when she has felt the need in the past. Two of the most controversial politicians in Uttar Pradesh, Amar Nath Tripathi and Hari Shankar Tiwari, were key members of the

BSP cabinet during her third term in office. Dreaded Uttar Pradesh don, D.P. Yadav was a prominent member of Parliament, representing the BSP in the nineties. Even more unacceptable was the induction into the BSP of two notorious brothers, Ramakant Yadav and Umakant Yadav, who were among the leaders of the mob that attacked Mayawati in the Lucknow guest house incident of 1995. Both have been subsequently thrown out of the party and one is now behind bars. But it is difficult to comprehend how and why she could even contemplate accepting into her fold persons who had showered her with filthy abuses and even tried to physically harm her. The only explanation can be that the Yadav brothers were useful feudal barons to spirit away from Mulayam Singh's camp and Mayawati is ready to use anyone whatever their past record as long as it suited her immediate political agenda. It betrays a complete lack of scruples that is quite disturbing.

The one quality that distinguishes Mayawati from other chief ministers who have ruled Uttar Pradesh is her identification with the lowest rung of the social ladder. Each time she came to power, there has been a sense of elation and relief among the poor, backward and deprived people in the state. Invariably, whether through a strict implementation of the Scheduled Caste and Scheduled Tribes (Prevention of Atrocities) Act, the distribution of pattas/chits giving ownership rights to precious land, or the provision of basic infrastructural facilities to Dalit villages, the people, oppressed and neglected for centuries and centuries, have gained. Her surprise inspection tours make field officers tremble. She introduced the practice of tehsil diwas many years ago, when every Tuesday public grievances can be brought to officials in each tehsil, and extra attention paid to those who are normally not heard. Schemes such as these are vital departures from the callous approach of other regimes. A Mulayam Singh, Kalyan Singh or Rajnath Singh would never empathize with those in need of administrative support as the following two examples from her latest stint in power illustrate.

A report in the *Hindu* in 2007 stated: 'Uttar Pradesh Chief Minister Mayawati on Tuesday suspended the District Magistrate of Gorakhpur, Rakesh Kumar Goel, for allegedly forcing members of the minority community to adopt family planning measures before applying for arms licences. Ms Mayawati has ordered an inquiry into the matter. The action followed the insistence by Mr

Goel on family planning measures for two members of the minority community when they applied for licences. Taking a strong view of Mr Goel's arbitrary action, Ms Mayawati said in a statement that the family welfare programme was voluntary. People had a right to apply for gun licences for security purposes. Adoption of family planning programme for getting arms licence did not figure in the policies of the Bahujan Samaj Party government, she said. She charged Mr Goel with dereliction of duty saying that his action amounted to misleading and pressuring the minority community, and contravened government directives.'[5]

In the second instance, in August 2007, the police arrested three women human rights activists, Roma, Shanta Bhattacharya and Malati, agitating on behalf of landless labourers in a remote district of eastern Uttar Pradesh. According to reports in the *Jansatta* newspaper, the police were acting on the orders of local upper-caste landlords who were upset with the activists for helping the labourers to fight for property rights. Although the agitation was peaceful, the police used the National Security Act to arrest the activists who they said were 'Maoists'. *Jansatta* also quoted one of the police officials as boasting that the women will be taught a 'lesson' in jail. Fortunately, word of the arrest reached chief minister Mayawati and the women activists were promptly released on her orders. The chief minister also asked for a full enquiry into the incident. The two examples cited above reveal that her sensitivity to the oppressed and exploited communities has been greater than that of other chief ministers and indicate that compared to other chief ministers she probably scores better as an administrator in a state with such vast social and economic disparities, even if on other counts she has followed similar practices on issues such as postings and transfers or the manipulation of state funds.

Has Mayawati evolved as a chief minister over four spells of governing Uttar Pradesh? There are some evident changes. She is definitely no longer the nervous and awkward debutante who had a permanent chip on her shoulder during her first term. Today, she is confident and successful, adept at manipulating the system and assisted by a well-oiled political and bureaucratic machine. A very significant difference seems to be her new-found ability to delegate administrative powers. The same leader, who stayed up late pouring over piles of files lest her bureaucrats try to fool her, nowadays tries to avoid them as much as possible.

The biggest beneficiary of Mayawati's less frenzied approach to governance is her chief administrative aide, Shashank Shekhar Singh. The cabinet secretary is perhaps the most powerful bureaucrat that Uttar Pradesh has ever seen under a democratically elected government. This transfer of power has percolated down the veins of the state bureaucracy, resulting in a far more balanced administrative style. It remains to be seen whether such powers will go to the head of Singh or not. So far he has been able to wield his clout with maximum effect and very little pomposity or bluster. In any case, with a boss as powerful as Mayawati sitting on his head, it appears unlikely that the pilot turned bureaucrat will overreach himself in a hurry.

The transfer raj that made Mayawati infamous in her first three stints as chief minister also appears to be a thing of the past. After a massive administrative drive in the first few days to purge the system of Mulayam Singh cronies, the chief minister astonished everyone by relinquishing her own powers to transfer at will. In less than a week after she formed the government, the cabinet secretary announced that henceforth 'all key appointments and transfers would be routed through the services establishment board and the chief minister would not deal with cases of officers below the rank of principal secretaries and additional directors general of police.' While the board has been part of the government system, it had become bit a joke over the past two decades as it was politicians who effectively controlled what had become known as the 'transfer industry'. According to Singh, transfers of departmental officers would be handled by their respective ministers, while those of junior Class I and Class II officers would be decided by principal secretaries, secretaries and heads of departments alone.

While several IAS and IPS officials have been transferred, the numbers have significantly come down compared to her earlier regimes as well as the previous Mulayam Singh government. An article in a national daily revealed that Mulayam Singh had transferred 160 IAS and 140 IPS officers in his first hundred days in office while Mayawati's score for the same period was ninety IAS and eighty IPS officers.[6]

Her mass sacking of nearly 18,000 police constables, recruited under dubious circumstances, allegedly for monetary bribes and, in the case of some women constables, sexual favours to police officers during the Mulayam Singh government, was a tough call on the policemen concerned, some of whom broke down in tears as they handed back their uniforms. But the exercise that also involved the suspension of twenty-five IPS officers of the rank of inspector general, deputy inspector general and senior superintendent of police and the departmental action ordered against fifty-eight police officers who were members of the recruitment boards was perceived as firm action against a recruitment scam that has been the bane of the police force in Uttar Pradesh and other poorly administered states. In an article Prakash Singh, former director general of the border security force, hailed Mayawati's move as 'the first time such stern action in a recruitment scam has been taken by any state government in the country.'[7]

With her politics now projecting sarvajana samaj, the coterie of scheduled caste officers has also vanished. There has been no Dalit bias in key postings in Mayawati's fourth term in office. If anything, upper castes have been given greater representation in top government posts in Lucknow than they had under other chief ministers in the recent past. This does not mean that Mayawati has forgotten her core constituency of Dalits, poorer backwards and the Muslim minority. She continues to appoint officers from these social groups in sensitive field posts across Uttar Pradesh so that justice is not denied because of caste or creed. For instance, one of her first administrative decisions was to order that twenty-three per cent of police officers working as inspectors in-charge and SHOs belonging to SCs/STs and twenty-seven per cent belonging to OBCs be posted in districts. Significantly, officers belonging to certain Muslim communities categorized as OBCs would also benefit from such a posting policy. What has clearly been abandoned is the past practice of encouraging a privileged Dalit cadre in the service. This change of approach must have caused some resentment among scheduled caste officers who were the chief beneficiaries of the earlier system. But they have to temper this disappointment with the pride sweeping the Dalit community at having their leader back at the helm with a full majority of her own. In any case, with Mayawati's stranglehold over Dalits as well as the administration, they have little choice. Meanwhile, the rest of the bureaucracy is visibly relieved that the hostility and suspicion between upper and lower castes that dogged the administration in the past is now virtually non-existent. 'It is a huge relief for bureaucrats like us who otherwise admired

Behenji's firm administrative style but felt that the constant caste bias needlessly got in the way of good administration,' said an upper-caste bureaucrat who has worked with Mayawati several times in the past. 'I don't believe in killing people who are already dead,' asserted Mayawati contemptuously when asked what she would do to her ancient enemy. The canny yadav leader is far from dead and nobody knows this better than Mayawati. But she has displayed new maturity as chief minister by not going after her predecessor thus denying him the opportunity of playing the political victim.

At the same time, she has not changed her stance on certain favoured projects. Her continuing obsession with Ambedkar Park provoked the first public controversy of her fourth term in office. Displaying flashes of her old disdain for urban middle class opinion she ordered the demolition of a popular sports stadium next to the Ambedkar Park to expand the complex. A spate of petitions by sports lovers in the city forced the courts to issue a stay on the demolition. The chief minister's aides later claimed that most of the petitions had been withdrawn after an offer to build a far better sports complex than the existing one.

Nor has Mayawati shed her fondness for imperial trappings. Her bungalow on the posh Mall Avenue in Lucknow has claimed several adjoining bungalows on the plea that the chief minister needs better security. Interestingly, the hijacking of such large tracts of public land in the name of VVIP security is similar to that of former chief minister Mulayam Singh who did the same in his residence on Vikramaditya Marg.

Mayawati's wish to ensure her place in history is also evident from an Uttar Pradesh cabinet decision to erect her statues, as well as those of her mentor, Kanshi Ram, across the state. The first such pair was unveiled some years ago inside the Prerna Kendra beside Kanshi Ram's last will and testament inscribed on the wall. The two statues were justified on the plea of honouring the late BSP leader's wish that he and Mayawati are always shown together. After Mayawati's return to power in May 2007, a move to honour Kanshi Ram by building his statues across Uttar Pradesh raised the question of whether to follow the model set by the Prerna Kendra. Mayawati, who kept completely quiet during deliberations at a meeting on this issue, finally spoke after it was proposed that she too should be immortalized along with Kanshi

Ram in statues across the state. 'If you people think so, I have no objections,' she is reported to have declared

So where does all this leave Mayawati's report card as an administrator? Will her record at governance now that she has the prospect of a full five-year term determine her political fate? Unfortunately, there is a huge disconnect between perceptions of what the urban intelligentsia consider good administrative qualities and that which the vast multitude, still struggling for basic rights and facilities, consider essential. For the chattering classes, the waste of public money on monuments and parks, arbitrary demolitions and her megalomania in general have been very controversial. For the poor and oppressed such issues hardly matter at all, since they identify and connect with her at their own level. The fact that Mayawati has rapidly increased BSP's electoral base in Uttar Pradesh, consolidating and further expanding her following among the poor and oppressed, underlines the political success of her stints in power. She has managed to do so despite the strident criticism of the media and the middle classes, who have only just started to accept her because they have come to realize they can ignore her success at their peril. It makes little sense, therefore, to link her political future with her administrative record which, as we have seen, appears differently from different perspectives. Clearly, in the case of Mayawati—and perhaps all mass leaders— it will be her politics that drives her administration, and not the other way around.

# ELEVEN

# A Party with a Difference

*The* phenomenal rise of the BSP under the leadership of Mayawati has baffled political pundits. Conventional wisdom suggests that a party rocked by so many defections should be struggling to find its feet. Mayawati hounded out virtually every party veteran who helped to build the BSP from its infancy, and this should—again, according to conventional wisdom—have led to her own political demise. The absence of senior and middle level leaders should have stunted the growth of the BSP. Leaders and activists are normally reluctant to remain in political parties where most of the tickets to state assembly and parliamentary elections are bartered to outsiders. Moreover, Mayawati is the leader of a party that claims to transform society; yet she has turned her back on mass political agitations. Yet the Mayawati juggernaut rolls on and on, grinding to dust these doubts and questions as well as the predictions that she would destroy the BSP and herself.

Consider the damaging evidence from the past. Very few parties have been as vulnerable to defections as the BSP has been in Uttar Pradesh, its main political field. In 1995, the then state chief minister, Mulayam Singh Yadav, almost succeeded in destroying Mayawati's chief ministerial career before it even started, by engineering defections from the BSP. He had managed to lure away thirteen of the BSP's sixty-six legislators and was on his way to grab at least a dozen more before his game was disrupted by BJP leader Atal Bihari Vajpayee and the state governor, Moti Lal Vora, under instructions from the then prime minister, Narasimha Rao. Mayawati was once again exposed to defections when the BJP pulled the plug on her short-lived first term in office. More than three dozen BSP legislators are believed to have promised support to Mulayam Singh if he managed to form an alternative government. This, however, never materialized because the governor kept the state assembly in suspended animation before ordering mid-term polls.

Defections tore the BSP apart once again in 1997 after Mayawati withdrew support from the Kalyan Singh government. She lost as many as seventeen out of her sixty-seven legislators—a dozen when he first engineered defections to stay in power and five more crossing over after he returned to power after the three-day coup by Jagadambika Pal fizzled out. In 2003 the number of defectors from the BSP went up to thirty-seven when Mulayam Singh formed an alternative government after Mayawati resigned as chief minister over the Taj Corridor case.

There has also been a steady procession of BSP veterans leaving the party after Mayawati started spreading her wings in the party from the early nineties. One of the first to leave was Dr Masood Ahmed, the first Muslim leader to join Kanshi Ram and the BAMCEF in the late seventies. Dr Ahmed who had been made minister of education in the Mulayam Singh led SP–BSP coalition government in 1993, left the party along with state BSP general secretary Sheikh Suleiman in June 1994, accusing Mayawati of being authoritarian. Later several high profile Muslim leaders would join the BSP only to be thrown out by her. They included Arif Mohammed Khan, Akbar (Dumpy) Ahmed and Rashid Alvi. While Khan later joined the BJP, Ahmed and Alvi joined the Congress. Significantly, while all three are still in politics, none of them have grabbed the headlines since they left the BSP.

Record numbers of BSP party presidents in Uttar Pradesh have left the party or have been dumped. They include Raj Bahadur, who led the team of defectors to Mulayam Singh in the summer of 1995. His successor, Jang Bahadur Patel, Kanshi Ram's first kurmi associate, left the party soon after Mayawati's government fell. In 1997 another state party president, Bhagwat Pal, was thrown out even as he was in Delhi complaining to Kanshi Ram of his ill treatment by Mayawati. His successor, Dayaram Pal, did not last very long either, and was expelled from the party. The list is endless.

With the sole exception of Mayawati, all the major associates that Kanshi Ram had chosen to build the BSP are no longer in the party. Others who were close to her fell out of favour as soon as they began to think they were leaders in their own right. For instance, Barkhu Ram Verma and R.K. Chaudhury were known to be Mayawati loyalists and were with her during the Lucknow guest house assault by Mulayam Singh's goons. As long as they were mere yes-men, the two were rewarded with ministerial berths and other perks. But both were swiftly dumped as soon they took an independent line on the BJP chief minister Rajnath Singh's quota-within-quota policy in 2001 when she briefly supported it. Ironically, they had adopted a stance similar to the one she had previously held and later returned to. But just that mere hint of political autonomy was enough for her to sack them peremptorily.

The constant departure of so many senior and middle-level leaders from the party has meant that the BSP organization has lacked the multi-tiered hierarchy of other political parties. This is quite unique since even in parties that have strong autocratic leaders who take most of the decisions, there are still rungs in the organizational ladder down which power percolates. Mayawati, on the other hand, has completely dispensed with this hierarchical structure. Internal organizational elections do take place in the BSP regularly in accordance with Election Commission regulations, but these are even more of a farce than those carried out by dynastic parties like the Congress.

Anyone with leadership ambitions in the BSP runs smack into the obvious lack of opportunity to represent the party in either the state assembly or Parliament. The overwhelming majority of the election tickets in state and national polls are distributed on a piecemeal basis to candidates depending on their caste, community and the financial resources at their command. They do not even have to be BSP members, let alone leaders or activists who have worked for the party for a long time. It means that those who belong to the party organization have little chance to further a career in the party. This is again quite different from other parties where even though top leaders distribute election tickets to favourites, most candidates are found from within the party and affiliated organizations.

The most distinctive trait that Mayawati and her party have displayed has been their reluctance to be involved in mass agitation. Strangely, despite the BSP's aggressive agenda representing the cause of deprived and oppressed Dalits, lower castes and minorities against the upper-caste establishment, party leaders and activists have stayed away from protests and demonstrations. They have, instead, devoted all their organizational energies towards promotional activities projecting the party and its leaders mostly in preparation for the next elections. During election campaigns these publicity exercises are turned into poll campaigns conducted with elaborate strategy and meticulous planning. But this formidable party machine and its charismatic leader are not available to agitate on behalf of, for instance, a group of Dalit labourers raped and murdered by upper-caste landlords. Not surprisingly, neither Kanshi Ram nor his protégé ever went to jail or clashed with the police despite perambulating for so many years across Uttar Pradesh with a missionary zeal to turn society upside down.

What is this political species that shows such disinterest for the normal preoccupations of politicians? More importantly, how have Mayawati and her party overcome these handicaps to become the role model of political success in India today?

We must remember that neither Kanshi Ram nor Mayawati belonged to the political mainstream of this country. There was no compulsion to observe the political conventions and codes which bound most national and regional parties. They have treated the BSP like a closely held private company without any larger institutional obligations. The two leaders regarded everyone who was involved in the growth of the BSP—activists, leaders, MLAs and MPs—as functional instruments who were dispensable. This cold-blooded approach by the BSP founder and his protégé made them nonchalant about defections, dissidence and expulsions that may have traumatized a party that valued its elected representatives and leaders more. Ever since a stroke crippled Kanshi Ram, there has been a tendency in political and media circles to view him as a gentler, idealistic visionary as compared to a scheming and ruthless Mayawati. But this is a figment of the imagination of politicians and journalists. Kanshi Ram wanted his disciple to be ruthlessly detached, and trained her to be so. In fact, it was Mayawati's uncanny ability to take the shortest route between two points that got her mentor to back her against more senior claimants to his mantle.

The uniqueness of Mayawati's and Kanshi Ram's political lineage, as compared to the leaders of other parties, also explains why they rejected a functional multi-tiered hierarchical party organization. As outsiders who carried no political baggage from other parties, Kanshi Ram and Mayawati could afford to knock off several rungs in the BSP's internal organizational ladder. In the early days while building the BSP organization brick by brick, Kanshi Ram was not completely averse to delegating authority to subordinates, but this changed as the party took off. Mayawati, who loves concentrating power in her hands, virtually eliminated the need for a ladder right from the outset.

Mayawati's antipathy towards customary forms of political organization is illustrated by the ease with which she banned student elections in all educational institutions of Uttar Pradesh on the plea that they were interfering with academic studies, just a few months after she took charge of the state in 2007. Most political leaders, Mulayam Singh for instance, would never dream of making such a move because it would mean closing down the primary source of their party cadre. But BSP recruitment follows completely different lines, and for Mayawati herself it is an unfamiliar route, even though it is one traversed by most politicians who climb from student politics to district to state and finally to the national arena.

The same logic guides BSP's policy of choosing candidates for state assembly and parliamentary polls. Most other leaders are compelled by their organizational structure to search for candidates primarily from within the party, even though parties like the Congress and the BJP have increasingly introduced a quota of outsider candidates, most notably film stars. In the case of the BSP, there is no such organizational imperative for Mayawati since nobody in the party is encouraged to even think that they will move upwards in the hierarchy. After all, if there is no ladder worth the name, it is impossible to climb.

Paradoxical as it may seem, the reason this party of the oppressed shies away from public agitations to push social reforms lies in the ideological line adopted by Kanshi Ram very early on in his career. The BSP founder had single mindedly focussed on the pursuit of Ambedkar's 'master key of political power' which he felt was essential to have before he could change society. The BSP leadership has over the years scrupulously eschewed any kind of mass action that would pit the party cadre against the state, instead emphasizing the priority of political power over social reforms. Significantly, both Kanshi Ram and Mayawati have viewed agitational methods that are normally used by most parties to further their political interests, as damaging to the purpose of capturing power through elections. Of all the differences between the BSP and other parties and movements, this distinctive attitude to mass agitation is the most fascinating.

Amazingly, these drastic departures from normal democratic political behaviour by Mayawati and her party have worked in their favour rather than to their disadvantage. Having a marginalized subaltern group like the Dalits as her core constituency, she has been able to get away with authoritarian methods that may have been unacceptable to more socially secure communities. It is ironic that the wretched of the earth, particularly those who are oppressed on the basis of race, creed or caste, have been historically prone to hero worship a dominant figure who brooks no dissent. Kanshi Ram had deliberately cast his protégé in the mould of such a goddess cleverly packaged in the more familiar reassuring form of 'Behenji' (Respected Sister). Mayawati has played this role superbly, far exceeding her mentor's expectations, managing to wield unlimited power in the BSP by making the party synonymous with herself.

The association of an individual leader or even a dynasty with a party is not unusual in India and is in fact fast becoming the norm, with the exception of a few parties like the communists and the BJP. Mayawati, however, unlike other political supremos, has been able to establish a direct bond with her constituency without depending on party subordinates. She was initially able to do so by drawing on the fierce loyalty of her chamar kinfolk in Uttar Pradesh, and has steadily increased the size of her constituency. The tendency of Dalits to repose their faith in the icon they revere, instead of getting swayed by voices of several less imposing figures, has clearly worked to her advantage.

A crucial component of Mayawati's complete dominance in the party has been her remarkable ability to capture power, even if her chief ministerial stints have been brief in the past. It started from 1993 when she became the 'super chief minister' in the guise of coordinating the Mulayam Singh-led SP–BSP coalition government; and through her four subsequent stints as chief minister she has built an aura that makes her appear destined for power. This is very powerful magic for a subjugated group like the Dalits in Uttar Pradesh, to whom the capture of state power by a leader and party of their community was an impossible dream till Mayawati came along. She has shrewdly used the halo acquired from her repeated successes to dwarf everyone else in the party— a strategy that has become the accepted norm rather than a fissiparous tendency.

Not surprisingly, not a single BSP leader who has left the party has met with any success. A few have tried to float parallel organizations and most of them have joined established parties such as the Samajwadi Party, the Congress and the BJP. But not a single BSP rebel has been able to launch even a remote challenge to Mayawati who grows bigger each time she humiliates an upwardly mobile leader. Party insiders still laugh about what happened to Uttar Pradesh BSP president Bhagwat Pal, who was expelled while in Delhi complaining to Kanshi Ram about Mayawati. To add insult to injury, he was simultaneously evicted from his official bungalow in Lucknow and his belongings strewn all over the road outside. Instead of getting sympathy from the party cadre, the hapless leader became an oft-quoted example of what happens to those who cross Behenji's will. At one point in the late nineties Kanshi Ram had showed some signs of anxiety about whether his party could fall apart because of his protégé's domineering ways. But ultimately he accepted Mayawati's style of functioning, not just out of his personal fondness for her, but because he genuinely felt that the BSP needed a heavy hand on the reins. Kanshi Ram's admiration for Mayawati's toughness is reflected in an introduction he wrote for a book about her, written by one of her admirers Mohammed Jameel Akhtar in 1999. '. . . Success created more problems for her. The seniors in the movement could not tolerate her rise. They tried to put pressure on me to curtail the opportunities I was giving to her. On refusal, most of the seniors left the BSP movement, started on their own. But none of them is visible today, whereas Mayawati became a success as chief minister of the largest state of India. . . . About the feelings of her other opponents only they may be knowing, but I know full well that these initial oppositions hardened her and made her the iron lady of this book.'[1]

The elimination of an organizational ladder and the deliberate castration of party leaders have allowed Mayawati full freedom to prepare for her primary objective—winning elections. Unlike in other parties, when the time comes to distribute election tickets, there are no jostling party aspirants to handicap her. In election after election over the past decade, she has firmly established that candidates, regardless of their caste, community, political background and criminal history, can be chosen without a revolt in the party. The remarkable flexibility shown by the BSP in accommodating different social groups in a particular constituency and the option of striking a deal with individual candidates commanding the right kind of resources, is based on this complete acquiescence of the party to whatever Behenji wants. Needless to say, she has managed to command such blind obedience within the organization because of her phenomenal success ratio in state and parliamentary polls in Uttar Pradesh.

Mayawati's personal charisma, a captive core constituency, frequent bouts of political power and a high success ratio in winning elections are clearly all factors that have helped her throw the political rule book out of the window. Nevertheless, some key questions still remain. How can a party with such a top-heavy organizational structure show sustained growth that is the envy of other political groups? And how has the BSP managed to retain the loyalty of oppressed groups without agitating on their behalf?

The BSP leader has addressed both these questions with remarkable innovative skill. She has supplemented a hollow shell of a party with a formidable election machine that runs on its own steam. For instance, the most impressive aspect of the BSP's campaign in 2007 was its organizational infrastructure—elaborate yet meticulously efficient. It was directed by coordinators, each one in charge of five districts, which in turn were headed by district presidents supervising those in charge of specific assembly segments. Those in charge of assembly segments were backed up by a lower ring of cadre who controlled clusters of booths each of which was the responsibility of an individual BSP worker who brought up the bottom-most rung of this formidable change of electoral command. Mayawati herself dealt directly with the coordinators and the district presidents, while they were responsible for the lower rungs of the organizational infrastructure.

Significantly, the election machine has a purely functional dynamic and forbidden from acquiring an identity of its own. This means that it is preoccupied with specific targets and tasks that need to be implemented. These are obvious during an election campaign; when there are no polls in the offing, the energies of this vast organizational machine is used to promote Mayawati herself, whether in Opposition and even more so while she occupies the chief ministerial chair. There is little scope for any individual leader or activist involved in this enterprise to promote personal agendas or parallel centres of power. Since there is no linkage drawn between this vast missionary army promoting Behenji and elected office or party posts, there are no incentives either for the political factionalism that is the bane of other parties.

The main motivation for the hundreds of thousands who have joined the BSP is the extra clout they acquire in their social circle by doing so. This is especially true among Dalits who still form the bulk of party cadre, but also among poorer backward castes and Muslims. The reflected glory they get from being associated with Behenji and her party helps in many tangible ways, whether in villages or urban ghettos. In the beginning this helped them enhance their stature mainly among their families and within their ethnic group. But as Mayawati grows from strength to strength, earning the fear and respect of all castes and communities across Uttar Pradesh, joining the BSP increased the party member's standing in society at large.

Mayawati has been able to separate her quest for political power from grass roots agitations and yet keep her constituency of the oppressed because of 'the complex and intricate web of relations between the political and non-political forces in the process of Dalit empowerment in Uttar Pradesh', as French political scientist Nicolas Jaoul described in a recent essay. 'The question of the "division of political labour" ... echoes an ongoing discussion among the Dalits in UP, concerning the "political" versus the "non-political" means of emancipation. This popular debate, which I witnessed during fieldwork, deals with some of the felt contradictions of Indian democracy. The attainment of political power is acknowledged as an essential step, but also regarded as a potential trap for an authentic people's movement. ... Dalit mobilizations in UP reflect this dilemma through a combination of electoral politics and a grass roots socio-cultural movement. While the latter concentrates the social and economic resources of the Dalit government employees, the former (BSP) has been able to gather the electoral resources of the community (the Dalit votebank).'[2]

Former activists of the BAMCEF, DS4 and even the Dalit Panthers and Naxalite groups are the ones who fight the daily battles of oppressed groups in the state against the upper-caste establishment. These radicals have a love–hate relationship with Mayawati and her party. They are wary and sometimes hostile to her single-minded pursuit of power that has often led the BSP to ally with forces inimical to its core constituency. At the same time, all activists and groups who are involved in social reform acknowledge that their task becomes much easier when Mayawati is in power and that her growing clout has put the upper-caste establishment on the defensive.

In many ways this is the realization of her mentor Kanshi Ram's ambition of creating a three-tiered movement, with a political party, an agitational wing and a government employees' organization. With Mayawati's capture of the bureaucratic apparatus, the government employees do not matter any more. But the two separate tiers of party devoted to capturing power through elections and a parallel social reform movement have complemented each other, even though the relationship between them remain tentative.

For Mayawati, the existence of non-political activists who agitate on behalf of her core constituencies is a great boon. Since she is not formally associated with these radical groups, the BSP leader has been able to negotiate her upper-caste alliances and in recent years even turn ideological somersaults by promoting 'sarvajana samaj' instead of 'bahujan samaj'. Had her own party been involved in violent agitations against upper-caste groups in the countryside, it may have been difficult for Mayawati to widen her electoral net. She has therefore been able to project the image of a responsible leader who would not turn society upside down if put in a position of power. Indeed, it is this distance maintained by Mayawati with the day to day struggles of the Dalit masses that encouraged upper-caste-dominated parties, as for instance, the BJP and the Congress, to initially prop her up as chief minister. The same acceptability to different social segments facilitated her sweeping win in the 2007 state assembly polls.

On the other hand, Dalits would have been far more nervous

about their interests being abandoned by Mayawati had it not been for her tacit support to the radicals who fight on behalf of the oppressed. By posting police officers belonging to the same caste and community as victims of social oppression, the BSP leader has ensured that social reform activists operating at an NGO level are not harassed and victimized. There have been occasional clashes of interest. But on the whole the two have learnt to tolerate and help each other, and this relationship has the wholehearted support of their target constituencies.

Mayawati and her party represent a unique political phenomenon that has no parallels in India and perhaps in the world. Its extraordinary success in Uttar Pradesh, however, does not mean it can be replicated elsewhere in the country. The far lower success ratio of the BSP in other states where the party has tried to grow indicates that Uttar Pradesh may be a special case, not least because of the larger-than-life image of Mayawati in the state.

Today, Mayawati is faced with a complex dilemma as she seeks to spread her wings across other northern states and even further in the country. The highly centralized command structure of the BSP makes it difficult for it to facilitate the growth of parallel power centres that are bound to emerge if the party is to mushroom in other states. She has for the moment asked her closest political aide, Satish Mishra, to resolve this problem, but it is difficult to see how he will do so. It is one thing for Mayawati to delegate powers to Mishra or a handful of appointees to implement tasks that she has assigned them—much like a schoolteacher gives homework to her students. This is quite different from allowing smaller replicas of herself to come up in the states of Madhya Pradesh, Chhattisgarh, Rajasthan, Punjab, Maharashtra and Delhi. Without a dominant local leader the BSP cannot become a major political force in any of these states and will have to remain content to being a bit player. It is a tough call for Mayawati and raises a question mark over the BSP's march forward beyond Uttar Pradesh.

# TWELVE

# Mayawati, Social Engineer

$\mathcal{M}$ayawati's surprise victory in the 2007 Uttar Pradesh assembly polls has spawned a rash of psephological theories. Some see her electoral success entirely through the caste calculus, laying huge emphasis on the BSP's overtures to brahmins in the run up to the polls. 'The BSP's victory in the UP polls was as much due to the caste coalition stitched by Mayawati as to voter disgust with the law and order situation,' wrote the *Times of India* in its main editorial a day after the Uttar Pradesh assembly election results were announced. Others have waxed eloquent on the Dalit leader's invention of a rainbow coalition that has magically merged the top and bottom rungs of society. 'Emerging from the shadow of her political mentor and BSP founder Kanshi Ram, Mayawati fought single-handedly aided by a rainbow coalition to decimate her opponents and become Chief Minister of Uttar Pradesh for the fourth time,' said the *Indian Express* on 11 May 2007 quoting agencies on her victory. A letter in the *Hindu* declared, 'Ms Mayawati's rainbow coalition of social groups has stolen the thunder in India's politically most watched State.' Virtually all of them attribute Mayawati's historic triumph to a drastic shift from the politics of isolation and confrontation to that of collaboration and compromise between different castes and communities.

This sudden discovery of Mayawati the social engineer is

rather belated. As we noted earlier in our chronological narrative of the evolution of Kanshi Ram, Mayawati and the bahujan samaj movement, right from the outset their entire thrust was towards building a wider coalition of different segments in Indian society. There is perhaps no other political leader who spoke so persistently on the vital importance of social collaboration as Kanshi Ram, even though initially he saw this encompassing eighty-five per cent of the population—the bahujan samaj—against a thin band of upper-caste rulers at the top. In fact, his distaste for the Republican Party of India and impatience with many of his BAMCEF colleagues was that they did not sufficiently appreciate the value of building coalitions and got bogged down in a narrow Dalit agenda. He specially chose Mayawati as his political successor because unlike most of his associates, she was ready to be as flexible as possible in both tactics and strategy to widen the BSP's support base. Both of them over the years made a series of adjustments in their outreach to various ethnic groups and subgroups. The social engineering skills of Mayawati and her party are, therefore, definitely not new.

There have been three distinct phases in the BSP's coalition-building strategy since the party was formed in 1984. The first phase lasted for a decade—till the mid-nineties—and mainly targeted Dalits, backward castes and minorities who comprised the bahujan samaj. It is during this period that the party indulged in a war of words against upper castes, carrying on the momentum set by its previous apolitical avatars, BAMCEF and DS4. On the other hand, the BSP went out of its way to espouse the cause of the Mandal classes that comprised the backward castes, including the upper echelons—the yadavs. The party also managed to get sizeable support up to the 1996 Uttar Pradesh assembly polls from the kurmis, a middle-rung backward caste that had initially responded to the idea of a bahujan samaj movement with considerable enthusiasm because they felt neglected by intermediate- and backward-caste parties as, for instance, the jat-dominated Lok Dal and the yadav-dominated Samajwadi Party. This phase reached its peak with a formal pre-electoral alliance with Mulayam Singh Yadav's Samajwadi Party before the 1993 Uttar Pradesh assembly polls, which led to the formation of a coalition government of the two parties.

The second phase of the party's coalition experiment started after the breakdown of both political and social relations between the BSP and the Samajwadi Party and their respective core constituencies of Dalits and yadavs, a breakdown that ultimately led to the collapse of the coalition government in the summer of 1995. This was followed by large-scale desertions from the party by kurmi leaders, both because of their personal differences with the rising star of Mayawati, and also because of clashes between Dalit agricultural labourers and kurmi landlords; a very similar situation arose with the yadavs. Kanshi Ram and Mayawati responded to these setbacks to their bahujan samaj coalition by wooing a section of the upper castes, particularly brahmins, not directly but through their political leaders and parties. It is with the help of dominant brahmin leaders, including Atal Bihari Vajpayee of the BJP and P.V. Narasimha Rao of the Congress, that Mayawati was given the chance of becoming chief minister several times in Uttar Pradesh. The governments ruled by Mayawati with the support of the BJP were not a result of a pre-poll pact, nor was it a genuine social alliance between Dalits and upper castes. But they did mark a toning down of the party rhetoric against the upper castes, indicating they were no longer anathema to the BSP. From the late nineties, the party also started to give an increasing number of tickets in state and parliamentary polls to upper- and intermediate-caste candidates—a bid to build a winning combine by adding the upper-caste personal vote base to the BSP's captive Dalit vote bank in specific constituencies. It is important to recognize that these were piecemeal transactions with individual candidates and did not represent a wider social alliance.

As in the first phase, the second instalment of social engineering lasted for about a decade, petering out after the end of Mayawati's third term in office. With the induction of Satish Mishra as her political adviser, the BSP embarked on an ambitious third phase that directly appealed to sections of the upper castes, particularly the brahmins and the banias. Mayawati encouraged them to join hands with the Dalits and the poorer backward castes to fight the rising domination of a whole range of landed, prosperous castes, such as the thakurs, yadavs, jats, kurmis and lodhs, whose muscle power was increasing by the day.

The new strategy was motivated by several factors. Firstly, Mayawati could no longer operate through powerful brahmin friends in the two national parties. The Congress had become irrelevant in Uttar Pradesh and the state BJP had been hijacked by thakur, kurmi and lodh leaders, none of them kindly disposed towards her. Besides, the brahmins, along with some other upper castes like the banias, had themselves become victims of the muscle and money power of the thakur, yadav, kurmi and lodh warlords in the countryside. The fact that it was no longer electoral adjustments or political deals but grassroots social compulsions that were driving the dynamics of this emerging alliance made it qualitatively different from earlier dalliances between the BSP and the upper castes. This phase, which is still in its infancy, is a major leap forward for Mayawati and her party, not least because it seeks to even replace the name of the movement from 'bahujan samaj' to 'sarvajana samaj'—shifiting the emphasis of the movement from the majority to one that encompasses all of society.

Having traced the various phases of the BSP's dogged efforts over the past two-and-a-half decades to widen its electoral base, we also need to identify the different social layers of this base and determine the roles they have played in the growth of the party. There are broadly three layers: firstly, a core constituency of Dalits who form the backbone of the BSP's electoral support; secondly, an auxiliary constituency of middle- to lower-backward castes, comprising both Hindus and Muslims, who have tended to vote sizeably but not substantially for the BSP; and thirdly, an emerging constituency of upper castes led by the brahmins and supported by banias and kayasthas, who have recently taken a new interest in the party.

A closer examination of the different roles played by these three layers in the BSP's rise in Uttar Pradesh reveals some basic truths. Firstly, despite Kanshi Ram's grandiose visions of a grand social alliance between Dalits, backward castes and minorities, it is the consolidation of the Dalit chamar sub-caste behind the BSP that first set the party on the road to success in Uttar Pradesh. Slowly but surely, other Dalit sub-castes followed suit and now the entire community votes en masse for Mayawati and her party. The Dalit vote for the BSP in the past three state assembly polls rose from sixty-two per cent in 1996 to sixty-nine per cent in 2002 to an incredible seventy-seven per cent in 2007. There is no other party in India that has ever received nearly eighty per cent of the vote from a single ethnic group.

There has also been a steady rise in the BSP vote from its auxiliary constituency of poorer backward castes and Muslims. The non-Yadav backward castes increased their vote percentage for the BSP from thirteen per cent in 1996 to twenty per cent in 2002 to twenty-seven per cent in 2007. Muslims, whose support for the party actually dipped from twelve per cent in 1996 to ten per cent in 2002, have registered a whopping increase with seventeen per cent voting for the BSP in 2007.

## BSP: CASTE SUPPORT 1996–2007[1]
*(figures in percentage)*

| Year | Upper Caste | OBC (non-Yadav) | Muslims | Dalits |
|------|-------------|-----------------|---------|--------|
| 1996 | 4 | 13 | 12 | 62 |
| 2002 | 5 | 20 | 10 | 69 |
| 2007 | 16 | 27 | 17 | 77 |

*Source:* Figures for 1996 and 2002 refer to the assembly election held in those years and are drawn from surveys done by the Centre for the Study of Developing Societies. Figures for the 2007 survey are from an *Indian Express–CNN IBN–CSDS* post-poll survey.

*Note:* All figures are per cent of voters from a community who voted for BSP in the relevant election. The vote share for major parties in that election has weighed the data for each of these surveys.

The upper-caste vote has registered a dramatic rise, but obviously lags way behind in volume from the core and auxiliary constituencies of the BSP. After languishing at an inconsequential four to five per cent in 1996 and 2002, the upper-caste vote nearly quadrupled to seventeen per cent in the latest state assembly polls of 2007. This is an incredible achievement considering that the third phase of the BSP's coalition strategy started less than three years before the elections.

However, it would be incorrect to view the BSP's meteoric rise in Uttar Pradesh as merely the result of a clever caste combine crafted by Mayawati. There is a very strong element of poor versus rich behind the party's growth in the state. Social scientist Yogendra Yadav of the Centre for the Study of Developing Societies (CSDS) has pointed out that 'the class slope of the BSP's vote is not different from the textbook illustration of the social basis of the communist parties: the vote share shoots up sharply from fifteen to forty-one as you go from the rich to the poor.' This is not just because the core voter base of the BSP is the Dalits, a majority of whom are poor. Even among upper castes and backward castes, the poorer sections have voted far more enthusiastically for the BSP. For instance as many as twenty-seven per cent of the poor brahmins voted for Mayawati compared to a mere twelve per cent among the rich. This was true for the jats and kurmis as well, with poorer segments of these groups turning out for the BSP in double the number of the prosperous segment rooting for the party.

## BSP: CLASS-BASED SUPPORT[2]

| Caste | All | Rich | Poor |
|---|---|---|---|
| All | 31 | 15 | 41 |
| Brahmin | 17 | 12 | 27 |
| Rajput | 12 | 10 | 14 |
| Jat | 13 | 11 | 22 |
| Kurmi | 16 | 12 | 20 |
| Yadav | 05 | 05 | 05 |
| Non-yadav  OBC | 34 | 27 | 34 |
| Lower OBC | 28 | 18 | 30 |
| Jatav | 85 | 73 | 86 |
| Other Dalits | 55 | 30 | 56 |
| Muslims | 17 | 12 | 18 |

*Source:* Figures for 1996 and 2002 refer to the assembly election held in those years and are drawn from surveys done by the Centre for Study of Developing Societies. Figures for the 2007 survey are from an *Indian Express*–CNN IBN–CSDS post-poll survey.

*Note:* All figures are per cent of voters from a community who voted for BSP in the relevant election. The vote share for major parties in that election has weighed the data for each of these surveys.

Behenji's solid support base among women voters has also to be taken into account. According to surveys done by the CSDS, there was a definite gender bias in favour of BSP candidates in the 2007 polls that may have gained the party an extra two per cent of the vote. While this is hard to prove in the absence of empirical evidence, the extra few percentile points contributed by the women may well have facilitated a full-fledged majority for Mayawati, who otherwise could have fallen short by a handful of seats.

Can Mayawati sustain support from her widening electoral base drawn from across the caste spectrum with so many varied social groups clamouring for attention and benefits? The answer may lie in the juggling skills she has already displayed in keeping all her social support bases in play. This is how the BSP leader has managed to retain her core Dalit constituency, which has had to watch more and more of their space in elections occupied by competing social segments from the backward castes and minorities and, more recently, even by sections of the upper castes.

Undoubtedly, the rock-solid backing for Mayawati from the Dalits, even as she has made overtures to other social groups, gives her a huge advantage. The heady elixir of a 'Dalit ki beti' ascending the throne of Lucknow again and again, is one constant factor in her favour. Most Dalits are also convinced that she is doing the right thing by expanding her social base—a move that has the backing of a majority of the community, regardless of what some rebel factions say. But it would be inaccurate to suggest that Mayawati has been able to retain the loyalty of her flock merely by symbolic gestures and by inspiring trust in her political judgement. Even in the limited period she has been at the helm of government, the BSP leader has brought many tangible benefits to the Dalit community, both in urban and rural areas.

For instance, the chamars who have supported the BSP through thick and thin right from the mid-eighties when the party was established, have been compensated by a lion's share of government jobs in various categories because of the rigorous implementation of the quota system whenever Mayawati has been in power. While this has primarily helped middle class chamars living in cities and towns because of their high literacy, other Dalit sub-castes along with rural chamars have benefited from amenities and welfare schemes implemented through the Ambedkar

Villages Programme. Some have been given fresh plots of fallow land while others have been given pattas/chits granting ownership rights on plots they have already occupied. And most importantly, the nightmarish ordeal that most Dalit families have to confront on the law and order front, particularly in rural areas, lessens considerably when Behenji holds the reins of power.

In return, Mayawati's core constituency has allowed her to grant similar benefits to the BSP's auxiliary constituency of poorer backward castes and Muslims. Many of the most backward castes share with Dalits the same impoverishment and vulnerability to atrocities by upper and intermediate caste landlords. Many poor Muslims, too, can draw comfort from programmatic benefits and security measures that have flowed from successive editions of Mayawati's raj. The minority community has good reason to be even more grateful for her impeccable record in protecting its lives and shrines from Hindu zealots.

Both the core and auxiliary constituencies of the BSP appear to have accepted the need for the party to reach out to an emerging potential constituency of sections of the upper castes to ensure the electoral triumph of the party. It is a moot point that had Mayawati's auxiliary constituency of the lower backward castes and Muslims consolidated behind her as solidly as Dalits, she may not have needed the upper castes to win elections. But the myriad numbers of scattered backward caste groups and the complex psyche of the Muslim groups, make the prospect of such a consolidation very doubtful. The move to recruit groups and individuals from the upper castes, therefore, is widely perceived by the BSP's other support bases as a sensible and pragmatic move. 'Behenji is right in getting support from upper castes. It will be good for all of us,' said Barkhu Ram, a cobbler in Sitapur, as he surveyed a row of brahmins wearing sacred threads and with sandalwood paste smeared on their foreheads, pass him by on their way to a BSP rally to be addressed by Mayawati during the 2007 state assembly elections.

During the second phase of the BSP's social engineering campaign for the parliamentary polls of the late nineties, the 2002 assembly poll, and the 2004 parliamentary polls, upper castes were drawn to the party only where they had their own candidates. Their high success ratio because of support from the BSP's Dalit vote banks, offered upper castes a whole range of patronage benefits once their candidates were elected. In a society where even basic rights and needs are met only through kinship networks, most caste groups feel it necessary to have their own caste candidates elected for patronage. Since many upper castes are often unable to have their kinfolk elected on their own steam, the BSP's winning formula was tempting, even though the party was run by Dalits. However, since these candidates had neither long-term stakes in the BSP, nor any empathy with Mayawati herself, their loyalty remained suspect. Indeed a large number of them abruptly left the BSP taking their support base along with them, when enticed by parallel offers from other parties. The upper-caste component of the party, therefore, was at best a temporary asset.

The dynamic of the BSP's relationship with upper castes has definitely changed in the third phase. There have been concerted efforts to project Mayawati as a protector of upper castes, particularly brahmins and banias, against the depredations of thakurs, yadavs and other marauding castes. She has also reached out to poorer segments of the upper castes by promising them job quotas, even petitioning the prime minister on their behalf. The spectacle of the leader of a party that not so long ago spat venom at the upper castes now fighting for their protection and rights, may seem paradoxical. But sections of the upper castes, particularly brahmins, who feel that they no longer enjoy political clout in any party, have been touched by Mayawati's gestures ever since her brahmin adviser lifted the BSP's social engineering to a different level.

The most heartening aspect of the BSP's social engineering enterprise today is the transparent and matter-of-fact manner in which it is implemented. All the three different tiers of support for the party are acutely aware of their diverse identities, but are pragmatic enough to acknowledge that they need to join hands with each other for mutual benefit. This is a refreshing contrast to parties like the BJP that had sought to trick a whole range of backward castes and sections of the Dalits to fall in line behind an upper-caste-dominated party in the name of religion during the early nineties. As long as Mayawati is able to engage in coalition building through honest transactions of give and take between different social segments, her support base is likely to grow and grow.

It is also significant that the BSP's historic triumph in 2007 was not the result of an emotional public upsurge sparked by a specific issue or event. There has been systematic work done over a number of years across Uttar Pradesh to implement an audacious strategy. This makes the party's winning formula more durable than the factors that helped the Congress in the 1984 parliamentary polls, and allowed the BJP to score sweeping victories in the state assembly polls in Uttar Pradesh in 1991 and Gujarat in 2002. This is why the popular surge for the BSP in Uttar Pradesh witnessed in the 2007 assembly polls may grow stronger rather than dissipate, since it is not dependent on simple anti-incumbency or on an emotive issue. There is a strong possibility of a large influx of Muslims from the Samajwadi Party and a steady increment of poorer upper castes, along with even deeper consolidation of the Dalit and lower backward caste vote, taking place. Considering that the BSP, apart from winning 206 seats, came second in over one hundred seats, losing sixty of them by five thousand or less votes, it will not be surprising if the party wins up to fifty to sixty seats in next Lok Sabha polls from Uttar Pradesh alone.

At the same time, it would be naïve to expect the BSP to replicate its successful social engineering experiment across the country. There will inevitably be some impact in states adjoining Uttar Pradesh and possibly Maharashtra, where the party has shown growth in recent years. However, it is difficult to envisage the BSP getting more than fifteen Lok Sabha seats beyond Uttar Pradesh in the next general elections, since it would take years— perhaps decades—before the party spreads its wings all over India, although its national vote percentage is bound to grow steadily. The real challenge for Mayawati and her party if they want to grow fast, is to replicate the two essential ingredients that have contributed to their success in Uttar Pradesh in several other states as well. One is a leader who has the courage, magnetism and political acumen to build a coalition from different segments of civil society. The other is a core constituency with a substantial vote share that consolidates en masse behind the leader and her party. It is only then that the BSP juggernaut can roll beyond the borders of Uttar Pradesh.

# THIRTEEN

# The Importance of Dalit Identity

𝓜edia hype on Mayawati's electoral triumph in 2007 and growing speculation about whether she will be the next prime minister has tended to divert public attention from the enormous impact of her rise for Dalits throughout the country and especially in Uttar Pradesh. She has collaborated in her appropriation by the urban intelligentsia by showing a recent inclination to speak in a caste-neutral language. The BSP leader no longer accuses anyone of being 'Manuvadi' and has switched from speaking on behalf of the 'bahujan samaj' to representing the wider interests of the 'sarvajana samaj'. When she negotiated an economic package for her state with the prime minister in Delhi shortly after assuming office in Lucknow, among the demands laid on the table were economic reservations for poorer upper castes. Asked at a press conference what she had asked on behalf of her Dalit community, Mayawati wrinkled her brow in mock annoyance thundering, 'We don't think in terms of caste or creed!'

Contrast Mayawati's purposeful efforts to publicly detach herself from a Dalit identity to an incident that happened in a remote village of Uttar Pradesh shortly after she became chief minister of the state for a fourth time, this time with a full-fledged majority. *Tehelka* magazine carried the following report:[1]

> Two years ago, in a village in Jaunpur district in eastern Uttar Pradesh, Thakur Devendra Singh cheated Phulpatti

Devi, a 45-year-old Dalit widow, of Rs 10,000. He told her he needed it to pay a bribe to ensure a Rs 60,000 bank loan for her daughters' weddings—the loan never materialized and Phulpatti Devi had to manage with what meagre resources she could muster. Over the next two years, she often asked Singh for her money. He would put her off, telling her the bank had not yet processed her request. Sometimes, though, he would take her to the bank, some kilometres away, and make her wait there for hours, returning her to their village after dark. On at least two such occasions, he attempted to rape her but she escaped. On May 18 this year, he came to her house at 8 at night to tell her that her loan would be issued in two days. Naturally, Phulpatti Devi wanted to know, 'Why couldn't you have waited till morning to give me this news?'

'I was passing by,' said Singh, 'I thought you'd be glad to know.' He then began to insist that she see him off, walking him to a neem tree some distance away. She didn't want to, but her children said she shouldn't be rude to someone who was helping them get money. Once at the tree, Singh tried to molest her once again. This time, however, Phulpatti Devi was prepared. She told him he needn't use force and that she would give in voluntarily. Singh undressed, upon which Phulpatti Devi put a hand to her waistband, took out a knife and castrated him.

The next morning, Phulpatti Devi went to the police station with the knife and Singh's amputated penis, and was arrested. After a few days of recuperation, the Thakur was also sent to jail, charged with attempt to rape. Unlike others in the village, local Thakurs don't find the incident funny, and its repercussions may have to be faced by all the village's Jatavs. How then did Phulpatti Devi collect the courage to do this, *Tehelka* asked her in Jaunpur Central Jail.

'I thought,' she said, 'that now that Mayawati is in power, she will save me.'

The Dalit widow's childlike faith in 'Behenji' is a poignant pointer to what this chief minister really means to her own community.

This is regardless of the electoral deals Mayawati may strike with other social segments, including upper castes, to get her candidates past the winning post. It is not affected by the smug assertions of the social elite that the BSP leader has been finally incorporated into the establishment. Even Mayawati's fresh image-building exercise projecting her as the benign ruler of all sections of society, has failed to shake the Dalits' sense of pride that it is their 'beti' who is on the throne of Lucknow.

One of the most remarkable qualities about Kanshi Ram, and later Mayawati, has been their supreme cockiness about mustering support from Dalits for every political adventure they embarked on. Had the duo been worried at having to maintain their credentials in the Dalit constituency, Kanshi Ram would not have relegated Dalits to only one component of his target bahujan samaj coalition encompassing eighty-five per cent of society. Nor could Mayawati think of building bridges with the hated brahmin caste after abusing them for so many years as the Dalits' public enemy number one. In contrast, other parties and groups, such as the Republican Party of India and the Dalit Panthers, who also depended on a core constituency of Dalits, obsessively clung on to the latter as their sole political lifeline.

The BSP did not get landslide Dalit support during elections right from the outset. The party received only a section of the scheduled caste vote in various states. Even in Uttar Pradesh it was only the chamars who voted in very large numbers for Mayawati, and she belonged to their own sub-caste. But she and Kanshi Ram were convinced that the entire Dalit vote would in time come to their party. They were both nervous and tentative about how to get the backing of other sections of the bahujan samaj such as the backward castes and the minorities. Yet, when it came to Dalits, the BSP leadership invariably had their finger on the pulse of the community.

In Uttar Pradesh, this confident approach with the Dalits has worked wonders. The chamars who comprise fifty-five per cent of the scheduled caste vote, were the first to root for the BSP as we have noted earlier. Within a few years the pasis, another major sub-caste, who comprise a little under twelve per cent of the Dalits, followed suit. The rest of the Dalit community, including the dhobis, koris, khatiks, dhanuks, slowly but surely climbed on to the BSP bandwagon. Even the valmikis, considered among the lowest ranks among Dalits, most of them scavengers by occupation, who used to vote for the BJP because they hated the uppity chamars and their leaders, have now switched loyalties. The BSP in the last assembly poll in the state commanded nearly eighty per cent of the total Dalit vote, an unprecedented consolidation of electoral support by any ethnic group for any party in the country.

The runaway success of the BSP in Uttar Pradesh provides an interesting contrast to the failure of the Dalit Panthers, a radical activist group that came up just around the time that Kanshi Ram launched his bahujan samaj movement. Both groups shared common perspectives on the decline in the only established Dalit political outfit, the Republican Party of India (RPI), as well as the betrayal by mainstream scheduled caste politicians in parties like the Congress. The two, however, differed sharply in the alternatives they offered to the Dalits. Kanshi Ram, as we have seen, moved towards capturing political power through the democratic process, a strategy that necessitated coalition building across the social spectrum, or at least a very large bandwidth.

The Dalit Panthers following the example set by their role model, the Black Panthers in the United States, chose a path of agitation and protest. Their radical politics veering towards the extreme Left, viewed democratic institutions, including elections, as promising far more than they delivered. It also meant that their appeal was limited to a highly oppressed niche constituency that would go along with their fiery agenda. This, in turn, shut the door on coalition building and made the Dalit Panther movement, by intention and in substance, a minority enterprise.

While the Panthers did play a key role in laying down the ideological foundations for the BSP by their pioneering efforts to arouse Dalit consciousness, their decision to confront the state without either support from any social groups than the Dalits or from political parties, exposed this band of dedicated activists to severe police repression. They were further handicapped by the terrain: they operated in the cities, towns and villages of the Uttar Pradesh plains. This hardly offered the scope for guerrilla warfare that the Naxalite groups adopted in the more inaccessible jungles of Bihar, Chhattisgarh, Orissa and Andhra Pradesh. In the end the Panthers were forced to decide whether to carry on their struggle for Dalit rights from outside the system, like the Naxalites, or to emulate the BSP and plunge into electoral battle. It did not take very long for the group to lose momentum and melt away.

Interestingly, many former Panther activists, along with those of the BAMCEF and DS4, continue to work for Dalit rights. They operate through NGOs, for instance, the Dynamic Action Group and the Savitri Bai Phule Dalit Mahila Sangharsh Morcha, that take up atrocity cases against Dalits because the BSP stays away from direct social work and agitation. The Panthers used to despise the BSP as an opportunist party that exploited Dalits as vote banks. But today the same activists acknowledge that their fight for Dalit rights gets a big boost whenever Mayawati sits in the chief ministerial chair.

The overwhelming majority of Dalits approve of this division of work between the political and apolitical streams of what they see as a common movement, although there is no formal link between the two. As French scholar Nicolas Jaoul points out, 'The combination of Mayawati's efficient pragmatism with an Ambedkarite movement that carries their democratic and equalitarian aspirations in a deeper and more uncompromising manner is thus considered safer than the risk of dividing the Dalit vote and harming the BSP's chances of gaining power.'[2] Clearly, the BSP leadership as well as Dalit activists of myriad scattered groups are both guided by the collective wisdom of the community. Activist groups are conscious of the enormous popularity of 'Behenji' in the community and and do not dare to work against her or the party. At the same time, Dalits across Uttar Pradesh expect the BSP government to support the many voluntary groups that have mushroomed all over the state to fight for them in their daily struggle for a better life.

It is significant that the pragmatic and democratic route to power adopted by Kanshi Ram and Mayawati has so decisively triumphed over the more romantic revolutionary path proposed by the Dalit Panthers. The success of the BSP over the Panthers is not just because the latter were hunted down by repressive state machinery, while the former played a safer brand of politics. It is also linked to what Dalits themselves want—a sustained battle of attrition that is flexible in both tactics and strategy, rather than an idealistic outburst of agitation that delivers no tangible benefits but brings even more tyranny by the oppressors. 'We trust Behenji because she knows when to fight and when to make peace. That is why she has been so successful,' declared Ram Piyari, a sweeper in Lucknow. Subjugated for centuries and centuries, the community is ready to wait for major social transformation as long as it is sure that efforts are being made in that direction. Much like the BSP election symbol, the elephant, the measured but weighty steps taken by Kanshi Ram and Mayawati have won them the unwavering loyalty of Dalits, belying the predictions of many experts that they would come to perceive their leaders' tactics as a brand of political opportunism, and turn against them.

Mayawati makes a forceful plea in her autobiography on the superiority of the peaceful democratic way to capture power through elections over the violent struggle to overthrow the state, as suggested by Naxalites and other radical groups. Discussing the choice before oppressed groups between the bullet and the ballot, the BSP leader says that while she has no ideological inhibitions in using bullets to liberate her people, this would be the wrong choice. She points out that while the oppressors had far more resources than the victims to manufacture bullets, it was the other way around when it came to ballots. The outcome of the 2007 polls in Uttar Pradesh has certainly vindicated her reliance on the ballot and further swelled the ranks of the faithful among Dalits and other marginalized groups.

There have been two main critiques that question Mayawati's claim to speak on behalf of the Dalits. One comes from human development economists like Santosh Merhotra, who point out that despite the growing political domination by the BSP in Uttar Pradesh over the past one-and-a-half decades, there has been no commensurate rise in the socio-economic indicators of the poorest in the state, who also happen to be Dalits. The other critique is from Dalit radicals, most of them secular leftists. They fear that Mayawati may barter the short-term gains she has made for her oppressed community, for a long-term compromise with the upper-caste establishment for her own personal advantage. Soon after the BSP's famous victory in the 2007 Uttar Pradesh assembly polls, Anand Teltumbe, the radical Dalit intellectual asserted: 'If the elections were a game, then there is no doubt that Mayawati has grounded all the veteran players. If they were a medium of securing personal power, then there is again no doubt that she has left everybody far behind in the race. But if they were taken as a vehicle to bring about a change in the caste/class relations to the benefit of oppressed and poor people, then Mayawati's unscrupulous handling of them throws up a galore of serious suspicions.'[3]

The human development economists cite grim facts and figures that show a yawning gap between Dalit political ascendancy in Uttar Pradesh and their woeful economic and social conditions. They feel that this makes a mockery of assertions of Dalit empowerment by parties like the BSP. Merhotra, who works with the Planning Commission, illustrates this by comparing conditions of Dalits in Uttar Pradesh with the southern state of Tamil Nadu. In Tamil Nadu, three out of four Dalit children are delivered in hospitals. In Uttar Pradesh, the number of scheduled caste babies delivered in hospitals is less than one in five. The infant mortality rate in Tamil Nadu for Dalit children is forty-two per thousand births, while they rise as high as 110 per thousand in Uttar Pradesh. Merhotra provides a whole range of statistics, all underlining the better living standards of Tamil Dalits compared to their northern counterparts.

Merhotra blames what he describes as 'programmatic bankruptcy of caste-based political mobilization' by parties like the BSP as the reason that Dalits in Uttar Pradesh lag so far behind those in Tamil Nadu. He claims that except for a Dalit minority, the community as a whole has not gained significantly from the repeated political triumphs of the BSP. Merhotra is particularly critical of Mayawati's drive to build memorials, rename roads and universities, and create new districts to honour important leaders of the Dalit movement. He describes this exercise as 'the least valuable programme' of the BSP that eats into precious financial resources of the government without bringing in concrete benefits. The statistical superiority of the Tamil Dalit over his counterpart in Uttar Pradesh is linked to the more broad-based social reform movements that swept the south in the early part of the twentieth century, and also to specific technical interventions that helped raise health and educational standards in the south.[4]

Unfortunately, statistical surveys and detached academic studies, in their anxiety to map the terrible living conditions of the oppressed group from under a microscope, often lose sight of the fact that they are real individuals with raw emotions coursing through their psyche. This is particularly true for Dalits, who have been browbeaten and demoralized for many centuries. They have, in fact, been robbed of their very identity after being cast out of caste Hindu society. It is, therefore, a mistake to see the plight of Dalits purely through the human development prism or through some charts listing indicators of health, nutrition, education and so on. This is not to suggest that these indicators are unimportant—they do highlight the deprivations suffered by groups that exist on the edge of Indian society like beasts in the wilderness. But ironically, despite living like animals, the primary angst for Dalits relates not to physical well being, but to their sense of dignity that has been snatched away. As a noted Dalit scholar explained, 'Dalits feel no nostalgia for the past, all they remember is a history of humiliation and exploitation.'

Shivam Vij, a journalist who has written extensively on Dalits in north India, pointed out in an article, 'The Mayawati-led BSP is often criticized for giving Dalits pride but little else'. The party exploits caste for power, it is said, mesmerizing Dalits with Ambedkar statues. Pyasaa and his neighbours in the largely Dalit slum of Bheemnagar in Varanasi, counter that this critique does not take into account what it means to be a Dalit in Hindu society and how grave are the effects of untouchability on Dalit minds.'[5]

Mayawati's campaign to inculcate a sense of identity and pride among Dalits by reminding them of their history and leaders through monuments and renaming drives, therefore, is the most valuable programme for Dalits, even though it may bring no physical comfort. Right from the outset, she and Kanshi Ram were acutely aware of this yearning of the Dalit to find his own self, perhaps because it touched a chord in their own souls. The two leaders, along with the urban educated Dalits who joined BAMCEF in the seventies, rediscovered their identity through the teachings of Ambedkar. When the unfamiliar, complex Ambedkarite idiom did not instantly appeal to the rural Dalit masses, Mayawati created monuments and parks; she renamed public thoroughfares, institutions and districts, projecting them as palpable symbols of Dalit identity drawn from a pantheon of leaders through history. Ambedkar's writings may not be accessible to the illiterate Dalit villager, but his presence is more than visible in suit, tie and glasses immortalized in statues that have come up over the past two decades in hundreds of thousands in villages and towns across Uttar Pradesh. The Dalit Panthers pioneered this trend of building Ambedkar statues in the state, but the BSP turned it into a giant enterprise. This is nothing less than the creation of a new religion—with idols and rituals—for a community that had been denied access to the gods themselves.

The BSP also showed great inventive skills in capturing the imagination of an audience that could only be reached through their ears. According to Dr Badri Narayan who runs the Dalit Resource Centre of the Gobind Ballabh Pant Institute of Social Sciences in Allahabad, party cadre liberally used local memories, histories and cultural symbols of Dalits in their political mobilization. The 'jati katha' or protesting caste narratives were an oral counter to the Puranas, which have remained the sacred religious and cultural preserves of the upper castes. Similarly, Eklavya, the famous untouchable archer from the Mahabharata, Sant Ravi Das, the fifteenth-century cobbler saint from Varanasi who was revered by upper and lower castes alike, and above all, the Buddha, were valorized to restore a sense of self-esteem to the Dalits.

In an attempt to look for more contemporary role models, Dalit freedom fighters from the days of the 1857 Sepoy Mutiny have been discovered. Interestingly, with Mayawati as their leader, there is special emphasis on Dalit heroines who blazed a trail of glory and sacrifice during India's first struggle for independence. Their heroic deeds have been recorded by Dr Narayan and they include Mahaviridevi of Muzaffarnagar in western Uttar Pradesh and Avantibai Lodhi from the bordering areas of Madhya Pradesh. Another concerns Jhalkaribai of Bundelkhand in central UP, who, along with her husband, Makka Pasi, laid down her life in the revolt at Sikendarabagh in Lucknow.[6] The oral narratives and statues glorifying these Dalit women, have helped create further aura around Mayawati, who is projected as their modern avatar.

To suggest, as Merhotra has done, that these symbolic gestures and cultural messages are unimportant because they do not improve the living conditions of Dalits is to miss the wood for the trees. The time will no doubt come when Dalits in Uttar Pradesh will be sufficiently self confident to give more importance to material benefits over symbolic gestures. But that is still ahead. Interestingly, in its political mobilization of Dalits, the BSP has chosen to use images of past heroes and heroines, scholars, sages and warriors, rather than dwell excessively on the daily misery of Dalit lives. The obvious popularity of this approach underlines how memories of a heroic past often give fresh confidence about a brighter future to a downtrodden community.

The relative merits of being a Dalit in Tamil Nadu rather than in Uttar Pradesh, as claimed by Merhotra, cannot be deduced from mere facts and figures. We need to look at other indicators as well. Dalits in Tamil Nadu are targets of some of the worst cases of caste atrocities in the country. The impact of these is compounded by the absence of a powerful charismatic leader or an influential party representing the community in the state. The Dravidian movement was launched a century ago to remove the iniquities of the caste system. But over the years it has degenerated and today actively acquiesces in discrimination and oppression by a whole range of supposedly backward castes of their subordinate castes. The worst victim of this caste conundrum is the lowest rung, the Dalits. In Uttar Pradesh, at least, the caste has had the satisfaction of witnessing the rise of their daughter to the highest office. In recent years the sight of the highest brahmin caste falling at her feet, appealing for protection, has further thrilled them. Undoubtedly, Dalits in Uttar Pradesh continue to live in miserable conditions, even worse than their counterparts in Tamil Nadu. Yet, in a hypothetical scenario that gave a choice to Dalits from the two states to swap locations, I strongly suspect that the one from Tamil Nadu would choose to travel to Uttar Pradesh and not the other way around.

The criticism of Mayawati by some radical Dalit intellectuals belongs to a different category. They acknowledge she and Kanshi Ram have politically empowered the Dalits as well as other impoverished and exploited sections of society. What they fear is her unreliability as an agent of social transformation over the long term. Radicals see her political opportunism, ideological frivolity, personal profligacy and, above all, the conspicuous absence of a land reforms programme, as quite inimical to the social revolution that the BSP should be launching in the country's largest state. In earlier years, these intellectuals also worried about Mayawati's repeated cohabitations with communal parties like the BJP. But this threat has receded with the rapid decline of the Sangh Parivar in Uttar Pradesh and the BSP's achievement of a majority of its own.

Shortly after the BSP's 2007 victory, prominent Dalit intellectual Anand Teltumbe bucked the trend of Dalit celebrations across the country by launching a frontal attack in an article questioning her credentials both as a Dalit leader and a progressive politician. At the end of his article Teltumbe wrote: '. . . no doubt, it would be a matter of great delight for the entire progressive world to see a daughter of a humble Dalit dislodging the traditional upper castes from the throne of the most unequal country on the planet. But would it be a Dalit Raj? Would it be a revolution? The answer to such questions may sadly be all negatives.'[7]

These critiques have some value in the seminar circuit of big metros, but do not make much sense in the world that Mayawati occupies. The little Dalit schoolgirl who wanted to be famous like Ambedkar, has travelled the distance through a combination of spunk, an ability to think out of the box and a liberal dose of good fortune. Politically correct postures of the Leftist variety are not a part of her success story. In this she has the backing of Dalits, who could not care less about theoretical constructs on how Mayawati should deliver them from exploitation and deprivation. They are just grateful that 'Behenji' is back in the saddle, this time for an assured five-year term. 'Till now she never got a chance. She came only for short stints. Now she has returned decisively, she will do in five years what others could not do in fifty years,' a Dalit voter told correspondents from the television channel NDTV in Meerut after the results of the 2007 Uttar Pradesh assembly polls gave her a clear five-year term. If she does deceive or betray them in the future, Dalits will certainly take a second look at her. Until that happens, Behenji has the confidence of her kinfolk, much like a real sister.

It is unfair to expect Mayawati to create a Dalit Raj or instigate a revolution, when all she may be capable of doing is generate a momentum of social change in one of the most feudal regions of the country to benefit its most wretched groups. As another Dalit intellectual, Chitibabu Padawala, in an article replying to Teltumbe wrote: 'The question is not what Mayawati can do to UP Dalits, but what they can do to themselves with BSP around. It is here the role of organizations, social movements and intellectuals become important. Will the Dalit intellectual class provide such a direction, inspiration and participation for the Dalits on the street or field, or it simply waits for the government to do everything is the question. It also opens up a unique and unprecedented opportunity for Dalits: Dalits are the only group whose emancipation cannot be achieved without enlightening the entire society. It is in the best interests of the Dalits to lead the rest of the society towards enlightenment.'[8]

# FOURTEEN

# A Rags-to-Riches Fairy Tale

$\mathcal{T}$here is another side to the amazing rise of Mayawati, quite apart from politics and social transformation. It is also literally a rags-to-riches fairy tale, an insight into the kind of personal wealth that successful politicians can accumulate in this country. From a very humble beginning in the lower middle class home of a government clerk with many dependants, in a relatively brief period Mayawati has acquired a phenomenal number of properties along with extremely substantial amounts of jewellery, cash and financial assets. Her immediate family, parents, brothers and sisters, have also prospered beyond their dreams.

When we started our story of Mayawati, all that she and her family owned was a poky little place in the west Delhi ghetto of Inderpuri, along with a modest amount of ancestral village land. They could not have had much money in the bank considering her father, Prabhu Das, was depending on his daughter's government schoolteacher's salary to provide for her dowry and wedding expenses. Contrast this with the list of assets for Mayawati and her family filed in 2003 by the CBI in the Supreme Court: seventy-two houses, plots and shops, and fifty-four bank accounts. She is supposed to have bought her most expensive properties after that, which indicates that her assets have quadrupled.

The CBI list gave a break up of the immovable assets of Mayawati and her family: forty-one agricultural plots, sixteen residential plots, seven shops, three orchards and two shop-cum-residences. Most of these, according to the investigative agency, are located in and around Delhi and the adjoining Noida region. Soon after the CBI filed its list in 2003, the Uttar Pradesh government, then under Mulayam Singh Yadav, came out with another list of 131 properties owned by the Mayawati family. Giving details of the properties, the state chief secretary, Akhand Pratap Singh, said in a press conference that they were mostly located in Lucknow, Noida, Ghaziabad, Bulandshahr and Bijnore. 'While we received photocopies of documents relating to 100 of these properties, the rest were verified from official records,' the chief secretary said. And the *Times of India* reported on 14 September 2003 that the Income Tax department was digging into the files of properties allegedly bought by Mayawati in the name of her relatives in Shimla, Ambedkarnagar, Saharanpur, Bulandshahr, Khurja, Meerut, Ghaziabad, Noida and Delhi.

It is difficult to ascertain whether this entire list is of properties actually owned by Mayawati, her parents, brothers, sisters and their families. But the properties for which there is substantial proof can certainly be examined. We should start with Inderpuri where she grew up, and with which she obviously still has a strong bond. Unlike many other self-made billionaires, the BSP leader has not abandoned her childhood playground. She has bought four plots, C-57, 58, 74 and 75, in the colony that—like all land in Delhi, even those located in former lower middle class shanty towns like Inderpuri—have shot up astronomically in value. The combined worth of these plots was valued in her affidavit filed with the Election Commission as a candidate for the 2004 Lok Sabha polls at twelve-and-a-half million rupees.

She has also built a mansion in her ancestral village of Badalpur. There was a flurry of media reports about her village home in the summer of 2006. The television channel NDTV described it on 27 June 2006 as a mini Taj Mahal built on a sprawling 30,000 square yard estate with a twenty-five-foot-high roof, Italian marble floors, teak doors, imposing pillars and Rajasthani frescoes. Annoyed at this publicity, Mayawati took a group of select journalists to her Badalpur bungalow, which turned out to be very spacious, but still very much under construction, and without most of the lavish trappings reported by the media. The BSP leader, of course, saw the media coverage as 'another Manuvadi conspiracy' to malign her.

The *Indian Express* on 19 July 1997 carried an account of a farmhouse acquired by Mayawati at Maman Road, situated on the Bulandshahr–Moradabad bypass in Uttar Pradesh. It encompassed nearly eight-and-a-half acres of agricultural land. The BSP leader's private residence in Lucknow—3, Nehru Road—is spread over 1,200 sq. m. She bought it in 2005 from an army officer, Gullu Chandani, for nearly ten million rupees. Today, it is worth more than double that amount. The building has undergone elaborate renovations carried out over a number of years.

Her really valuable properties are bunched around the elite residential area of New Delhi's Sardar Patel Marg where embassies and state guest houses are located, and in the prime commercial centre of Connaught Place that boasts of some of highest land rates in the world. In 2003, Mayawati bought bungalow No. 11 on Sardar Patel Marg from the Dehlvis, a famous Muslim business family of Delhi. It was reportedly bought with a bank draft of fifty million rupees from the Parliament Street branch of the Bank of India and allegedly an unknown sum under the table. The actual market value of the bungalow was estimated in 2007 to be several times the original price paid by bank draft. The house was bought in the name of the BSP and a large metal placard at the entrance proclaims 'BSP House'.

In 2006, Mayawati bought another bungalow on 2, Sardar Patel Marg, located next to bungalow No. 11. According to a report by Shishir Gupta in the *Indian Express* on 30 June 2007, she paid 170 million rupees and another ten million in stamp and transfer duty to buy the 2194.4 sq. yard property. Giving specific details of the property deal, the newspaper reported:

> The sale agreement was executed between Mayawati and Homender Arora, Director of M/s HMP Delhi Enclave Private Limited. Mayawati paid fifty million rupees through cheque number 563141 (Bank of India, Parliament Street) on July 14, followed by another 120 million rupees pay order (No: 062024) on July 17 on the same bank. Again, the actual value of the property is estimated to be many times more than the bank draft amounts recorded in the deal.

The same report in the *Indian Express* has also catalogued the purchases made by Mayawati from 2004 onwards of properties in

Connaught Place, New Delhi's oldest and most famous commercial centre, located in the heart of the capital. The detailed transactions reported by the newspaper are as follows:[1]

- In 2004, Mayawati made her first big property deal in Delhi buying 3268.2 sq. ft of commercial space in B-15, Inner Circle, Connaught Place. She bought the ground and a portion of mezzanine floor from one Mr Hari Om Gulati at the cost of 19 million rupees on December 20, 2004. The payment for the property was done through cheque number 558798, drawn on Bank of India, Parliament Street, New Delhi.

- The original owners of this space were M/s I.A.G. Promoters and Developers Private Limited, who had partly rented this property to M/s Bata India Limited. I.A.G. Promoters sold the above space to Hari Om Gulati by a sale deed executed on November 29, 2004. Gulati, in turn, sold it to Mayawati the very next month. The fact is that M/s Bata India is a tenant of Mayawati as she is getting rent since the day she purchased the property.

- A year later, Mayawati purchased the first floor of the same building with an area of 4535.02 square feet from M/s A.R.D. Developers Private Limited through a sale deed dated November 15, 2005. While the deed was for Rs 12 million rupees Mayawati shelled out another Rs. 720,000 towards transfer duty.

- On November 7, 2006, Mayawati let out this space to M/s DLF Home Developers Limited for a monthly rent of Rs 680,000. Significantly, the right to construct the mezzanine floor, records show, has been gifted by one Rati Ram to Mayawati's brother, Anand Kumar, through gift deed on February 10, 2004. The value of the gift is eight million rupees. This area is also given on rent to the developer company.

Mayawati's other commercial property is located in the Okhla industrial area of Delhi, where she owns a fairly large area of 34,112.26 sq. ft valued at 155 million rupees.

Significantly, all these properties are investments for Mayawati as she already has several official bungalows in which to live. She retains the MP's bungalow, 11 Humayun Road, in New Delhi that has been her Delhi base and that of Kanshi Ram till his death in 2006, for over one-and-a-half decades. In Lucknow, she has the sprawling official chief ministerial residence on 5 Kalidas Marg. Mayawati also retains the bungalow given to her as former chief minister on 13 Mall Avenue. She is now busy expanding the existing house into a much larger private estate by razing surrounding bungalows, on the plea that she needs more security.

We turn now to Mayawati's financial holdings, jewellery and moveable assets, and those of her close relatives. According to the CBI list filed in 2003, she had assets worth 36.5 million rupees in account number 9195 at the Moti Bagh branch of the Union Bank of India. In another account in the State Bank of India, Parliament Street branch, 2.345 million rupees was found. The investigative agency also found bank accounts and fixed deposits in different bank branches in Greater Noida and Bulandshahr belonging to her parents, brothers, sisters and their families that amounted to just under twenty-four million rupees.

Some more details of Mayawati's moveable assets are available from the affidavits filed by her in the 2004 Lok Sabha polls and in the 2007 Uttar Pradesh Legislative Council polls. In 2004, Mayawati said that she had 150,000 rupees in cash, Rs 97.8 million rupees in bank deposits and jewellery worth 3.09 million rupees. In 2007, her moveable assets included 5.02 million rupees in cash, 128.8 million rupees in bank deposits and jewellery worth 5.08 million rupees. Giving further details of her jewellery, she had listed 1034.260 grams of gold, 76.040 grams of diamond and 18,500 kilograms of silver that included a very elaborate and fancy dinner set. Mayawati also admitted owning murals worth one-and-a-half million rupees.

According to Mayawati's own self-valuation from the two affidavits, her financial worth including both moveable and immoveable assets jumped from 160.7 million rupees in 2004 to 520 million rupees in 2007. This dramatic rise in fortunes of the BSP leader in the space of three years was entirely due to the high-value residential mansions, one in Delhi and the other in Lucknow, and the commercial properties in Delhi that she listed in 2007, compared to just the four Inderpuri plots shown in 2004.

The list above is by no means exhaustive or comprehensive. It does not include every single asset owned by Mayawati and has to take into account the full wealth of her immediate family. But even if we were to accept Mayawati's self-valuation of 520 million rupees, it is indeed a stupendous amount for an individual politician to own. Of course, there are stray industrialist members of Parliament and perhaps a few ministers at the state and central level, whose business empires are worth far more. But obviously, they cannot be compared to Mayawati who has no other occupation but politics. According to affidavits filed by various political leaders in recent years with the Election Commission, in north India, Prakash Singh Badal, the rich kulak chief minister of Punjab comes closest with assets worth ninety-two million rupees, which is way below that of his Uttar Pradesh counterpart. She does have some competition in south India led by another powerful woman leader, Jayalalithaa, who valued herself at 240 million rupees followed by M. Karunanidhi with 220 million rupees, both from Tamil Nadu, and Chandrababu Naidu from Andhra Pradesh with 210 million rupees. None of them, however, have even half the wealth of Mayawati.

The BSP leader offers three basic explanations for her rags-to-riches story. She sources most of the funds she has used to acquire her wealth to contributions from her followers who 'want to see a Dalit ki beti rich as well as powerful.' Mayawati also claims that quite a bit of the immovable and financial assets are actually for her party and in some cases, like her bungalow at 11 Sardar Patel Marg, the ownership documents mention the BSP. Finally, she has also asked the CBI, which is investigating the disproportionate assets case against her, not to include properties and financial holdings owned by her family members.

In 2004, the CBI strongly contested Mayawati's plea that a large portion of her wealth came from voluntary contributions from her fans. Investigating 130 such donors who had contributed sums of about 130.8 million rupees into bank accounts operated by Mayawati and members of her family, the CBI tracked down around fifty sweepers, hawkers and rickshaw pullers who claimed that for a 'few hundred rupees', they were asked to open bank accounts and sign blank cheques. The CBI revelations were incorporated in a status report filed to the Supreme Court on 26 October 2004 in connection with the disproportionate assets case against Mayawati.

Considering the scale of donations required to accumulate mansions, commercial estates, bank deposits, and stockholdings worth millions of rupees, the BSP leader's claim that it all came from ordinary party workers may have few takers. Unsurprisingly, there has been speculation that a large portion of the donations came from aspiring bureaucrats and election candidates, who had good reason to keep Mayawati happy. This is not to suggest that ordinary Dalits are reluctant to empty their pockets for their leaders. Kanshi Ram, as we noted earlier, did find it very difficult to collect funds in the beginning. But once his movement caught the imagination of Dalits in the late eighties, they started contributing generously.

Both Kanshi Ram and Mayawati routinely collected donations from their followers on every possible occasion. In contrast to other party leaders who spent money to get crowds for their public meetings, the BSP leaders actually charged entry fees to those who wanted to come and hear them speak. In the late eighties, Kanshi Ram started charging a flat rate of fifty-two thousand rupees per meeting. He was known to raise his rates when his schedule was fully booked, encouraging his followers from different regions to bid against each other for the privilege of getting him for a meeting.

Nor were Kanshi Ram and Mayawati coy accepting birthday presents from their flock. In the late nineties the BSP ran a year-long collection drive so that they could give birthday gifts of 650,000 rupees and 420,000 rupees to Kanshi Ram and Mayawati to celebrate their sixty-fifth and forty-second birthdays. The money was handed over at a function held on 14 April 1999 at Constitution Club in New Delhi.

There is also no credible explanation why these large donations, even if contributed by party workers, have been used for mansions, farmhouses, commercial plots, jewellery and bank deposits in the name of Mayawati and her close relatives. For a party with such ambitious plans across the country, would not the money have been better spent for more obvious political purposes, for instance, on election campaigns and promotional activities of the BSP? This holds true for Mayawati's plea that some of the properties were bought in the name of the party. For instance, what earthly use would a mansion in the corner of a posh residential enclave like Sardar Patel Marg have for the BSP?

It is difficult to be convinced by Mayawati's efforts to distance herself from the assets owned by members of her family. Everybody knows that her relatives are quite dependent on the one big success story in the family. It would have been virtually impossible for any of them to acquire the wealth they have on their own steam. The fact that a large bulk of the undeclared assets of 280 million rupees that the CBI is investigating happens to be in the name of her relatives underscores this obvious subterfuge.

Are Mayawati's vast assets illegal and can she be prosecuted for it? Ironically, the Taj Corridor case that provoked the CBI enquiry into her assets has collapsed because of extremely flimsy evidence against the BSP leader. After four years of investigations it has become amply clear that there is no real case against her under the Prevention of Corruption Act. In any case, after the Uttar Pradesh Governor T.V. Rajeshwar's refusal to sanction the CBI's further pursuit of the case, Mayawati is completely safe.

The disproportionate assets case looked quite dangerous for her a few years ago, but the threat appears to have receded. After sustained counselling from her aide Satish Mishra, Mayawati seems to have got her papers in order and her assets reorganized. As a matter of fact, the declaration of 520 million rupees in moveable and immoveable assets in her affidavit for the 2007 Uttar Pradesh Legislative Council elections, reflects her new confidence since she is up to date with her tax payments on this wealth.

Her family, on the other hand, would have been in serious trouble had they been required to explain how they came to be in possession of tens of millions of rupees worth of assets. But the relatives appear to have saved themselves in the nick of time. The *Indian Express* reported on 1 June 2007 that a number of Mayawati's relatives had approached the Income Tax Settlement Commission to declare their undeclared assets and pay the penalties. The Commission has the powers to grant immunity from any prosecution in connection with these assets. Interestingly, the family members made it just in time to beat an amendment in the Income Tax Act that bars the Commission from granting immunity to those whose residential and commercial premises have been raided and searched by investigative agencies.

If the CBI is still keen to pursue the case rigorously, Mayawati and her relatives can be harassed. The various transfers of properties within the family over the past few years, as well the vast sums of money that her relatives will have to pay in penalties, can be investigated, raising embarrassing questions. However, considering the Uttar Pradesh chief minister's rising political clout, it is unlikely that any government agency is to seriously trouble her in the near future.

A major reason why Mayawati has accumulated so much wealth with such impunity is that there is no political liability to what the media and the urban intelligentsia consider improper. The BSP leader's own constituency backs her to the hilt. An overwhelming majority of Dalits instead of being critical are proud that a political leader of their community possesses even more wealth than the upper castes. Amazingly, her riches have become a symbol of Dalit empowerment. In a manner of speaking, therefore, Mayawati is not lying when she claims that she has acquired her wealth on behalf of the people.

The same blind adulation has allowed her to throw some of the most lavish birthday bashes in Indian politics. Her forty-seventh birthday, celebrated when she was chief minister of Uttar Pradesh for the third time in 2003, created a stir when an estimated one hundred million rupees of official funds were spent on the festivities. Covered with glittering diamonds Mayawati pranced around on a stage measuring forty feet by sixty feet, with sets copied from the Bollywood blockbuster *Mughal-e-Azam*. A fifty-one-kilogram cake, 100,000 ladoos, sixty quintals of marigold flowers and around 5,000 bouquets, were some of the highlights. She has failed to match the scale and glitz of that particular birthday party in subsequent celebrations, but Mayawati is not a leader who shies away from ostentatious show of her power and wealth. The fact that her supporters like this approach is enough justification for her. It has also allowed the BSP leader to elevate these splurges on a political pedestal, naming her birthday, for instance, as *swabhiman diwas* or self-respect day for Dalits.

Condemnation of Mayawat's vast wealth and lavish spending must be tempered with the recognition of the general absence of any kind of moral code in Indian politics when it comes to money. There are innumerable political leaders who may not be as transparently ostentatious as Mayawati, but they also have extraordinarily deep pockets. Most of them, if investigated as rigorously as the BSP leader, would also stand exposed of accumulating properties, money and jewellery beyond their obvious means. Clearly, it is a malaise that afflicts the country's political system as a whole, rather than just an individual leader, as her detractors suggest. As long as the rules of the political game remain the same, Mayawati will continue to view her journey from poverty to affluence as a fairy tale and not a dirty story.

# FIFTEEN

## *Prime Minister Mayawati?*

*M*ayawati has always conquered the odds, snatching success from the jaws of overwhelming challenges. Her father threw her out for switching from the safe IAS highway to the tortuous, risky path of politics; yet she came up trumps. Seniors in the BSP waited for the young firebrand to fall on her face, but it was they who were sent packing. Mulayam Singh Yadav tried to scare her, and ended up a big loser. The Sangh Parivar wanted to patronize her, but are now at her mercy. Kanshi Ram's cronies expected the BSP to collapse after he was crippled; she took the party to a new level. Pundits and pollsters declared a hung assembly in the 2007 Uttar Pradesh polls, and promptly had to eat their prophecies. The list of miracles performed by Mayawati is endless.

Despite this formidable record, her political peers and the media have persistently underestimated Mayawati and her party. Throughout her career she has been regarded as an unguided missile that has explosive intent, but no sense of direction. Ironically, this tendency to underestimate the BSP leader has actually facilitated the phenomenal growth of the party under her leadership. One by one, the Samajwadi Party, BJP and the Congress struck deals with the BSP in the misplaced confidence that they would be able to manipulate the fledgling political outfit and its maverick leader. In the process they ceded precious political turf in Uttar Pradesh, allowing Mayawati to spread her wings. It was too late by the time they realized it was she who was calling the shots.

There is a big change in the perception of Mayawati after her sweeping victory in the 2007 polls. Having underrated her for so long, political and media circles are now jumping to the other extreme. They are busy inflating the BSP leader's image to larger-than-life proportions. Her party's triumphant Dalit–brahmin alliance in Uttar Pradesh has overnight become a blueprint for electoral success across the country. Some commentators are predicting the BSP will make rapid gains through this winning combine elsewhere in India as well. They are convinced that Mayawati would be a frontrunner for the prime minister's job if neither the UPA nor the NDA is in a position to form a government in the next Lok Sabha.

Does Mayawati have a realistic chance of becoming the next prime minister? Under normal circumstances it would be ludicrous to suggest that the leader of a party with less than twenty seats in a Lok Sabha of 542 members can form the government in the space of one general election. Even if the BSP were to more than double their present tally from Uttar Pradesh, getting a maximum of fifty seats, it will still fall short of constituting a tenth of the elected Lower House. If in addition, the party won twenty seats from other states—a best-case scenario—it would get a total of seventy seats. This will take the BSP to third position behind the Congress and the BJP.

Obviously, the next general elections need to usher in a period of considerable instability if Mayawati is to have a crack at the top job. In the past, the BSP leader has shrewdly used political turmoil to leapfrog rival claimants to power, even though she lacked the numbers. Her first two stints in power as Uttar Pradesh chief minister came when she had only sixty-six members in a 400-member assembly and a third term in office when her numbers went up to ninety-eight. Each time she was well short of a majority. She was able to grab power because other parties prevented each other from forming the government. A political deadlock in New Delhi similar to that which prevailed in Lucknow in 1995, 1997 and again in 2002 will certainly see Mayawati in business.

As the year 2007 neared its end, national politics did seem to be heading towards confusion if not commotion. The Congress-led

United Progressive Alliance (UPA) government formed after the last general elections looked increasingly in disarray with the prime minister, Manmohan Singh, locked in battle with the Left Front over the Indo-US nuclear deal. With the leftists whose support is vital for the ruling coalition's survival threatening to pull the plug if the prime minister did not abandon the deal with the US, there is still speculation whether the government will survive till the summer of 2009, when the next general elections are due.

To complicate matters, for the first time perhaps in the recent history of Indian politics, troubles in the ruling alliance have not been accompanied by a corresponding rise in fortunes of the Opposition. The main opposition alliance, the National Democratic Alliance (NDA) led by the BJP, is languishing because of the party's inability to fill the leadership vacuum left by its aged and semi-retired leader, Atal Bihari Vajpayee. A younger generation of leaders is locked in a power struggle, which is compounded by the insistence of former deputy prime minister, Lal Krishna Advani, that he too is in the race. The sense of drift within the BJP has quickly transferred to the rest of the NDA. This was underlined by the inability of the alliance to put up a common candidate for the 2007 presidential elections.

Spotting the disorder in the two main national coalitions, a bunch of regional parties, Telegu Dasam and the All India Anna Dravida Munnetra Kazagam (AIADMK) in the south, Samajwadi Party and Indian National Lok Dal in the north and Asom Gana Parishad in the east, formed a third front, the United National Progressive Alliance (UNPA) in the summer of 2007. But after some rhetorical flourishes aimed at the UPA government, the new alliance has developed cracks. They were unable to put up a candidate for the presidential polls with each alliance partner adopting an independent posture. Since then, factional squabbles have broken out with the mercurial AIADMK supremo, Jayalalithaa, taking personal swipes at Samajwadi Party leader Mulayam Singh's deputy, Amar Singh.

Significantly, the prospects of none of the alliances seem particularly bright in the next elections. The Congress is expected to gain some seats from the BJP in Rajasthan, Madhya Pradesh, Chhattisgarh and a few from the Left Front in Kerala. But the party and it allies are likely to lose heavily in Andhra Pradesh,

Tamil Nadu and Bihar. A few media opinion polls in the middle of 2007 predicted an overall gain for the Congress, but the accuracy of these polls have been badly punctured by their totally innacurate predictions for elections to the last Lok Sabha in 2004 and the Uttar Pradesh assembly in 2007.

There is also considerable confusion in the Congress on who would be the next prime ministerial candidate. The party supremo, Sonia Gandhi, had refused the job in 2004 citing an 'inner voice' warning her not to do so. She had chosen her most trusted aide, the apolitical Dr Manmohan Singh, as India's first appointed prime minister. He was widely expected to hold the job till the Gandhi heir, Rahul Gandhi, was ready to take charge. Unfortunately for the Congress and its leader, the young scion appears nowhere near ready and has only recently taken up the post of party general secretary. In his few forays into election campaigning, Rahul Gandhi has not met with much success. In the 2007 Uttar Pradesh polls, the political debutant drew large crowds to his road shows, but the Congress slipped further from its pathetic twenty-five-seat tally in the previous elections.

Clearly, Rahul Gandhi will not be ready to be prime minister if Congress is able to form a government after the next elections. So will Dr Manmohan Singh be appointed for a second term? Congress insiders maintain that Sonia Gandhi is reluctant to do so lest he gets too fond of his chair and becomes a parallel centre of authority to her. Dr Singh is believed to be aware that he will not be made prime minister again and his aggressive run-in with Left leaders over the nuclear deal may have been a deliberate bid to force a mid-term poll on the issue. The calculation was that if such an election were held with Dr Singh's sacrifice of the government to protect the nuclear deal as a backdrop to the polls, it would have been difficult for Sonia Gandhi not to project him as the prime ministerial candidate.

If the Congress president refuses to oblige Dr Singh, the question still remains of whom she will put in his place after the elections. Will she forget her 'inner voice' and become prime minister herself? Or is there another trusted aide she can turn to? Finally, how long can the Congress and Sonia Gandhi wait for Rahul Gandhi to take charge?

Normally, the BJP would have wasted no time in taking advantage of the political angst within the Gandhi family and in the Congress. But the party that in the nineties was poised to become an alternative to the Congress, looks a pale shadow of its former self. The defeat in the 2004 general elections knocked the BJP off its perch, but it was the humiliation suffered in the 2007 Uttar Pradesh state polls that has traumatized the party. Relegated to the role of a bit player in its former bastion, expected to lose heavily in the adjoining north Indian states where it rules, and likely to face the anti-incumbency factor, the BJP is not expected to make a serious bid for power in the next elections.

Its partners in the NDA are better placed with both the Janata Dal (U) in Bihar and the Biju Janata Dal in Orissa expected to hold their own. But they no longer look to the BJP for leadership. Other former allies, the Telegu Dasam, AIADMK and the Trinamul Congress, for instance, may also improve their vote share considerably in the polls, but they are not even in an alliance with the BJP. With the party's individual tally likely to come down to less than a hundred, its relevance in the post-election scenario may be that of just a spoiler, wanting to prevent a Congress-led alliance from coming to power.

Another political alliance likely to take a toss in the next Lok Sabha polls is the Left Front, which is in serious distress in its only two regional bastions Kerala and West Bengal. The Left had wielded considerable influence in national politics after doing phenomenally well in the 2004 polls. Their interventions in economic and foreign policy over the past three years have undermined this clout. Expected to lose at least a third of their seats in the next elections, they will no longer be the political force they were. The plight of the Left's closest ally, the Samajwadi Party, which is likely to lose heavily in its main political arena of Uttar Pradesh, is a double blow. This means that the parliamentary bloc of the Left and Samajwadi Party, with a combined strength of around a hundred members in the Lok Sabha, nearly a fifth of the Lower House, may be reduced to half its size and lose most of its political manoeuvrability.

Mayawati's chances of becoming prime minister depend on how the political melting pot described above gets stirred. She knows that if her party manages to get fifty seats or more in the next Lok Sabha, any alliance that comes to power will have to turn to her for support. A supreme opportunist who has always managed to exploit other people's compulsions and vulnerabilities to her advantage, the BSP leader is capable of doing business with both the Congress and the BJP and, if required, with various regional parties as well—all except Mulayam Singh's Samajwadi Party, of course.

The fact that neither the Congress nor the BJP has a clear prime ministerial candidate is in Mayawati's favour. She has an excellent personal rapport with Sonia Gandhi. The BSP leader is also a favourite of the Sangh Parivar, including powerful sections of the RSS, who are strong supporters of her Dalit–brahmin alliance. It is not totally impossible in a hopelessly muddled post-Lok Sabha poll scenario, that she manages to get one side or the other to propose her as a compromise candidate to head the government. This may seem far-fetched and smack of political suicide by the Congress and the BJP, but stranger things have been known to happen in politics.

Mayawati herself is supremely focussed to take the big leap forward. With characteristic candour she announced almost immediately after winning the Uttar Pradesh polls, that her next challenge was to capture power at the centre. She has started making elaborate preparations to get the maximum number of seats in the next parliamentary polls. Long before the 2007 assembly polls in Uttar Pradesh, Mayawati had meticulously planned for each of the 400-odd assembly constituencies in the state. She is doing a similar exercise for the 542 parliamentary constituencies that will go to polls.

These plans will naturally be of particular relevance in Uttar Pradesh where Mayawati hopes to win as many as sixty out of eighty seats. She is planning to virtually obliterate the Congress and the BJP, and reduce Mulayam Singh's party to single digits in the next Lok Sabha. There is little scope for the BSP to add to its core Dalit vote, since this is already near saturation—close to eighty per cent. But the party should attract a much larger component of the poorer backward caste and Muslim vote, along with a substantial section of the brahmin and bania vote. BSP election managers are, however, aware that they may need a larger percentage of votes in the next elections, since politics in Uttar Pradesh is increasingly polarized between the BSP and the Samajwadi Party, which is also likely to receive the consolidated backing of its supporters.

The real challenge for the BSP in the general elections will come in the adjoining states of Madhya Pradesh, Chhattisgarh, Rajasthan and Delhi, where the party needs to pick up seats if Mayawati is to make a serious bid for power after the next general elections. Her return to power with a full majority in Uttar Pradesh is bound to have an impact on these states. Undoubtedly, there will be a major consolidation of Dalit votes behind the BSP next time, but can the party commensurately increase its votes from tribals and poorer backward castes? It would also need to replicate the alliance with brahmins beyond the borders of Uttar Pradesh. This will not be easy because Mayawati and the BSP are on a completely different level in Uttar Pradesh compared to other states, where the party's winnability ratio is far less.

It is a similar story in Maharashtra, which is the only state outside north India where the BSP has realistic chance of winning a few seats. The party does enjoy support in some Dalit pockets of Vidarbha region, but these by themselves will not be enough to win seats. Much would depend on whether the party will be able to stitch up the right kind of alliances with other sections of society.

Satish Mishra, Mayawati's brahmin lawyer aide, who set her on the road to a historic alliance with brahmins, has been given the responsibility of networking with brahmins across the country to enlist their support for the next Lok Sabha polls. He is an extraordinarily resourceful man, who has contacts with a variety of opinion makers, mostly brahmins, but some other upper castes as well. Many of them are reported to have told Mishra that they were tired of the present political options, and willing to try a radically different leader like Mayawati now that she is no longer against the upper castes.

There is often a subterranean current in favour of a political leader or movement that is not fully visible on the surface. Mayawati comprehensively proved that in Uttar Pradesh. It is possible that she will do so again in a larger national arena. Certainly, for a long time no other leader has been talked about with as much excitement and anticipation across social strata— from upper class living rooms to working class slums. There is a certain weariness cutting across class and caste barriers today, with the minimalist politics practised by mainstream political parties, whether it is the Congress or the BJP. This is why the idea of a prime minister like Mayawati appeals to more people than one would normally imagine. The hype about provincial politicians like Mayawati by proliferating television channels, newspapers, and periodicals has made her an instantly recognizable national figure. We should not underestimate the novelty of this image.

Even if Mayawati were not to make it as prime minister after the Lok Sabha polls, she would remain a strong contender for the post in future electoral battles. With a secure bastion in the country's largest state and an emotional stranglehold over a countrywide group like the Dalits, she has extremely strong political cards to play in an increasingly fractured polity. It is perhaps just a matter of time before she does become the prime minister of this country.

# Notes

## 1. Early Years

1. Kumari Mayawati, *My Life of Struggle and the Path of the Bahujan Movement*; Bahujan Samaj Party, 2006.
2. Ibid.
3. Interview to the *Indo-Asian News Service*, 11 May 2007.
4. Singh, Gurmukh: 'Power of Maya', *Times of India*, 11 June 1995.
5. Kumari Mayawati, *My Life of Struggle*.

## 2. Kanshi Ram

1. Jaffrelot, Christophe, *India's Silent Revolution*, Permanent Black, 2003.
2. Ibid.
3. Ram, Kanshi, *Aaj ke neta/Alochanatmak adhyayanmala*, Raj Kamal Prakashan, 1997 (Hindi).
4. Quoted in Anandan, Sujata, 'Messaiah of the Few', *Outlook*, 6 September 1999.
5. Ram, Kanshi, *Chamcha Age: An Era of Stooges*, New Delhi, 1982.
6. Kumar, Vivek and Sinha, Uday, *Dalit Assertion and the Bahujan Samaj Party*, Bahujan Sahitya Sansthan, 2001.

## 3. Behenji and Saheb

1. Kumari Mayawati: *My Life of Struggle and the Path of the Bahujan Movement*, Bahujan Samaj Party, 2006.
2. Ibid.

3. Ram, Kanshi, *The Incomparable Lady—Kumari Mayawati*, www.dalitindia.com, 24 March 2001.
4. Akhtar, Mohammed Jameel, *Iron Lady—Kumari Mayawati* (Foreword by Kanshi Ram), 25 February 1999.

## 4. The Quest for Political Power

1. Ram, Kanshi, *Chamcha Age: An Era of Stooges*, New Delhi, 1982.
2. Quoted in Kumar, Vivek and Sinha, Uday, *Dalit Assertion and the Bahujan Samaj Party*, Bahujan Sahitya Sansthan, 2001.
3. Ram, Kanshi, *The Incomparable Lady—Kumari Mayawati*.
4. Interview with Jayant Malhoutra cited in Mendelsohn, Oliver, and Vicziany, Marika, *The Untouchables: Subordination, Poverty and the State in Modern India*, Cambridge University Press, 1998.

## 5. A Doomed Alliance

1. Kumari Mayawati, *My Life of Struggle and the Path of the Bahujan Movement*, Bahujan Samaj Party 2006.
2. Jaffrelot, Christophe, *India's Silent Revolution*, Permanent Black, 2003.
3. Ram, Kanshi: *The Incomparable Lady—Kumari Mayawati*.
4. Sharma, Amit: 'The man whom both Maya and Mulayam love', *Indian Express*, 29 August 2003.

## 6. Chief Minister Mayawati

1. *Dainik Jagaran*, 8 December 1995.
2. *Dainik Jagaran*, 6 September 2004.
3. *Outlook*, 11 September 1996.

## 7. The Second Coming

1. Dasgupta, Swapan: 'Beyond Sanctimoniousness', *Indian Express*, 22 March 1997.
2. *Times of India*, 21 August 1997.
3. On 10 April 1997 a group of Shia activists sat on a hunger strike to press their demand to take out religious processions in Lucknow that had been banned two decades ago. When the government refused to give in to their demands, three Shia youths immolated themselves on 13 April 1997 at Dargah Hazrat Abbas in Lucknow. They died on 16 April 1997 in Safdarjung Hospital, New Delhi.
4. *Indian Express*, 18 May 1997.
5. *India Today*, 29 December 1997.

## 8. Third Time Unlucky

1. Naqvi Bhowmik, Saba, 'Big hit on Chotte Raja', *Outlook*, 10 Februrary 2003.
2. Joshi, Poornima, 'A few sharp dog bytes', *Outlook*, 21 April 2003.

## 9. A Historic Triumph

1. *Times of India* (Lucknow edition), 10 June 2005.
2. Ramakrishnan, Venkitesh, 'Votes and hopes', *Frontline*, November 2006.
3. Bose, Ajoy, 'Crossing the caste line', *Pioneer*, 18 April 2007.
4. Jerath, Arati R., 'Maya goes to Janpath', *Daily News and Analysis*, 27 May 2007.

## 10. Iron Lady Versus Transfer Rani

1. Mukherjee, Sutapa, 'Queen Maya's pawns', *Outlook*, 10 June 2002.
2. Jaffrelot, Christophe, *India's Silent Revolution*, citing figures published in *India Today*, July 1995.
3. Chandra, Atul, 'Mayawati the reformist', *Times of India*, (Lucknow edition), 13 October 2002.
4. Pradhan, Sharat, 'Cracks in the coalition', *Indian Express*, 23 May 1997.
5. The *Hindu*, 18 July 2007.
6. '100 day dash—Mulayam versus Mayawati', *Indian Express*, 25 August 2007.
7. *Hindustan Times*, 3 October 2007.

## 11. A Party with a Difference

1. Akhtar, Mohammed Jameel, *Iron Lady—Kumari Mayawati*.
2. Jaoul, Nicholas, 'Political and Non-political Means in the Dalit Movement', in *Political Process in Uttar Pradesh*, Pearson Longman, 2007.

## 12. Mayawati, Social Engineer

1. Yadav, Yogendra, and Kumar, Sanjay, 'How Parties Caste Their Votes in UP', CNN IBN, 8 May 2007.
2. Ibid.

## 13. The Importance of Dalit Identity

1. Vij, Shivam, 'Sister Act—the first quarter', *Tehelka*, 8 September 2007.

2. Jaoul, Nicholas, 'Political and Non-political Means in the Dalit Movement', in *Political Process in Uttar Pradesh*, Pearson Longman, 2007.
3. Teltumbe, Anand, 'Judging Mayawati', *Economic and Political Weekly*, 9 June 2007.
4. Merhotra, Santosh, 'Why Uttar Pradesh is not like Tamil Nadu', in *Political Process in Uttar Pradesh*, Pearson Longman, 2007.
5. Vij, Shivam, 'Icon for an icon', *Tehelka.com*, 17 March 2007.
6. *Tehelka*, 17 March 2007.
7. Teltumbe, Anand: 'Judging Mayawati', *Economic and Political Weekly*, 9 June 2007.
8. Ibid.

## 14. A Rags-to-Riches Fairy Tale

1. Gupta, Shishir, 'Maya began buying prime Delhi land after CBI sealed assets case', *Indian Express*, 30 June 2007.

# Index